POWER/KNOWLEDGE

Selected Interviews and Other Writings 1972–1977

POWER/KNOWLEDGE

*Selected Interviews and Other Writings
1972–1977*

Michel Foucault

Edited by
COLIN GORDON

Translated by
COLIN GORDON, LEO MARSHALL
JOHN MEPHAM, KATE SOPER

 Pantheon Books, New York

LIBRARY OF CONGRESS CATALOGING IN PUBLICATION DATA

Foucault, Michel.
    Power/knowledge.

    Bibliography: p.
    1. Power (Social sciences)   I. Gordon, Colin.
II. Title.
HM291.F59   303.3'3   79-3308
ISBN 0-394-51357-6
ISBN 0-394-73954-x (pbk.)

Manufactured in the United States of America
FIRST AMERICAN EDITION

CONTENTS

PREFACE

Michel Foucault's name, at least, must now be a familiar one to English-speaking readers, since this is the tenth volume of his writings to have been translated within the last dozen years. But perhaps the distinctive features of his work have not always been easy for us to discern from among that gyrating nebula of Gallic luminaries which we have been so arduously and querulously observing during the span of Foucault's career to date. One of the motives for fabricating, in translation, this further Foucault 'book' has therefore been the hope that it will facilitate access to works that are, at least in principle, already available: to construct a sort of non-didactic primer made up of texts in which the author himself explains in straightforward and informal terms some stages and facets of his work and the preoccupations that traverse it. By bringing into clearer focus the political and intellectual environment in which this work has been carried out, this volume should help to undo some of the obfuscating effects commonly produced by the use of such vague and polemical labels as 'structuralism' and 'post-Marxism', and hence make possible a more informed estimate of its significance within contemporary thought, or, to speak less grandly, of the interest, utility and pleasure it offers us.

A few words about the material selected. All the pieces date from since Foucault's election, following a brief spell as one of the founders of the experimental University of Vincennes, to the chair of History of Systems of Thought at the Collège de France; within his published output, they succeed his two methodological and programmatic texts, *The Archaeology of Knowledge* (1969) and *The Order of Discourse* (1970). With the exception of Chapter 1, which is a discussion occasioned by an episode in post-1968 revolutionary French politics, all of the book is closely linked to the themes and arguments of Foucault's two most recent works, *Discipline and Punish* (1975) and *The Will to Know: History of Sexuality 1* (1976). We have sought to minimise internal redundancies, and have omitted items already widely available in English. The resulting pattern is that of an aleatory, open-ended collage in which, from point to point and in changing contexts and perspectives, a certain number of figures and motifs recur. The forms and occasions of the pieces, the identity of the interlocutors and the origin and point of the questions posed are numerous and diverse. Some texts are more or less direct oral transcripts, others are writings in a more orthodox sense. Some have never appeared in France, or are no longer available there.

The diversity of this volume's sources (documented in a separate note below) gives an indication of the remarkable impact of Foucault's books in France and elsewhere, an impact by no means confined to the literary *beau monde*. What are in essence historical essays, albeit unconventional ones in their scope and form, have encountered a wide and receptive audience among the proliferating intellectual and militant action groups, campaigns, currents and publications which have been a feature of the international terrain since the 1960s. One should note that this volume does not represent Foucault's important and extensive journalistic output on topics including capital punishment, abortion, suicide, prison revolts and the recurring scandals of justice and psychiatry (not to speak of their everyday norms), crime and punishment in the Soviet Union, China and Iran, and the popular uprising in the latter country. Some of his articles, notably those on the application of the guillotine by Presidents Pompidou and Giscard, have a philippic force rare in contemporary writing. What is striking about the discussions collected here is the way in which the dimensions of history and philosophy are brought to intersect and interact with this same detailed confrontation of present actuality.

It would nevertheless be misplaced to set about installing Foucault within the lineage of Voltaire, Zola and Sartre, French tradition of great intellectual paladins of justice and truth. For reasons which his analysis of the twilight of the 'universal intellectual' (see p. 126ff) makes clear, Foucault has persistently and dexterously avoided the canonical roles of revolutionary guru, great-and-good writer or 'master-thinker'. This feature of his personal trajectory, while making it less readily visible from afar than those of other illustrious contemporaries and predecessors, may perhaps turn out to be as seminal as any system of theoretical positions to be extracted from his books. At any rate, part of the interest of the present volume lies in the complex relationship it documents between a singular intellectual venture and some common issues posed by our recent historical experiences. Collaborative, consciously pro-visional, often fragmentary and digressive, abounding in hypotheses and sparing in conclusions, these dialogues manifest their own kind of rigour through an abiding concern, constant throughout Foucault's work, to question and understand the fluctuating possibilities, the necessary or contingent historical limits of intellectual discourse itself. The problematic of *'pouvoir-savoir'*, power and knowledge, which has given this book its title, is a fundamental theme of Foucault's historical studies of the genealogy of the human sciences: it is also, ineluctably, a fundamental question concerning our present.

This also means that these discussions, given their location in time and space, have to do with the events of May 1968 and the transformations of political thought and practice which these events were seen as inaugurating. Now, some years later, one can tentatively identify the years around 1972–1977 in France as an unusual and fascinating, albeit confused, period, during which new lines of investigation and critique emerged on the intellectual scene in a relation-ship of mutual stimulation with new modes of political struggle conducted at a multiplicity of distinct sites within society. This is not of course to say that France has been unique in this respect, nor that the relationship in question should be understood as having provided these new zones of militancy with a set of perfect and reciprocal political and theoretical legitimations. In France, moreover, many would now see this period of intellectual ebullition and pervasive 'local struggles' as over, ended—at the latest—by the electoral débâcle of 1978. But if these years' climate of immediate optimism has for the moment given way—and not only in France—to one of *morosité*, something of their vitality will, we hope, be transmitted through the present texts.

The chapters in this book are arranged in approximate chronological order. Readers new to Foucault may however prefer to start with Chapters 5 and 6, for a general overview, and Chapters 2 and 10, for presentations of the recent books. Foucault is his own best expositor and his writings are intractable material for the commentator's arts; I have, however, added as an appendix an essay in which I attempt a speculative summary of the philosophical background to Foucault's enterprise and its main conceptual architecture.

COLIN GORDON

TRANSLATIONS AND SOURCES

Chapter 1 is translated by John Mepham, Chapter 5 by Kate Soper, Chapter 10 by Leo Marshall and the remainder by Colin Gordon. Original titles and sources of the pieces are as follows:

Chapter 1: 'Sur la justice populaire: débat avec les maos', in *Les Temps Modernes* 310 *bis*, 1972: a special issue entitled *Nouveau fascisme, nouvelle démocratie*. Pierre Victor is co-author with Jean-Paul Sartre and Philippe Gavi of *On a raison de se révolter* (Paris, 1974).

Chapter 2: From *Magazine Littéraire* 101, June 1975, reprinted as 'Les jeux du pouvoir' in D. Grisoni (ed.) *Politiques de la Philosophie* (1976).

Chapter 3: 'Pouvoir et Corps', in *Quel Corps?*, September/October 1975, reprinted in *Quel Corps?* (Petite collection maspero, Paris, 1978), a selection of material from this Marxist journal on physical education and sport.

Chapter 4: 'Questions à Michel Foucault sur la géographie', in *Hérodote* 1 (1976). Issue 4 of this Marxist geographers' journal contains responses to questions posed in return by Foucault.

Chapter 5: These two lectures, which have not appeared in French, were transcribed and translated by Alessandro Fontana and Pasquale Pasquino in Michel Foucault, *Microfisica del Potere* (Turin, 1977).

Chapter 6: 'Intervista a Michel Foucault', in *ibid*. A (shortened and mutilated) French version appeared as 'Vérité et Pouvoir' in *L'Arc* 70 (1977).

Chapter 7: 'Pouvoirs et Stratégies' in *Les Révoltes Logiques* 4 (1977). The journal is produced by the Centre de Recherches sur les Idéologies de la Révolte.

Chapter 8: 'L'Oeil du Pouvoir', published as a preface to Jeremy Bentham, *Le Panoptique* (Paris, Belfond, 1977). This comprises a facsimile of the French version (Paris, 1791) and a translation of the first part of the English version (Dublin and London) of Bentham's *Panopticon*, together with a postface by Michelle Perrot on Bentham and the Panopticon which has a useful bibliography. Michelle Perrot's works include *Les ouvriers en grève* (1974). The full English version of Bentham's text is contained in Volume IV of the Bowring edition of his works (Edinburgh 1838–43; Russel & Russel, New York, 1971).

Chapter 9: 'La politique de la santé au XVIIIe siècle', in Michel Foucault, Blandine Barret-Kriegel, Anne Thalamy, Francois Beguin, Bruno Fortier, *Les Machines à Guérir (aux origines de l'hôpital moderne)* (Institut de l'Environnement, Paris, 1976).

Chapter 10: 'Les rapports de pouvoir passent à l'intérieur des corps', in *Quinzaine Littéraire* 247, 1–15 January 1977.

Chapter 11: 'Le jeu de Michel Foucault' in *Ornicar?* 10 July 1977. The journal is published by members of the Department of Psychoanalysis at the University of Vincennes. A few preliminary remarks are omitted from this translation.

We are grateful to Michel Foucault for his friendly assistance and co-operation throughout the preparation of this volume. (It must be said that the Afterword is in no sense an authorised representation of his views.) We are also much indebted to Foucault's Italian editors and translators, Alessandro Fontana and Pasquale Pasquino, whose work formed the basis for this volume. We gratefully acknowledge permission from the Princeton University Press to quote in the Afterword from Albert O. Hirschman's *The Passions and the Interests: Political Arguments for Capitalism before its triumph* (1977). I would like to thank John Mepham for helping to organise the translations, Meaghan Morris and Paul Patton for kindly showing me their versions of Chapters 6 and 7 (see Bibliography), and Graham Burchell and Nikolas Rose for advice on the Afterword. Earlier versions of Chapter 2 and part of Chapter 6 appeared in *Radical Philosophy* 16 and 17, Spring and Summer 1977.

COLIN GORDON

POWER/KNOWLEDGE

Selected Interviews and Other Writings 1972–1977

1 ON POPULAR JUSTICE: A Discussion with Maoists

In the following discussion Michel Foucault and some Maoist militants attempt to identify the basic issues in a debate which had been initiated in response to the project of June 1971, to set up a people's court to judge the police.

FOUCAULT: In my view one shouldn't start with the court as a particular form, and then go on to ask how and on what conditions there could be a people's court; one should start with popular justice, with acts of justice by the people, and go on to ask what place a court could have within this. We must ask whether such acts of popular justice can or cannot be organised in the form of a court. Now my hypothesis is not so much that the court is the natural expression of popular justice, but rather that its historical function is to ensnare it, to control it and to strangle it, by re-inscribing it within institutions which are typical of a state apparatus. For example, in 1792, when war with neighbouring countries broke out and the Parisian workers were called on to go and get themselves killed, they replied: 'We're not going to go before we've brought our enemies within our own country to court. While we will be out there exposed to danger they'll be protected by the prisons they're locked up in. They're only waiting for us to leave in order to come out and set up the old order of things all over again. In any case, those who are in power today want to use against us—in order to bring us back under control—the dual pressure of enemies invading from abroad and those who threaten us at home. We're not going to fight against the former without having first dealt with the latter.' The September executions were at one and the same time an act of war against internal enemies, a political act against the manipulations of those in power, and an act of vengeance against the oppressive classes. Was this not—during a period of violent revolutionary struggle—at least an approximation to an act of popular justice; a response to oppression, strategically effective and politically necessary? Now, no sooner had the executions started in September, when men from the Paris Commune—or from that quarter—intervened and set about staging a court: judges behind a table, representing a third party standing between the people who were 'screaming for vengeance', and the accused who were either 'guilty' or 'innocent'; an investigation to establish the 'truth' or to obtain a 'confession'; deliberation in order to find out what was 'just'; this form was imposed in an authoritarian manner. Can we not see the embryonic, albeit fragile form of a state apparatus reappearing here? The possibility of class oppression? Is not the setting up of a neutral institution standing between the people and its enemies, capable of establishing the dividing line between the true and the false, the guilty and the innocent, the just and the unjust, is this not a way of resisting popular justice? A way of disarming it in the struggle it is conducting in reality in favour of an arbitration in the realm of the ideal? This is why I am wondering whether the court is not a form of popular justice but rather its first deformation.

VICTOR: Yes, but look at examples taken not from the bourgeois revolution but from a proletarian revolution. Take China: the first stage is the ideological revolutionisation of the masses, uprisings in the villages, acts of justice by the peasant masses against their enemies: executions of despots, all sorts of reprisals for all the extortions suffered over the centuries, etc. The executions of the enemies of the people spread, and we would all agree in saying that these were acts of popular justice. All this is fine: the peasant has a good eye for what needs to be done and everything goes just fine in the countryside. But a new stage in the process develops, with the formation of a Red Army, and then it is no longer simply a matter of the masses in revolt against their enemies, for now we have the masses, their enemies, plus an instrument for the unification of the masses, namely the Red Army. At this point all of the acts of popular justice are supported and disciplined. And it is necessary that there be some legal authority so that the diverse acts of vengeance should be in conformity with law, with a people's law which is now something entirely different from the old system of

feudal law. It has to be decided that this particular execution
or that particular act of vengeance is not simply a matter of an
individual settling of accounts, that is, purely and simply an
egotistical revenge against all the oppressive institutions
which had themselves equally been based on egoism. In this
case it is true that there is what you call a neutral institution
which stands between the masses and their immediate
oppressors. Would you argue that at this point in the process
a people's court is not only not a form of popular justice but
is a deformation of people's justice?

FOUCAULT: Are you certain that in this example a 'neutral
institution' came to intervene between the masses and their
oppressors? I do not think so: I would say that, on the
contrary, it was the masses themselves which came to act as
intermediary between any individual who might become
separated from the masses, from the aims of the masses, in
order to satisfy an individual desire for vengeance, and
some other individual who might well, in fact, be an enemy
of the people but whom the former individual might be
aiming to get at simply as a personal enemy . . . .

In the example which I was discussing, the people's court,
as it functioned during the Revolution, did tend to act as a
'neutral institution' and, moreover, it had a very precise
social basis: it represented a social group which stood
between the bourgeoisie in power and the common people
of Paris (*la plèbe*); this was a petty bourgeoisie composed
of small property owners, tradesmen, artisans. This group
took up a position as intermediary, and organised a court
which functioned as a mediator; in doing this it drew on an
ideology which was up to a certain point the ideology of the
dominant class, which determined what it was 'right' or 'not
right' to do or to be. This is why, in this court, they
convicted not only refractory priests or people involved in
the events of 10 August—quite a small number of people—
but they also executed convicts, that is, people who had
been convicted by the courts of the Ancien Regime. They
executed prostitutes, and so on . . . . So it is clear that it had
reoccupied the 'median' position of the judicial institution
just as it had functioned under the Ancien Regime. Where
there had originally been the masses exacting retribution
against those who were their enemies, there was now

substituted the operation of a court and of a great deal of its ideology.

VICTOR: This is why it is interesting to compare cases of courts during the bourgeois revolution with cases of courts during the proletarian revolution. What you have described comes down to this: between the masses at the base—what then constituted 'the people' on the one hand, and their enemies on the other—there was a class, the petty bourgeoisie (a 'third party') which was an intermediary, which took something from the common people and something else from the class which was becoming dominant: it thereby played the role of a median class, it coalesced these two elements, and this gave to the people's court what was, from the point of view of the development of popular justice which was being conducted by the common people, an element of internal repression, thus a deformation of popular justice. So if there is a 'third party', this does not arise from the court itself, it comes from the class which took over the courts, that is, from the petty bourgeoisie.

FOUCAULT: I would like to take a brief look backwards, at the history of the state judicial apparatus. In the Middle Ages there was a change from the court of arbitration (to which cases of dispute were taken by mutual consent, to conclude some dispute or some private battle, and which was in no way a permanent repository of power) to a set of stable, well defined institutions, which had the authority to intervene and which were based on political power (or at any rate were under its control). This change was accomplished in conjunction with two underlying processes. The first was the fiscalisation of the judicial system: by means of fines, confiscations, distraints, by granting expenses and all sorts of allowances, operating the judicial system became profitable; after the breakdown of the Carolingian state the judicial system became, in the hands of the nobles, not only an instrument of appropriation—a means of coercion—but a direct source of revenue; it produced an income over and above feudal rent, or rather it became an aspect of feudal rent. To be a judge was to have a source of income, it was property. Judgeships became a form of wealth which could be exchanged, circulated, which were sold or inherited as part of, or sometimes separately from, fiefs. They became an integral part of the circulation of wealth and of the feudal levy. For those who owned them they constituted rights (in addition to those of quit-rent, mortmain, tithe, tonnage, banalités, etc.); and for those who came under their jurisdiction they amounted to a kind of taxation which was not systematised but to which it was nevertheless in certain cases certainly necessary to submit. The archaic operation of the judicial system had become inverted: one could say that in earlier times justice was a right for those to whom it was applied (the right to demand justice when the disputants agreed to do so) and a duty for those who made the judgments (the obligation to exercise their prestige, their authority, their wisdom, their politico-religious power). It was to become from this point on a (lucrative) right for those in power, and a (costly) obligation for those who had to submit to it. At this point we can see the convergence with the second of the processes which I mentioned earlier: the increasing link between the judicial system and armed force. To replace private wars by a compulsory and lucrative judicial system, to impose a judicial system where one is— at one and the same time— judge, party to the dispute and tax collector, instead of a system of deals and settlements, to impose a judicial system which secures, guarantees and increases by significant amounts the levy on the product of labour, all this implies the availability of the power of constraint. It could not be imposed without armed force: wherever a feudal lord disposed of sufficient military power to enforce his 'peace' it was possible for him to impose juridical and fiscal levies. Having become a source of income, judgeships developed in the direction of the division of private property. But supported by the force of arms they developed in the direction of its ever increasing concentration. This dual development led to the 'classical' result: when, during the fourteenth century the feudal lords were faced with the great peasant and urban revolts, they sought the support of a centralised power, army and taxation system: and in this emergency there arose, together with the provincial High Courts, the King's Procurators, official prosecutions, legislation against beggars, vagabonds, idlers, and before long the early rudimentary forms of police and a centralised judicial system. This was an embryonic state

judicial apparatus which was superimposed upon, duplica-
ted and controlled the feudal judges and their fiscal rights,
but which allowed them to continue to function. There thus
sprang up a 'judicial' order which had the appearance of the
expression of public power: an arbitrator both neutral and
with authority, of whom the task was both to 'justly' resolve
disputes and to exercise 'authority' in the maintenance of
public order. It was on these foundations, of social struggles,
the levying of taxes and the concentration of armed force,
that the judicial apparatus was erected.

We can understand, then, why it is that in France and, I
believe, in Western Europe, the act of popular justice is
profoundly anti-judicial, and is contrary to the very form of
the court. In all the great uprisings since the fourteenth
century the judicial officials have regularly been attacked,
on the same grounds as have tax officials, and more
generally those who exercise power: the prisons have been
opened, the judges thrown out and the courts closed down.
Popular justice recognises in the judicial system a state
apparatus, representative of public authority, and instrument of class power. I would like to put forward a hypothesis, though I'm not certain about it: it seems to me that a
certain number of habits which derive from the private war,
a certain number of ancient rites which were features of
'pre-judicial' justice, have been preserved in the practises of
popular justice: for example, it was an old Germanic custom
to put the head of an enemy on a stake, for public viewing,
when he had been killed 'according to the rules', or 'juridi-
cally', in the course of a private war; the destruction of the
house, or at least the burning of the timber-work, and the
ransacking of the contents of the house, is an ancient rite
which went together with being outlawed: now, these are
acts which predate the setting up of a judicial system and
which are regularly revived in popular uprisings. The head
of Delaunay was paraded around the captured Bastille;
around the symbol of the repressive apparatus revolves,
with its ancient ancestral rites, a popular practice which
does not identify itself in any way with judicial institutions.
In my view the history of the judicial system as state
apparatus enables us to understand why, in France at least,
acts of justice which really are popular tend to flee from the

court, and why, on the other hand, each time that the bourgeoisie has wished to subject a popular uprising to the constraint of a state apparatus a court has been set up: a table, a chairman, magistrates, confronting the two opponents. Thereby the judicial system is reborn. That is my view of things.

VICTOR: Yes. You see things up to 1789, but what I'm interested in is what happens later. You have described the birth of a class idea and how this class idea was materialised in practices and apparatuses. I perfectly well understand how it was possible, in the French Revolution, for courts to become instruments of indirect deformation and repression of the acts of popular justice of the common people. If I've understood, this was because there were several social classes involved, on the one hand the common people, on the other hand the traitors to the nation and to the revolution, and between them a class which attempted to play out to the full the historical role which was open to it. Therefore I cannot draw any definitive conclusions about the form of the people's court from this example—in any case, for us there are no forms which are incapable of historical development—but merely see how the petty bourgeoisie as a class picked up from the common people some scrap of an idea and then, being dominated as it was, especially in this period, by the ideas of the bourgeoisie, crushed the ideas drawn from the common people under the form taken by courts at that time. I cannot draw from this any conclusions about the practical problem we are faced with today, concerning people's courts in the present-day ideological revolution, nor, *a fortiori*, in the future people's armed revolution. This is why I would like us to compare this example from the French Revolution with the example which I mentioned just now, that of the people's armed revolution in China.

Now you would say 'In this example there are only two elements—the masses and their enemies'. But the masses in a way delegate some part of their power to an element which, while being deeply attached to them, is nevertheless distinct, the People's Red Army. Now this figure, military power/judicial power, which you pointed out, can be seen again here with the People's Army helping the masses to organise regulations covering the trial of class enemies. I myself do not find anything surprising about this, given that the People's Army is a state apparatus. So I would put the following question to you: are you not dreaming up the possibility of going straight from present-day oppression to communism without any transition period—that which is traditionally called the dictatorship of the proletariat— during which there is a need for a new type of state apparatus, of which we must define the content? Is it not this which lies behind your systematic refusal of the people's court as a form?

FOUCAULT: Are you certain that it is merely the *form* of the court that is involved here? I do not know how these things are done in China, but look a bit more closely at the meaning of the spatial arrangement of the court, the arrangement of the people who are part of or before a court. The very least that can be said is that this implies an ideology.

What is this arrangement? A table, and behind this table, which distances them from the two litigants, the 'third party', that is, the judges. Their position indicates firstly that they are neutral with respect to each litigant, and secondly this implies that their decision is not already arrived at in advance, that it will be made after an aural investigation of the two parties, on the basis of a certain conception of truth and a certain number of ideas concerning what is just and unjust, and thirdly that they have the authority to enforce their decision. This is ultimately the meaning of this simple arrangement. Now this idea that there can be people who are neutral in relation to the two parties, that they can make judgments about them on the basis of ideas of justice which have absolute validity, and that their decisions must be acted upon, I believe that all this is far removed from and quite foreign to the very idea of popular justice. In the case of popular justice you do not have three elements, you have the masses and their enemies. Furthermore, the masses, when they perceive somebody to be an enemy, when they decide to punish this enemy—or to re-educate him—do not rely on an abstract universal idea of justice, they rely only on their own experience, that of the injuries they have suffered, that of the way in which they have been wronged, in which they have been oppressed; and finally, their decision is not an authoritative one, that is, they are not backed up by a state apparatus which has the power to enforce their decisions, they purely and simply carry them out. Therefore I hold firmly to the view that the organisation of courts, at least in the West, is necessarily alien to the practice of popular justice.

VICTOR: I do not agree. Whereas you discuss concretely all revolutions up to the proletarian revolution, you become completely abstract when talking about modern revolutions, including those that have occurred in the West. That's why I'll now take a new case, coming back to France. During the Liberation there were a variety of acts of popular justice. I will deliberately take an ambiguous example of popular justice, an act of popular justice which was both real yet ambiguous, that is, an act which was in effect manipulated by the class enemy; we can draw a general conclusion from this so as to locate more exactly the theoretical criticism which I am making.

I want to discuss those young women whose heads were shaved because they had slept with the Germans. In one way this was an act of popular justice: for intercourse (in the most physical sense of the term) with Germans was something which was offensive to the deepest, bodily, sense of patriotic feeling: this really was an emotional and physical injury to the people. However, it was an ambiguous act of popular justice. Why? Quite simply because while the people were being entertained by shaving the heads of these women, the real collaborators— the real traitors— remained untouched. So the enemy was allowed to exploit these acts of popular justice; not the old enemy— the Nazi occupation forces, now disintegrating militarily— but the new enemy, the French bourgeoisie, with the exception of a small minority who were too compromised by the occupation and who could not come out into the open too much. What can we learn from this ambiguous act of popular justice? Not at all the conclusion that this mass movement was unreasonable, because there was in fact a reason for this act of retaliation against young women who had slept with the German officers, but that if the mass movement is not given proletarian unity and direction it can disintegrate from within and be exploited by the class enemy. In short, the mass movement on its own is not enough. This is because there are contradictions among the masses. These contradictions within a popular movement can easily cause its development to take a wrong course, to the extent that the enemy takes advantage of them. So it is necessary for there to be an organisation to regulate the course of popular justice, to give it direction. And this cannot be done directly by the masses themselves, precisely because what is needed is an organisation which is able to resolve the masses' internal contradictions. In the case of the Chinese revolution the organisation which enabled these contradictions to be resolved (and which played the same role once again after state power had been seized, at the time of the Cultural Revolution) was the Red Army. Now the Red Army is different from the people even though it is linked to them, even though the people love the army and the army loves the people. Not all the Chinese were in the Red Army, and they are still not so today. The Red Army represents a delegation of the power of the people, it is not the people themselves. This is also why there is always the possibility of a contradiction between the army and the people, and there will always be the possibility that this state apparatus will repress the popular masses, and this opens up the possibility and the necessity for a whole series of cultural revolutions, precisely in order to abolish contradictions which have become antagonistic between the state apparatuses such as the army, the Party or the administrative apparatus, and the popular masses.

Therefore, I would be against people's courts, I would find them completely unnecessary or detrimental if the masses—once set in movement—were a homogeneous whole—that is, in short, if there were no need, in order to keep the revolution moving ahead, for institutions which could discipline, centralise and unify the masses. In other words I would be against people's courts if I did not think that to make the revolution it is necessary to have a Party, and, for the revolution to keep going, a revolutionary state apparatus.

As for the objection which you put forward on the basis of

the analysis of the spatial arrangement of courts, my reply is as follows: on the one hand we are not forced to adopt any particular form—in the formal sense of spatial arrangement —for any particular court. One of the best of the Liberation courts was that at Béthune. Hundreds of miners had decided to execute a 'boche'—that is, a collaborator—and they left him in the central square for seven days; each day they turned up, and they said: 'We'll execute him', and then went away again. The lad was still there, and they still didn't execute him. At that point somebody marginal, I'm not sure who exactly, with some vestige of authority left, said, 'Let's get it over with, lads. Either kill him or let him go, we can't go on like this', and they said 'OK. Come on comrades, we'll execute him', and they took aim and fired, and before dying the collaborator cried out 'Heil Hitler!', which allowed everyone to say that the decision had been a just one . . . . In this example there was not the spatial arrangement that you describe.

What forms should the judicial system take under the dictatorship of the proletariat? This is an unanswered question, even in China. Things are still at an experimental stage on this question, and there is a class struggle around the question of the judiciary. You can see from this that it is not a matter of once again adopting the table, the magistrates, etc. But here I'm only touching on the superficial aspect of the problem. Your example went much further. It pointed to the problem of 'neutrality'; as far as popular justice goes what happens to this necessarily neutral 'third element' which is purportedly in possession of a truth different from that of the popular masses, and by virtue of this acting as a shield?

FOUCAULT: I identified three elements: (i) a 'third element'; (ii) reference to an idea, a form, a universal rule of justice; (iii) decisions with power of enforcement. It is these three characteristics of the courts which are represented in anecdotal fashion by the table, in our society.

VICTOR: The 'third element' in the case of popular justice is a revolutionary state apparatus—for example, the Red Army in the early stages of the Chinese Revolution. In what sense is it a 'third element', a repository of a *law* and of a *truth*? This is what needs to be explained.

There are the masses, there is this revolutionary state apparatus, and there is the enemy. The masses express their grievances and compile an inventory of all the extortions, of all the suffering caused by the enemy; the revolutionary state apparatus takes note of this inventory, and the enemy interjects, 'I don't agree about such-and-such a point'. Now, the truth as far as the facts are concerned can be established. If the enemy has betrayed three patriots, and if the whole population of the commune is present and are agreed on a verdict, then it must be possible to establish the facts of the matter. If it is not then there must be some problem: if there is no agreement that he is guilty of such-and-such an extortion then the least that can be said is that the desire to execute him is not an act of popular justice but a settling of accounts between some minority fraction of the masses with egotistical ideas and this enemy, or this alleged enemy.

The facts of the matter have been established, the role of the revolutionary state apparatus is not yet over. Already, during the investigation of the facts, it has played a role, since it has allowed the whole of the actively participating population to list the charges against the enemy, but its role does not stop here; it still has a contribution to make when it comes to deciding on the sentence. Say the enemy is the owner of some moderately large factory; the fact can be established that he really did exploit the workers abominably, that he was responsible for quite a few accidents at work; is he to be executed? Let us suppose that it is desirable that the middle bourgeoisie be rallied to the cause of the revolution, that it is said that only the very small handful of archcriminals should be executed, and that these can be identified by objective criteria; then this enemy would not be executed even though the factory workers whose friends had been killed have a violent hatred of their boss and would perhaps like to execute him. This could constitute a perfectly correct policy, as was, for example, during the Chinese revolution, the deliberate minimising of the contradictions between the workers and the national bourgeoisie. I don't know if it would happen like that here, but I will give you a hypothetical example. It is probable that not all the bosses would be liquidated, particularly in a country like France where there is a large number of small-

and medium-sized firms so that this would amount to too many people . . . . All this comes down to saying that the revolutionary state apparatus, representing the general interests which have priority over those of any particular factory or any particular village, applies objective criteria in sentencing. I'll go back again to the example of the early stages of the Chinese revolution. At a certain point in time it was correct to attack all landowners, while at other points there were some landowners who were patriots and who had to be spared; it was necessary to educate the peasants, and so to go against their natural inclinations with regard to these landowners.

FOUCAULT: The procedures you've described seem to me completely alien to the very form of the court. What role is played by this revolutionary state apparatus, in this case the Chinese army? Is its role to choose between two sides, for one rather than the other, between the masses who represent one particular will or one particular interest, and an individual representing a different interest or will? Obviously not, because it is a state apparatus which is engendered by the masses, which is under the control of the masses, and which will carry on being controlled by them, and which in fact has a positive role to play, not in making decisions as between the masses and their enemies, but in guaranteeing the education, the political training, the broadening of the political vision and experience of the masses. So is the job of this state apparatus here to determine sentences? Not at all, but to educate the masses and the will of the masses in such a way that it is the masses themselves who come to say, 'In fact we cannot kill this man' or 'In fact we must kill him'.

You can see clearly that this is not at all the way that courts operate, as they exist at the present time in France — where they are of an entirely different order — in which it is not one of the parties which is in control of the judicial system and where the judicial system has no educative role to play. To go back to your earlier example, if people went rushing after women to shave their heads it was because the collaborators who should have been their natural targets and against whom they should have exercised popular justice, were presented to the masses as being too difficult to deal with in that way: it was said, 'Oh, those people's crimes are too great, we'll bring them before a court'. They were put in prison and were brought before the courts, and they, of course, acquitted them. In this case the courts were just used as an excuse for dealing with things other than by acts of popular justice.

Now I've arrived at the basic point of my thesis. You speak about contradictions among the masses and you say that there is a need for a revolutionary state apparatus to help the masses resolve these contradictions. Now, I don't know what happened in China: perhaps the judicial apparatus was like those in feudal states, an extremely flexible apparatus, with little centralisation, etc. In societies such as our own, on the contrary, the judicial apparatus has been an extremely important state apparatus of which the history has always been obscured. People do the history of law, and the history of the economy, but the history of the judicial system, of judicial practices—of what has in fact been a penal system, of what have been systems of repression—this is rarely discussed. Now, I believe that the judicial system as a state apparatus has historically been of absolutely fundamental importance. The penal system has had the function of introducing a certain number of contradictions among the masses, and one major contradiction, namely the following: to create mutual antagonism between the proletarianised common people and the non-proletarianised common people. There was a particular period when the penal system, of which the function in the Middle Ages had been essentially a fiscal one, became organised around the struggle to stamp out rebellion. Up until this point the job of putting down popular uprisings had been primarily a military one. From now on it was to become taken on, or rendered unnecessary by a complex system of courts–police–prison. It is a system which has basically a triple role; and depending on the period, depending on the state of struggles and on the conjuncture, it was one or other of these roles which was dominant. On the one hand it is a factor in 'proletarianisation': its role is to force the people to accept their status as proletarians and the conditions for the exploitation of the proletariat. It is perfectly obvious that from the end of the Middle Ages up until the eighteenth century, all the laws against beggars, vagabonds and the idle, all the police organisations designed to catch them, forced them—and this was of course their role—to accept, at the particular place where they were, the conditions imposed on them, which were extremely bad. If they rejected these conditions, if they went away, if they took to begging or 'to doing nothing', then it was prison and often forced labour. On the other hand, this penal system was aimed, very specifically, against the most mobile, the most excitable, the 'violent' elements among the common people: those who were most prepared to turn to direct, armed action, including farmers who were forced by debts to leave their land, peasants on the run from tax authorities, workers banished for theft, vagabonds or beggars who refused to clear the ditches, those who lived by plundering the fields, the small-time thieves and the highwaymen, those who, in armed groups, attacked the tax authorities and, more generally, agents of the State, and finally those who—on days of rioting in the towns or in the villages—carried weapons. There was widespread plotting, a whole network of communications, within which individuals could adopt different roles. It was these 'dangerous' people who had to be isolated (in prison, in the Hôpital Général, in the galleys, in the colonies) so that they could not act as a spearhead for popular resistance. This fear was great in the eighteenth century, and it was greater still after the Revolution, and at all the times of commotion during the nineteenth century. The third role of the penal system: to make the proletariat see the non-proletarianised people as marginal, dangerous, immoral, a menace to society as a whole, the dregs of the population, trash, the 'mob'. For the bourgeoisie it is a matter of imposing on the proletariat, by means of penal legislation, of prisons, but also of newspapers, of 'literature', certain allegedly universal moral categories which function as an ideological barrier between them and the non-proletarianised people. All the literary, journalistic, medical, sociological and anthropological rhetoric about criminals (and we are all familiar with examples of all these in the second half of the nineteenth century and the beginning of the twentieth century) play this role. Finally, the distance which the penal system creates and sustains between the proletariat and the non-proletarianised people, all the pressures which are put upon the latter, enable the bourgeoisie to make use of certain of these plebeian elements against the proletariat; they mobilise them as soldiers, policemen, racketeers and thugs, and use them for the surveillance and repression of the proletariat (it is not only fascism which has provided examples of this).

At first sight these are at least some of the ways in which the penal system operates as an anti-seditious system, as a variety of ways of creating antagonism between the pro-letarianised and the non-proletarianised people, and there-by introducing a contradiction which is now firmly rooted. This is why the revolution can only take place via the radical elimination of the judicial apparatus, and anything which could reintroduce the penal apparatus, anything which could reintroduce its ideology and enable this ideology to surreptitiously creep back into popular practices, must be banished. This is why the court, an exemplary form of this judicial system, seems to me to be a possible location for the reintroduction of the ideology of the penal system into popular practice. This is why I think that one should not make use of such a model.

VICTOR: You have surreptitiously forgotten one particular century, the twentieth. So I put to you the following question: is the principal contradiction among the masses that between prisoners and workers?

FOUCAULT: Not between prisoners and workers; between the non-proletarianised people and the proletariat: this has been one of the contradictions, one of the important contradictions, which the bourgeoisie has for a long time, and especially since the French Revolution, seen as a means of self-defence. For the bourgeoisie the main danger against which it had to be protected, that which had to be avoided at all costs, was armed uprising, was the armed people, was the workers taking to the streets in an assault against the government. They thought they could identify, in the non-proletarianised people, in those common people who rejected the status of proletarians, or in those who were excluded from it, the spearhead of popular rebellion. They therefore provided themselves with a certain number of methods for distancing the proletarianised from the non-proletarianised people. At the present time these methods are deficient; they have been or are being taken away from them.

These three methods are or were the army, colonisation and prisons. (Obviously the distancing between proletarianised and non-proletarianised people and the prevention of armed uprising were only one of their functions.) The army, with the 'proxy' (*remplaçants*) call-up system, made it possible to drain off significant numbers, especially from the peasant population which was over-numerous in the countryside and could not find work in the towns. It was this army which was used against the workers when the need arose. The bourgeoisie tried to maintain an antagonism between the army and the proletariat, and this often worked, though sometimes it failed when the soldiers refused to move or to shoot. Colonisation constituted another way of draining off these elements; those who were sent to the colonies did not take on a proletarian status. They were used as cadres, administrative functionaries, as tools of surveillance and control over the colonised peoples. And it was certainly in order to avoid the forming of an alliance between these 'lesser whites' and the colonised peoples—an alliance which would have been just as dangerous out there as proletarian unity would have been in Europe—that a rigid racialist ideology was foisted on them: 'Watch out, you'll be living among cannibals'. As for the third method of separating off these elements, this was organised around the prison system, and the bourgeoisie erected an ideological barrier around those who went to prison or who had been in prison (an ideology about crime, criminals, theft, the mob, degenerates, 'animals') which was in part linked with racialism.

But look what's happened; no overt form of colonisation is possible any longer. The army can't play the same role as it used to. As a result we have a reinforcement of the police and an overloading of the penal system; these now have to take on by themselves the whole burden of performing all these functions. Systematic police control of every quarter, the police stations, the courts (especially those dealing out summary judgments to those 'caught in the act'), the prisons, the parole and probation systems, the whole system of controls involved in making children wards of court, the social welfare system, reform schools, all these must now perform, here in France, all the roles that used to be taken on by the army and colonisation in geographically relocating people and in sending them abroad.

The Resistance, the Algerian war, May '68 have been crucial episodes in this story, involving the revival, in the various struggles, of clandestinity, of arms, and of action in the streets. At the same time there has also been the establishment of an apparatus for fighting internal subversion (an apparatus which has been strengthened, adapted and refined in response to each of these episodes, but from which, of course, all the corrupt elements have never been purged); an apparatus which has been in continuous operation now for thirty years. We can say that the techniques employed up to 1940 relied primarily on the policy of imperialism (the army/the colonies), whereas those employed since then are closer to a fascist model (police, internal surveillance, confinement).

VICTOR: Still, you haven't answered my question, which was: is this the principal contradiction among the people?

FOUCAULT: I am not saying that it is the principal contradiction.

VICTOR: You are not asserting that, but the way you tell the story speaks for itself: uprisings are the result of a fusion between the proletarianised and the non-proletarianised people. You have described for us all the mechanisms which operate to draw a dividing line between the proletarianised and the non-proletarianised people. So, obviously, given this dividing line, there are no uprisings, whereas were the fusion to be reestablished then there would be uprisings. Although you say that you don't consider this to be the principal contradiction, it in fact becomes the principal contradiction on your interpretation of history. I'm not going to respond to this in relation to the twentieth century. I'll stick to the nineteenth century, and introduce a little extra historical evidence, evidence which is somewhat contradictory, taken from a text by Engels on the development of large-scale modern industry.[1] Engels said that the first form of revolt of the modern proletariat against large-scale industry was criminality, that of those workers who killed their bosses. He made no attempt to discover the underlying causes of this criminality, nor the conditions in which it operated, and he did not write a history of the penal system. He was speaking from the point of view of the masses and not from the point of view of the state apparatuses, and he said that criminality was an initial form of revolt; then he went on quickly to demonstrate that this was very embryonic and not very effective. The second, and superior, form was machine-breaking. But here again it did not get very far, because as soon as the machines were broken others immediately took their place. This hit at one aspect of the social order but did not attack the root causes. Where revolt took on a conscious form it was with the formation of 'combinations', that is, of unions in the original sense of the word. Combination is the superior form of the revolt of the modern proletariat because it resolves the principal contradiction among the masses, namely the internal contradiction among the masses which results from the social system and from its core, the capitalist mode of production. It was, Engels tells us, simply the struggle against competition between the workers, and thus combination, to the extent that this united the workers, which made it possible to transfer competition to the level of competition among the bosses. It is in this context that he situates his early descriptions of union struggles over wages or for the reduction of the working day. This little extra historical evidence suggests to me that the principal contradiction among the masses is the opposition between egoism and collectivism, competition and combination, and that it is when you have combination, that is, the victory of collectivism over competition, that you have the working masses, and thus a unity among the proletarianised people, and that then there will be a mass movement. It is only then that the first condition for the possibility of subversion, for revolt, is achieved. The second condition is that these masses gain a hold on all people in revolt throughout the social system and do not confine themselves to the workshops and the factories as the site of revolt, and it is then that you will in fact find them coming together with the non-proletarianised people, and you will also find them joining together with other social classes, with young intellectuals, the self-employed petty bourgeoisie, small tradesmen, in the first revolutions of the nineteenth century.

FOUCAULT: I don't think I said that it was the basic contradiction. I meant that the bourgeoisie saw sedition as being the main danger. This is how the bourgeoisie viewed things: but this does not mean that things will happen in the way that they fear, and that the joining up of the proletariat with the marginal elements of the population will spark off the revolution. All that you have just said in relation to Engels I would by and large agree with. It does in fact seem that at the end of the eighteenth century and at the beginning of the nineteenth century criminality was perceived, by the proletarians themselves, to be a form of social struggle. By the time that struggles take the form of combinations criminality no longer has quite this role; or rather, breaking the law, the transitory and individual overturning of power and order which criminality represents, can no longer have the same meaning, nor the same function in struggles. But we should take note of the fact that the bourgeoisie, forced to retreat in the face of these proletarian forms of organisation, did everything that it could to divorce this new force from a segment of the population which was thought of as violent, dangerous, without respect for the law, and consequently liable to revolt. Among the methods employed some were of enormous consequence (as, for example, the morality taught in primary schools, that is, the gradual imposition of a whole system of values disguised as the teaching of literacy, reading and writing covering up the imposition of values) and some were rather smaller innovations, tiny and horrible machiavelianisms. (Since unions had no legal status those in power could use great ingenuity in getting them run by people who one fine day would run off with the funds; it was impossible for the unions to sue them; thus there was a backlash of hatred against thieves, a desire to be protected by the law, etc.)

VICTOR: I think that it is necessary to make a point of clarification, to be somewhat more accurate and dialectical in the use of this concept of the non-proletarianised people. The main, principal, cleavage introduced by the unions, which would turn out to be the cause of their degeneration, was not between the proletarianised people—in the sense of the fully formed, established proletariat—and the *lumpenproletariat*—that is, in the strict sense, the marginalised proletariat, those who had been thrown out of the proletariat. The principal cleavage was between a minority of the workers and the great mass of the workers, that is, the people who were being proletarianised. These latter were workers who were coming from the countryside; they were not hooligans, brigands, street brawlers.

FOUCAULT: I think I have never, in anything that I have just said, tried to show that this was a basic contradiction. I have described a certain number of factors and effects, and I have tried to show how they were all interconnected, and how the proletariat was able, up to a certain point, to come to terms with the moral ideology of the bourgeoisie.

VICTOR: You say: 'This is one factor among others, it is not the principal contradiction'. But all of your examples, the whole history of these mechanisms as you've described it, tend to put the emphasis on this contradiction. For you the proletariat first sold out to the devil in having adopted the 'moral' values by means of which the bourgeoisie established a divorce between the non-proletarianised people and the proletariat, between the hooligans and the honest workers. I reply, not so. The first selling out to the devil by the workers' organisations was to have made belonging to a trade a condition of membership. It was this which allowed the first unions to become corporations which excluded the mass of unskilled workers.

FOUCAULT: This restriction on membership which you mention was certainly the most fundamental one. But notice what its implications were: if workers who had no trade didn't belong to the unions this was all the more so for those who were not proletarian. So, once again, we can ask how did the judicial apparatus, and more generally the penal system, operate? My answer is that it has always operated in such a way as to introduce contradictions among the people. I am not saying (it would be ridiculous to do so) that the penal system introduced the basic contradictions, but I am rejecting the idea that the penal system is a nebulous superstructure. It has played a determining role in the divisions of present-day society.

GILLES: I am wondering whether we shouldn't distinguish

two different kinds of 'plebs' (or non-proletarianised common people) in this story. Can the 'plebs' really be identified as those who refuse to be workers, with the consequence of this being that the 'plebs' would then have a monopoly on violence, whereas the workers, the proletarians in the strict sense of the word, would be inclined to be non-violent? Isn't this the effect of a bourgeois view of the world, in that it classifies the workers as a group organised within the state, and similarly the peasants, and so on . . . whereas all the rest would be the 'plebs', a rebellious residue in this pacified, organised world as the bourgeoisie would have it, in which the judicial system has the mission of controlling the borders. But the 'plebeians' can themselves well be trapped within this bourgeois view of things, that is, they can conceive themselves as being of another world. And I am not sure that, being trapped within this view of things, their other world would not be a duplicate of the bourgeois world. Obviously this wouldn't be completely so, because there are traditions, but it would be so in part. Moreover, there is yet another fact; this bourgeois world, divided but stable, the realm of the familiar judicial system, does not exist. Is there not, behind the opposition between the proletariat and the 'plebs' who monopolise violence, the coming together of the proletariat and the peasantry, not the 'safe' peasantry, but the peasantry in potential rebellion? Isn't that which threatens the bourgeoisie then rather the coming together of the workers and the peasants?

FOUCAULT: I completely agree with you in saying that we must distinguish between the common people as they are seen by the bourgeoisie and the common people as they are in reality. But what we have been trying to see is how the judicial system operates. Penal law was not created by the common people, nor by the peasantry, nor by the proletariat, but entirely by the bourgeoisie as an important tactical weapon in this system of divisions which they wished to introduce. That this tactical weapon was not based on a true assessment of what the actual possibilities of revolution were is a fact, and a fortunate one at that. This is to be expected, because the bourgeoisie cannot have an accurate perception of real relations and real processes. And in fact, to speak of the peasantry, we can say that relations between workers and peasants were not at all the target of the Western penal system in the nineteenth century; the general impression is that the bourgeoisie in the nineteenth century were relatively confident about the peasants.

GILLES: If this is so then it is possible that the real solution to the problem of the relations between proletariat and plebs is contained in the capacity to resolve the problem of popular unity, that is, the fusion of proletarian methods of struggle and the methods of peasant warfare.

VICTOR: This would not be sufficient to resolve the problem of fusion. There is also the problem of methods suitable for those who are mobile. An army is the only solution to the problem.

GILLES: This means that the solution to the opposition between proletariat and non-proletarianised plebs involves an attack on the state, taking over state power. This is also why there is a need for people's courts.

FOUCAULT: If what has been said is true then the struggle against the judicial apparatus is an important struggle — I do not say a basic struggle, but it is as important as was that judicial system in the division which the bourgeoisie created and maintained between the proletariat and the plebs. This judicial apparatus has had specific ideological effects on each of the dominated classes, and there is in particular a proletarian ideology into which certain bourgeois ideas about what is just and what unjust, about theft, property, crime and criminals have infiltrated. This does not mean that the non-proletarianised plebs has remained unsullied and resolute. On the contrary, for one-and-a-half centuries the bourgeoisie offered it the following choices: you can go to prison or join the army, you can go to prison or go to the colonies, you can go to prison or you can join the police. So this non-proletarianised plebs has been racialist when it has been colonialist; it has been nationalist, chauvinist, when it has been armed; and it has been fascist when it has become the police force. These ideological effects on the plebs have been uncontestable and profound. The effects on the proletariat are also uncontestable. This system is, in a sense, very subtle and works relatively well, even though the bourgeoisie is blind to the basic relations and real processes.

VICTOR: From the strictly historical discussion we have

learned that the struggle against the penal apparatus constitutes a relative unity and that everything which you have
described as the introduction of contradictions among the
people does not represent a major contradiction but a series
of contradictions which have had great importance *from the
point of view of the bourgeoisie*, in its struggle against the
revolution. But with what you have just said we are now at
the heart of popular justice, which goes far beyond the
struggle against the judicial apparatus: beating up the
foreman has nothing to do with the struggle against the
judge. Similarly for the peasant who executes a landowner.
This is popular justice and it is far broader than the struggle
against the judicial apparatus. Even if we take the example
of the past year we can see that popular justice was put into
practice before the broad struggles against the judicial
apparatus, that it was the former which paved the way for
the latter: it was the first locking up of the bosses, and
beating up of their lackeys, which mentally prepared people
for the big struggle against injustice and against the judicial
apparatus, Guiot,[2] the prisons, etc. In the aftermath of May
'68 it was really this that happened.

Grosso modo what you're saying is this: the proletariat has
an ideology which is a bourgeois ideology and which
incorporates the system of bourgeois values, the opposition
between the moral and the immoral, the just and the unjust,
the honest and the dishonest, etc. Therefore there results
from this a corruption of ideology among the proletarianised people, and corruption of ideology among the
non-proletarianised people, brought about by all the
mechanisms of integration and the various tools of repression of the people. Now, and this is exactly the point,
the development of the unifying idea, the raising of the
banner of popular justice, is the struggle against alienated
ideas within the proletariat and elsewhere, hence also
among those sons of the proletariat who have been 'led
astray'. We must find a way of putting this so as to clarify
this struggle against these forms of alienation, this fusion
of ideas coming from all the different fractions of the
people—a fusion of ideas which enables the divided
fractions of the people to be reunited—because it is not
with ideas that history is made to move forward, but with a

material force, that of the people reunited in the streets. We can take as an example the slogan used by the Communist Party in the early years of the occupation, to justify the looting of shops, particularly those on the Rue Buci: 'Housewives, it is right to steal from the thieves'. This is perfect. You can see how the fusion works: you have a demolition of the system of bourgeois values (thieves contrasted with honest people) but it is a particular kind of demolition, because when you get down to it there are always thieves. But now we have a new classification. The whole people are reunited; they are the non-thieves: and it is the class enemies who are the thieves. This is why I have no hesitation in saying, for example, 'To jail with Rives-Henry'.[3]

If we look to fundamentals we see that the revolutionary process is always the fusion of the rebellion of those classes which are constituted as such, with that of classes which are fragmented. But this fusion comes about in a very specific direction. The 'vagabonds', and there were millions upon millions of them in semi-colonial and semi-feudal China, were the mass basis of the first Red Army. The ideological problems within this army derived precisely from the mercenary ideology of these 'vagabonds'. And Mao—from his red base where he was surrounded—sent appeals to the Central Committee of the Party, saying roughly, 'Send me just three cadres from a factory, to counteract a bit the ideology of all my "bare-foot" people'. The discipline of the war against the enemy was not enough. It was necessary to counteract mercenary ideology with ideology from the factory.

The Red Army under the leadership of the Party, that is, the peasant war under the direction of the proletariat, was the crucible which made possible the fusion between the fragmenting peasant classes and the proletariat. Therefore, in order to have modern subversion, that is, a rebellion as the first stage of a continuous revolutionary process, it is necessary for there to be a fusion of rebellious elements from among the non-proletarianised people with the proletarianised people, under the leadership of the factory proletariat and its ideology. There is an intense class struggle between ideas which come from the non-proletarianised people and those which come from the proletariat: the latter must be in command. The looter who joins the

Red Army must give up looting. At the beginning he was executed on the spot for stealing a single sewing needle belonging to a peasant. In other words, the fusion only develops with the setting up of rules, of a dictatorship. To return to my very first example, acts of popular justice coming from all the various strata of the people who have been subjected to material and emotional suffering at the hands of class enemies, do not develop into a broad movement which advances the cause of the revolution in ideology or in practice unless they are brought under a system of rules. This is why a state apparatus develops, an apparatus which derives from the masses of the people but which, in a certain way, becomes detached from them (which is not to say that it becomes cut off from them). And this apparatus, in a certain way, has the role of arbitrator, not between the masses and the class enemy, but between the warring ideas among the masses, with the aim of resolving the contradictions among the masses, so that the overall battle against the class enemy may be as effective, as focussed as possible.

Thus in periods of proletarian revolution it always comes about that a state apparatus of a revolutionary kind is set up, between the masses and the class enemy, of course always with the possibility that this apparatus might become repressive in relation to the masses. Therefore there would never be people's courts without these courts being controlled by the people, and hence the possibility of their being challenged by the masses.

FOUCAULT: I would like to respond to you on two points. You say that it is under the leadership of the proletariat that the non-proletarianised people will join in the revolutionary battle. I entirely agree. But when you say that this happens under the leadership of *the ideology of the proletariat*, then I want to ask you what you mean by the ideology of the proletariat.

VICTOR: I mean, by that, the thought of Mao Tse-tung.

FOUCAULT: Fine. But you will grant me that what is thought by the mass of the French proletariat is not the thought of Mao Tse-Tung and it is not necessarily a revolutionary ideology. Moreover, you say that there must be a revolutionary state apparatus in order to regulate this new unity between the proletariat and the marginalised people. Agreed, but you will also grant me that the forms of state apparatus which we inherit from the bourgeois apparatus cannot in any way serve as a model for the new forms of organisation. The court, dragging along with it the ideology of bourgeois justice and those forms of relations between judge and judged, between judge and the parties to the action, between judge and litigant, which typify bourgeois justice, seems to me to have played a very significant role in the domination of the bourgeoisie. When we talk about courts we're talking about a place where the struggle between the contending forces is willy-nilly suspended: where in every case the decision arrived at is not the outcome of this struggle but of the intervention of an authority which necessarily stands above and is foreign to the contending forces, an authority which is in a position of neutrality between them and consequently can and must in every case decide which party to the dispute has justice on its side. The court implies, therefore, that there are categories which are common to the parties present (penal categories such as theft, fraud; moral categories such as honesty and dishonesty) and that the parties to the dispute agree to submit to them. Now, it is all this that the bourgeoisie wants to have believed in relation to justice, to its justice. All these ideas are weapons which the bourgeoisie has put to use in its exercise of power. This is why I find the idea of a people's court difficult to accept, especially if intellectuals must play the roles of prosecutor or judge in it, because it is precisely the intellectuals who have been the intermediaries in the bourgeoisie's spreading and imposing of the ideological themes that I'm talking about.

This justice must therefore be the target of the ideological struggle of the proletariat, and of the non-proletarianised people: thus the forms of this justice must be treated with the very greatest suspicion by the new revolutionary state apparatus. There are two forms which must not under any circumstances be adopted by this revolutionary apparatus: bureaucracy and judicial apparatus. Just as there must be no bureaucracy in it, so there must be no court in it. The court is the bureaucracy of the law. If you bureaucratise popular justice then you give it the form of a court.

VICTOR: Then how is it to be regularised?

FOUCAULT: I'll reply to that by what is, of course, an evasion: it remains to be discovered. The masses—proletarian and non-proletarian—have suffered too much over the centuries from this judicial system for its old form to be reimposed upon them, even with a new content. They have struggled since the Middle Ages against this system of justice. After all, the French Revolution was a rebellion against the judiciary. The first thing that it got rid of was the judicial apparatus. The Commune was also profoundly against the judicial system.

The masses will discover a way of dealing with the problem of their enemies, of those who individually or collectively have harmed them, methods of retribution which will range from punishment to reeducation, without involving the form of the court which—in any case in our society, I don't know about China—is to be avoided.

This is why I was against the people's court as a solemn form, designed to synthesise, to replace, all other forms of struggle against the judicial system. This seemed to me to re-legitimate a form which drags along with it too much of the ideology imposed by the bourgeoisie, with the divisions which result from this between the proletariat and the non-proletarianised people. At the present time it is a dangerous weapon because it will act as a precedent, and will be dangerous later on, within a revolutionary state apparatus, because forms of legal proceedings will be subtly introduced into it which will threaten to reestablish these divisions.

VICTOR: I'm going to reply to you in a provocative way. It is likely that socialism will invent something different from the assembly-line. So if someone were to say 'put Dreyfus[4] on the assembly-line' this would be a politically inventive idea because Dreyfus doesn't work on the assembly-line, but it would be an invention heavily influenced by the past (the assembly-line). The moral is Marx's old idea: the new is born from the old.

You say, 'The masses will discover something'. But at the present time there is a practical problem to be solved. I agree that all the *forms* of the procedures of popular justice would need to be new, that there would no longer be either the bench or the robe. What remains is a regulatory instance. It is this that we call the people's court.

FOUCAULT: If you define the people's court as a regulatory instance—I would prefer to say, an instance of political elucidation—on the basis of which acts of popular justice can be integrated with the overall political line of the proletariat, then I entirely agree. But I feel some difficulty in calling such an institution a 'court'.

I think, just as you do, that acts of justice by which the class enemy is repaid cannot be limited to a kind of thoughtless, instant spontaneity, unintegrated into an over-all struggle. It is necessary to find forms through which this need for retribution, which is in fact real among the masses, can be developed, by discussion, by information . . . . In any case, the court, with its triple division into two disputing parties and the neutral institution, which comes to decisions on the basis of some concept of justice which exists in and for itself, seems to me a particularly disastrous model for the clarification and political development of popular justice.

VICTOR: If a States General were convened tomorrow, where all groups of citizens involved in struggles were to be represented (groups such as action committees, anti-racialism committees, committees for the investigation of the prisons, and so on, in short all those who happen to be at present representatives of the people, the people in the Marxist sense of the term) would you be against this on the grounds that it invoked an old model?

FOUCAULT: The States General have often enough at least functioned as an instrument, not of course of proletarian revolution, but of the bourgeois revolution, but we well know that there were revolutionary processes in the wake of this bourgeois revolution. After the States General of 1357 there was the peasant uprising; after 1789 there was 1793. Consequently this might be a good model. On the other hand, it seems to me that the bourgeois judicial system has always operated to increase oppositions between the proletariat and the non-proletarianised people. This is the reason that it is a bad instrument, not because it is old.

The very form of the court contains the statement to the two parties, 'Before the proceedings your case is neither just nor unjust. It will only be so on the day when I pronounce it so, because I will have consulted the law or the canons of eternal equity'. This is the very essence of the court, and it is in complete contradiction with the point of view of popular justice.

GILLES: The court says two things: 'There is a problem'. And then, 'Being a third party *I* will make a decision about this problem, etc.'. The problem is that the power to exercise justice is in the hands of forces which work against popular unity. This is why it is necessary for there to be a representation of this popular unity when it comes to exercise justice.

FOUCAULT: Do you mean that popular unity must represent and make manifest that it has—provisionally or definitively—taken possession of the power to judge?

GILLES: I mean that the question of the court at Lens[5] was not settled exclusively by the miners and the *Houillières* (National Coal Board). It was a matter which concerned all the popular classes.

FOUCAULT: The necessity that unity be affirmed does not have to take the form of a court. I would even say—though perhaps the analogy is a bit strained—that the court sets up again a kind of division of labour. There are those who judge—or who pretend to judge—with total tranquillity, without being in any way involved. This re-inforces the idea that for judicial proceedings to be just they must be conducted by someone who can remain quite detached, by an intellectual, an expert in the realm of ideas. When, into the bargain, the people's court is organised or presided over by intellectuals, who come along to hear what on the one hand the workers and on the other hand the bosses have got to say, and to pronounce: 'This one is innocent, that one guilty', then the whole thing is infused with idealism. When it comes to proposing this as a general model of what popular justice should be like, I'm afraid that the worst possible model has been picked.

VICTOR: I would like us to summarise the results of our discussion. The first conclusion is this: an act of popular justice is an action carried out by the masses—a homogeneous fraction of the people—against their immediate enemy identified as such . . . .

FOUCAULT: . . . In response to some specific injury.

VICTOR: The full range of present-day acts of popular justice includes all those subversive actions which are at the present time being led by the various strata among the people.

Second conclusion: the transition of popular justice to a higher form presupposes the setting up of regulations which aim to resolve the contradictions among the people, to distinguish between authentic cases of justice and cases which are merely settling of accounts, which can be manipulated by the enemy so as to discredit popular justice, to fracture the unity of the masses, thereby to impede the revolutionary movement. Do we agree?

FOUCAULT: Not quite when it comes to talking about regulations. I would prefer to say that an act of popular justice cannot achieve its full significance unless it is clarified politically, under the supervision of the masses themselves.

VICTOR: Acts of popular justice enable the people to start to seize power when they take place within the context of a coherent overall line, that is, when they are under political command, on condition that this political leadership is not external to the mass movement, and that the popular masses are unified around it. This is what I mean by the setting up of regulations, the setting up of new state apparatuses.

FOUCAULT: Imagine that in some factory or other there is a conflict between a worker and one of the bosses, and that this worker suggests to his comrades that some retribution is called for. This would not be a real act of popular justice unless the target and the potential outcome were integrated into the overall political struggle of the workers in that factory . . . .

VICTOR: Yes, but in the first place it must be that the action is a *just* one. This presupposes that all the workers agree that this boss is a sod.

FOUCAULT: This assumes that there will be discussion among the workers and a collective decision, before any action is taken. I can't see any embryonic state apparatus here, and yet we've gone from some particular demand for retribution to an act of popular justice.

VICTOR: It's a matter of stages. First there is rebellion, following that there is uprising, and finally revolution. What you are saying is correct for the first stage.

FOUCAULT: I had got the impression that you thought that only the existence of a state apparatus could change a desire for retribution into an act of popular justice.

VICTOR: At the second stage. At the first stage of the ideological revolution I'm in favour of looting, I'm in favour of 'excesses'. The stick must be bent in the other direction, and the world cannot be turned upside down without breaking eggs . . . .

FOUCAULT: Above all it is essential that the stick be broken . . . .

VICTOR: That comes later. At the beginning you say, 'Put Dreyfus on the assembly-line', later on you break the assembly-line system. At the first stage there can be an act of retribution against a boss which is an act of popular justice, even if not everyone in the workshop agrees with it, because there are informers and creeps, and even a small handful of workers who are shocked by the idea: 'He is the boss after all'. Even if things go too far, if he gets three months in hospital when he really only deserved two, it is still an act of popular justice. But when all these actions take the form of a movement, of the growth of popular justice— which for me only makes sense with the constitution of a people's army— then you have the setting up of regulations, of a revolutionary state apparatus.

FOUCAULT: I understand perfectly as far as the stage of armed struggle is concerned, but I'm not so sure that after-wards it will be so absolutely necessary for there to be a state judicial apparatus in order for the people to perform acts of justice. The danger is that a state judicial apparatus would take over acts of popular justice.

VICTOR: Let's restrict ourselves to questions which confront us here and now. Let's not talk about people's courts in France during a period of armed struggle, but about the stage we are actually at, that of ideological revolution. One thing that is typical of this is that as a result of rebellions there is an increase in acts of subversion, of justice, of real alternative power. And these are instances of alternative power in the strict sense, that is, where things are turned upside down, with that profoundly subversive message that it is we who are really powerful, that it is us who are setting things right way up, and that it is the world as it exists at present which is upside down.

What I say is that one kind of creation of alternative power among all the others is this, the setting up of people's courts in the place of bourgeois courts. In what context would this be justified? Not for the carrying out of acts of justice within a workshop, where there is an immediate confrontation between the masses and the class enemy. As long as the masses are mobilised to struggle against this enemy then justice can be carried out directly. The boss is judged, but there is no court. There are the two opponents and things are settled between them, and this involves ideological values; we're in the right, he's a sod. To say: 'He's a sod', is to assert a value which, in a way, makes reference to the system of bourgeois values (the hooligans against the honest people) but only in order to subvert it. This is how it would be understood at the level of the masses.

In the context of a city, where the masses are heterogeneous and where they must be unified by an idea—for example, the idea of judging the police—where, therefore, the truth has to be won, where the unity of the people has to be won, there it could be an excellent way of creating alternative power to set up a people's court to challenge the constant collusion between the police and the courts which legitimate their dirty work.

FOUCAULT: You are saying that it is a victory to exercise alternative power in opposition to, in the place of, an existing power. When Renault workers grab a foreman and stick him underneath a car and tell him, 'You're going to have to tighten the bolts yourself', this is fine. They are actually exercising alternative power. But when it comes to the courts we must ask two questions. What would it amount to exactly to exercise alternative power over the judicial system? And, what is the real power that is exercised in a people's court like that at Lens?

The struggle in relation to the judicial system can take various forms. Firstly it can be played according to its own rules. For example, one can sue the police. This is obviously not an act of popular justice, it is bourgeois justice caught in a trap. Secondly, one can conduct guerrilla operations against the power of the judicial system and prevent it from being exercised: for example, escaping from the police, heckling in the courts, demanding that a judge be made to account for what he's done. These are all anti-judicial operations, but they are still not a counter-justice. A *counter-justice* would be one that enabled one to put into operation, in relation to some person who would in the normal course of events get away with what he's done, some kind of judicial proceedings (that is, to seize him, bring him before a court, persuade a judge, who would judge him by reference to certain forms of equity, and who would effectively sentence him to some punishment which the person would be compelled to undergo). In this way one would precisely be *taking the place* of the judicial system.

In a court like that at Lens there was no real exercise of alternative judicial power but primarily of the power to disseminate information. Information which had been withheld from the masses was seized from the bourgeoisie, from the colliery management, from the technical staff. Secondly, the means for distributing information is in the hands of those in power, and the people's court made it possible to break this monopoly on information. So two important kinds of power were put into effect here, the power of knowledge of the truth and the power to disseminate this knowledge. This is very important, but it is not the same as the power to judge. The ritual form of the court was not in reality a true expression of the powers that were exercised. Now when a kind of power is exercised, the manner in which it is exercised—which must be visible, solemn, symbolic— must only refer us to that kind of power which is exercised in reality and not to some other kind of power which is not exercised in reality at that particular time.

VICTOR: Your example of *counter-justice* is completely idealist.

FOUCAULT: Exactly; I think that it is impossible for there to be a counter-justice in the strict sense. The judicial system as it operates, as a state apparatus, can only have the function of dividing the masses: therefore the idea of a proletarian counter-justice is a contradiction; there can be no such thing.

VICTOR: If we consider the court at Lens, in fact the most important thing was not the seizure of the power of knowledge and its dissemination. It was that the idea 'Colliery owners, murderers' became a powerful idea, which took the place in people's minds of the idea 'The blokes who threw the Molotov cocktails are the guilty ones'. I maintain that this power to pronounce an unenforceable sentence is a real power, which has its material expression in an ideological transformation in the minds of those people to whom it is addressed. It is not a judicial power, this goes without saying; it is ridiculous to imagine a counter-justice because there can be no such thing as a counter-judicial power. But there is a counter-tribunal which can operate effectively at the level of the revolution in people's minds.

FOUCAULT: I accept that the Lens court expressed one of the forms of anti-judicial struggle. It played an important role. In fact it took place at the very same time that another trial was going on, in which the bourgeoisie was exercising its power to judge, as it really can exercise it. At a single time it was possible to take word-by-word, fact-by-fact, everything that was said at this court in order to expose what was really going on. The court at Lens was the inverse of what was going on in the bourgeois court: what was black in the latter was made to look white by the former. This does seem to me a perfectly appropriate form for getting to know and to familiarise people with what really goes on in the factories on the one hand and in the courts on the other. It is an excellent means of informing people about the way that justice is exercised in relation to the working class.

VICTOR: So we agree on a third point: conducting a counter-trial, a people's court, in the very specific sense of one that operates as the inverse of the bourgeois court, as what the bourgeois press calls a 'parody of justice', is the exercise of a counter-power.

FOUCAULT: I do not think that the three theses which you have put forward adequately represent the discussion, or the points on which we are in agreement. For my part, the idea that I wanted to introduce into the discussion is that the bourgeois judicial state apparatus, of which the visible, symbolic form is the court, has the basic function of introducing and augmenting contradictions among the masses, principally between the proletariat and the non-proletarianised people, and that it follows from this that the forms of this judicial system, and the ideology which is associated with them, must become the target of our present struggle. And moral ideology—for what are our moral values but those which are over and over again associated with and re-confirmed by the decisions of the courts—this moral ideology, just like the forms of justice operated by the bourgeois apparatus, must be submitted to the scrutiny of the most rigorous criticism . . . .

VICTOR: But there can be created a counter-power in relation to morality as well: 'the real thief is not who you think he is . . .'.

FOUCAULT: Here the problem becomes very difficult. It is from the point of view of property that there are thieves and stealing. I would like to say in conclusion that re-employing a form like that of the court, with all that is implied in it— the third-party place of the judge, reference to a law or to impartiality, effective sentencing—must also be subjected to very rigorous criticism; and, for my part, I cannot see using this form as valid except in a case where one can, in parallel with a bourgeois trial, conduct an alternative trial which can expose as lies what is taken as truth in the former, and its decisions as an abuse of power. Apart from this situation, I can see thousands of possibilities on the one hand for anti-judicial guerrilla operations, and on the other hand for acts of popular justice; but neither of these involve using the form of the court.

VICTOR: I think we are in agreement about the interpretation of actual practices. But perhaps we have not really got to the bottom of our philosophical differences . . . .

5 February 1972

Notes

1 F. Engels, *The Condition of the English Working Class*, Chapter 11.
2 A *lycée* student arrested in Paris in February 1971 during a demonstration against the prisons.
3 A Gaullist deputy charged with fraudulent property speculations and saved from prison by his parliamentary immunity.
4 Managing Director of Renault.
5 A coal-mining town in Northern France where a group of Maoists, together with Jean-Paul Sartre, set up a people's court after a mining disaster to investigate the management's responsibility for the casualties.

2 PRISON TALK

Interviewer: J.-J. Brochier.

> One of the concerns of *Discipline and Punish* is to criticise certain blank areas in historical studies. You remark for instance that no one has ever written, or even thought of writing the history of the practice of examining. This is hard to believe.

Historians, like philosophers and literary historians, have been accustomed to a history which takes in only the summits, the great events. But today, unlike the others, historians are becoming more willing to handle 'ignoble' materials. The emergence of this plebeian element in history dates back fifty years or more. This means that I have fewer problems about talking to historians. You would never hear a historian say what someone or other wrote about Buffon and Ricardo in an incredible journal called *Raison Présente*: 'Foucault concerns himself only with mediocrities'!

> In your study of the prisons, you seem to regret the absence of a certain kind of source material, of monographs on particular prisons, for instance.

At the moment, people are returning increasingly to the monograph form, but no longer so much in terms of studying a particular object as of rendering apparent the point at which a certain type of discourse is produced and formed. What would it signify today to write a study of a particular prison or psychiatric hospital? Hundreds of such studies were written in the nineteenth century, mostly of hospitals, dealing with the histories of the institutions, chronologies of their directors, and so forth. Today, writing a monograph history of a hospital would involve making the

whole archive of the hospital emerge in the movement of its
formation as a discourse in the process of constituting itself,
and interacting at the same time with the development of
the hospital and its institutions, inflecting and reforming
them. What one would thus try to reconstitute would be the
enmeshing of a discourse in the historical process, rather on
the lines of what Faye has done with totalitarian discourse.[1]

Establishing a corpus of source data does indeed pose a
problem for my research, but this is undoubtedly a different
problem from the one encountered in linguistics, for
example. With linguistic or mythological investigations it is
first necessary to take a certain corpus, define it and
establish its criteria of constitution. In the much more fluid
area that I am studying, the corpus is in a sense undefined: it
will never be possible to constitute the ensemble of discourses on madness as a unity, even by restricting oneself to
a given country or period. With the prisons there would be
no sense in limiting oneself to discourses *about* prisons; just
as important are the discourses which arise within the
prison, the decisions and regulations which are among its
constitutive elements, its means of functioning, along with
its strategies, its covert discourses and ruses, ruses which are
not ultimately played *by* any particular person, but which
are none the less lived, and assure the permanence and
functioning of the institution. All of this has to be brought
together and made visible by the historian. And in my view
this task consists rather in making all these discourses visible
in their strategic connections than in constituting them as
unities, to the exclusion of all other forms of discourse.

> You determine one moment as being central in the
> history of repression: the transition from the inflicting
> of penalties to the imposition of surveillance.

That's correct—the moment where it became understood
that it was more efficient and profitable in terms of the
economy of power to place people under surveillance than
to subject them to some exemplary penalty. This moment in
time corresponds to the formation, gradual in some respects
and rapid in others, of a new mode of exercise of power in
the eighteenth and early nineteenth centuries. We all know

about the great upheavals, the institutional changes which
constitute a change of political regime, the way in which the
delegation of power right to the top of the state system is
modified. But in thinking of the mechanisms of power, I am
thinking rather of its capillary form of existence, the point
where power reaches into the very grain of individuals,
touches their bodies and inserts itself into their actions and
attitudes, their discourses, learning processes and everyday
lives. The eighteenth century invented, so to speak, a
synaptic regime of power, a regime of its exercise *within* the
social body, rather than *from above* it. The change in official
forms of political power was linked to this process, but only
via intervening shifts and displacements. This more-or-less
coherent modification in the small-scale modes of exercise
of power was made possible only by a fundamental structural
change. It was the instituting of this new local, capillary form
of power which impelled society to eliminate certain
elements such as the court and the king. The mythology of
the sovereign was no longer possible once a certain kind of
power was being exercised within the social body. The
sovereign then became a fantastic personage, at once
archaic and monstrous.

Thus there is a certain correlation between the two
processes, global and local, but not an absolute one. In
England the same capillary modification of power occurred
as in France. But there the person of the king, for example,
was displaced within the system of political representations,
rather than eliminated. Hence one can't say that the change
at the capillary level of power is absolutely tied to institutional changes at the level of the centralised forms of
the State.

> You show that as soon as the prison was constituted in
> its form as surveillance, it began to secrete its own raw
> material, namely delinquence.

My hypothesis is that the prison was linked from its
beginning to a project for the transformation of individuals.
People tend to suppose that the prison was a kind of refuse-
dump for criminals, a dump whose disadvantages became
apparent during use, giving rise to the conviction that the

prisons must be reformed and made into means of transforming individuals. But this is not true: such texts, programmes and statements of intention were there from the beginning. The prison was meant to be an instrument, comparable with—and no less perfect than—the school, the barracks, or the hospital, acting with precision upon its individual subjects.

The failure of the project was immediate, and was realised virtually from the start. In 1820 it was already understood that the prisons, far from transforming criminals into honest citizens, serve only to manufacture new criminals and to drive existing criminals even deeper into criminality. It was then that there took place, as always in the mechanics of power, a strategic utilisation of what had been experienced as a drawback. Prisons manufactured delinquents, but delinquents turned out to be useful, in the economic domain as much as the political. Criminals come in handy. For example, because of the profits that can be made out of the exploitation of sexual pleasure, we find the establishment in the nineteenth century of the great prostitution business, which was possible only thanks to the delinquents who served as the medium for the capitalisation of everyday, paid-for sexual pleasure.

Another example: everyone knows that Napoleon III was able to seize power only with the help of a group consisting, at least on its lower levels, of common-law criminals. And one only needs to see the workers' fear and hatred of criminals during the nineteenth century to understand that the criminals were being used against them, in social and political struggles, as agents of surveillance and infiltration, preventing and breaking strikes, and so forth.

So the Americans in the twentieth century weren't the first to use the Mafia for this sort of job?

Absolutely not.

There was the problem of penal labour as well: workers feared the undermining of their wages by competition from cheap prison labour.

Perhaps. But I wonder whether the issue of penal labour was not orchestrated precisely so as to constitute this hostility between delinquents and workers which was of such importance for the general workings of the system. What worried the bourgeoisie was the kind of amiable, tolerated illegality that was known in the eighteenth century. One should be careful not to exaggerate this: criminal punishments in the eighteenth century were of great ferocity. But it is nonetheless true that criminals, certain of them at least, were perfectly tolerated by the population. There was no autonomous criminal class. A man like Mandrin[2] was received wherever he went, by bourgeoisie and aristocracy as well as peasantry, and protected by all. But once capitalism had physically entrusted wealth, in the form of raw materials and means of production, to popular hands, it became absolutely essential to protect this wealth. Because industrial society requires that wealth be directly in the hands, not of its owners, but of those whose labour, by putting that wealth to work, enables a profit to be made from it. How was this wealth to be protected? By a rigorous morality, of course: hence the formidable layer of moral-isation deposited on the nineteenth-century population. Look at the immense campaigns to christianise the workers during this period. It was absolutely necessary to constitute the populace as a moral subject and to break its commerce with criminality, and hence to segregate the delinquents and to show them to be dangerous not only for the rich but for the poor as well, vice-ridden instigators of the gravest social perils. Hence also the birth of detective literature and the importance of the *faits divers*, the horrific newspaper crime stories.

You show that the poorer classes were the principal victims of crime.

And the more they were its victims, the more they feared it.

But criminals were recruited from among these classes.

Yes, and the prisons were the great instrument of recruit-ment. The moment someone went to prison a mechanism came into operation that stripped him of his civil status, and when he came out he could do nothing except become a criminal once again. He inevitably fell into the hands of a system which made him either a pimp, a policeman or an informer. Prison professionalised people. Instead of having nomadic bands of robbers— often of great ferocity— roaming about the countryside, as in the eighteenth century, one had this closed milieu of delinquency, thoroughly structured by the police: an essentially urban milieu, and one whose political and economic value was far from negligible.

> You rightly remark that penal labour has the peculiarity of being useless. One wonders then what its role can be in the general economy.

As it was initially conceived, penal labour was an apprenticeship not so much in this or that trade as in the virtues of labour itself. Pointless work, work for work's sake, was intended to shape individuals into the image of the ideal labourer. It was a chimera, perhaps, but one which had been perfectly worked out and defined by the American Quakers, with the founding of the workhouses, and by the Dutch. But then, from the late 1830s, it became clear that in fact the aim was not to retrain delinquents, to make them virtuous, but to regroup them within a clearly demarcated, card-indexed milieu which could serve as a tool for economic or political ends. The problem thereafter was not to teach the prisoners something, but rather to teach them nothing, so as to make sure that they could do nothing when they came out of prison. The futile character of penal labour, which was linked initially to a didactic plan, now came to serve a different strategy.

> Don't you find it striking that today people are returning from the schema of crime as delinquency to crime as an infraction, an illegality, reversing, that is, the course taken in the eighteenth century?

I believe that the great intolerance of the population for the delinquent, which the morality and politics of the nineteenth century set out to establish, is in fact now being eroded.

Certain forms of illegality or irregularity are becoming more and more accepted: not just those which were previously tolerated and accepted, such as fiscal and financial irregularities, things which the bourgeoisie had been able to get along with on the best of terms, but also the sort of irregularity that consists, for example, in stealing something from a shop.

> But isn't it because everyone has got to know about the first kind of irregularities, the fiscal and financial ones, that the general attitude to 'minor irregularities' has changed? Some time ago, *Le Monde* published statistics comparing the considerable economic damage caused by the first kind of offences and the small number of months or years of imprisonment with which they were punished, and the small amount of economic damage caused by the other sort of offences (including violent crimes such as hold-ups) and the substantial number of years of prison given the offenders. The article expressed a sense of scandal at this disparity.

This is a delicate issue, one which is currently under discussion among the ex-prisoners' groups. It is quite true that in popular consciousness, and also in the present economic system, a certain margin of illegality is not seen as a serious problem, but rather as perfectly tolerable. In America, people know that hold-ups are a permanent business risk for big stores. They work out roughly what it costs, and find that the cost of an effective surveillance and security system would be too high, and thus uneconomical. They leave things as they are. The insurance pays for it, it's all just part of the system.

Regarding this sort of illegality, which seems to be spreading, are we dealing with a questioning of the line of demarcation between tolerable, tolerated breaches of the law and serious crimes, or is this not rather a simple relaxation on the part of the system which, aware of its own solidity, can afford to accept at its margins something which after all poses absolutely no threat to it?

There has also clearly been a change in people's attitude to wealth. The bourgeoisie no longer has that proprietorial attitude to wealth which it had in the nineteenth century. Wealth is no longer what one possesses, but what one makes a profit out of. The accelerating flow of wealth, its ever-growing power of circulation, the abandonment of hoarding, the practice of credit, the decrease in the importance of landed wealth: all these factors tend to make theft seem no more scandalous to people than confidence tricks or tax evasion.

> There has also been another change. In discourses about crime, the straightforward condemnation of the nineteenth century: 'He steals because he is evil', has given way to explanation: 'He steals because he is poor', and also to the attitude that it is worse to steal when one is rich than when one is poor.

True. If that were all, perhaps one could feel confident and hopeful. But along with that, isn't there an explanatory discourse that involves a number of dangers? He steals because he is poor, certainly, but we all know that all poor people don't steal. So for this individual to steal there has to be something wrong with him, and this is his character, his psyche, his upbringing, his unconscious, his desires. And with that the delinquent is handed over either to the penal technology of the prison or the medical technology, if not of the asylum then of specialised supervision.

> The link you establish between penal and medical techniques and modes of repression may upset some people.

Well, maybe fifteen years ago it was still scandalous to say things like that. I've noticed that even today the psychiatrists still have not forgiven me for *Madness and Civilisation*. Not a fortnight ago I received yet another abusive letter. But I think today this sort of analysis is much more readily accepted, whatever offence it may still give, above all, to the psychiatrists who have been dragging their bad consciences around for so long.

> You show that the medical system has always served as an auxiliary to the penal system, even today when the

psychiatrist collaborates with the judge, the court and the prison. But perhaps this is unjust to some of the younger doctors who have tried to free themselves from this complicity.

Perhaps. Anyway, I was only trying to mark out a few paths in *Discipline and Punish*. At the moment I'm preparing a work on the role of psychiatric experts in penal matters. I intend to publish some dossiers, of which some go back to the nineteenth century but others are more contemporary, and are quite stupefying.

You distinguish between two sorts of criminality, one which ends up in the police and the other which lapses into aesthetics: Vidocq and Lacenaire.

I ended my analysis with these crucial years, the 1840s. It was then that the long cohabitation of the police and criminality began. The first assessments had been drawn up of the failure of the prison, people knew that it didn't reform, but on the contrary manufactured criminals and criminality, and this was the moment when the benefits accrued from this process of production were also discovered. Criminals can be put to good use, if only to keep other criminals under surveillance. Vidocq[3] is very characteristic of this. He came out of the eighteenth century and the Revolutionary and Imperial periods, in which he was for a while a smuggler, a pimp, and then a deserter. He was one of those nomads who circulated through towns, the country and the army. It was the old style of criminality. Then he became absorbed into the system. Sent to forced labour, he emerged as an informer, became a policeman, and ended up as head of a detective force. And, on a symbolic level, he is the first great criminal to have been used *as* a criminal by the apparatus of power.

As for Lacenaire,[4] he is the token of another phenomenon, different from but related to the first, that of the aesthetic or literary interest beginning to be felt in crime: the aesthetic cult of crime. Until the eighteenth century, crimes were only celebrated in two modes: a literary mode when, and because, they were the crimes of a king, and a popular mode, found in the broadsheets which narrate the exploits of Mandrin or of some great murderer. There are these two completely separate genres.

Then, around 1840, there appears the figure of the criminal hero who is a hero because he is a criminal, and is neither aristocratic nor plebeian. The bourgeoisie begins to produce its own criminal heroes. This is at the same moment when the separation is effected between criminals and the popular classes: the criminal cannot be allowed to be a popular hero, he must be an enemy of the poor. The bourgeoisie constitutes for itself an aesthetic in which crime no longer belongs to the people, but is one of those fine arts of which the bourgeoisie alone is capable. Lacenaire is the model of this new kind of criminal. True, his parents have been guilty of certain misdeeds, but he has been properly brought up, has been to school and has learned to read and write. This enables him to act as a leader in his milieu. The way he talks about other criminals is typical. They are brutal animals, cowards and incompetents; he, Lacenaire, is the cold, lucid brain. Thus the new hero is created, displaying all the signs and tokens of the bourgeoisie. That leads us in turn to Gaboriau and the detective story, in which the criminal is always of bourgeois origins. You never find a working class hero in nineteenth-century detective novels. The criminal is always intelligent, playing a sort of game on equal terms with the police. What is funny is that in reality Lacenaire was pathetic, ridiculous and inept. He always dreamed of killing, but never got as far as doing it. The one thing he could do was blackmail the homosexuals he picked up in the Bois de Boulogne. The only real crime he committed was a bit of dirty business with a little old man in prison. If Lacenaire came within a hair's breadth of being killed by his fellow forced-labour convicts, it was because they thought, no doubt with good reason, that he was an informer.

When you say criminals are useful, couldn't it be argued that many people view crime more as part of the nature of things than as a politico-economic necessity? It might appear that for an industrial society criminals are a less socially useful resource than working-class labour power?

In the 1840s, unemployment and short-time working were fixed economic conditions. There was a surplus of labour-power.

But to think that crime was part of the order of things was part of the cynical intelligence of nineteenth-century bourgeois thought. One had to be as naive as Baudelaire to think that the bourgeoisie is stupid or prudish. Rather it is intelligent and cynical. You only need to read what it said about itself and, better still, what it said about others.

At the end of the eighteenth century, people dreamed of a society without crime. And then the dream evaporated. Crime was too useful for them to dream of anything as crazy —or ultimately as dangerous—as a society without crime. No crime means no police. What makes the presence and control of the police tolerable for the population, if not fear of the criminal? This institution of the police, which is so recent and so oppressive, is only justified by that fear. If we accept the presence in our midst of these uniformed men, who have the exclusive right to carry arms, who demand our papers, who come and prowl on our doorsteps, how would any of this be possible if there were no criminals? And if there weren't articles every day in the newspapers telling us how numerous and dangerous our criminals are?

> You are very hard on criminology, its 'garrulous discourse', its 'endless repetitions'.

Have you ever read any criminological texts? They are staggering. And I say this out of astonishment, not aggressiveness, because I fail to comprehend how the discourse of criminology has been able to go on at this level. One has the impression that it is of such utility, is needed so urgently and rendered so vital for the working of the system, that it does not even need to seek a theoretical justification for itself, or even simply a coherent framework. It is entirely utilitarian. I think one needs to investigate why such a 'learned' discourse became so indispensable to the functioning of the nineteenth-century penal system. What made it necessary was the alibi, employed since the eighteenth century, that if one imposes a penalty on somebody this is not in order to punish what he has done, but to transform what he is. From this point, a penal judgment, in other words saying to someone 'We'll cut off your head, or put you in prison, or just fine you because you have done this or that', is an act which no longer has any meaning. Once you suppress the idea of vengeance, which previously was the act of a sovereign threatened in his very sovereignty by the crime, punishment can only have a meaning within a technology of reform. And judges themselves have gradually made the shift, without wanting to and without even taking cognizance of the fact, from a verdict which still retained punitive connotations to one which they cannot justify in their own vocabulary except on the condition of its being transformatory of the person condemned. Yet they know perfectly well that the instruments available to them, the death penalty, formerly the penal colonies, today imprisonment, don't transform anyone. Hence there is the necessity to call on those who produce a discourse on crime and criminals which will justify the measures in question.

> In short, criminological discourse is only useful for giving judges a semblance of good conscience?

Yes: or rather it is indispensable in enabling them to judge.

> In your book on Pierre Rivière,[5] it is a criminal who does the speaking and writing. But, unlike Lacenaire, he carried his crime through to the end. First of all, how did you come upon this astonishing text?

By chance, while systematically working through penal reports by medico-legal and psychiatric experts published in professional journals of the nineteenth and twentieth centuries.

> Isn't it extremely rare for an illiterate, or barely literate peasant to take the trouble to write forty pages narrating and explaining his crime?

It's a totally strange story. It can however be said, and this is what struck me, that in such circumstances writing one's life story, one's recollections and experiences, was a practice found in a fair number of cases, and particularly in the prisons. Someone called Appert, one of the first philanthropists to visit a large number of penal colonies and prisons, got some prisoners to write their memoirs and subsequently published some fragments of these. In America one also finds judges and doctors doing this. It was the first great burst of curiosity about the individuals whom it was desired to transform and for the sake of whose transformation it was necessary to acquire a certain *savoir*, a certain technique. This curiosity about the criminal certainly did not exist in the eighteenth century, when it was simply a matter of knowing whether the person accused had really done what he was accused of; once that was established, the tariff was fixed.

The question, 'What is this individual who has committed this crime?', is a new question. But this does not suffice for explaining the story of Pierre Rivière, because Rivière makes it clear that he had tried to begin writing his memoir even before committing his crime.

In this book we didn't want to conduct any kind of analysis of Rivière, whether psychological, psychoanalytical or linguistic, but rather to render visible the medical and juridical mechanisms that surrounded the story. The rest we leave to the psychoanalysts and criminologists. But what is astonishing is that this text, which left the experts silent at the time, has struck them equally dumb today.

> I came across a sentence in *Madness and Civilisation* where you say that we must 'free historical chronologies and successive orderings from all forms of progressivist perspective'.

This is something I owe to the historians of science. I adopt the methodical precaution and the radical but unaggressive scepticism which makes it a principle not to regard the point in time where we are now standing as the outcome of a teleological progression which it would be one's business to reconstruct historically: that scepticism regarding ourselves and what we are, our here and now, which prevents one from assuming that what we have is better than—or more than—in the past. This doesn't mean not attempting to reconstruct generative processes, but that we must do this without imposing on them a positivity or a valorisation.

Even though science has long shared the postulate that man progresses?

It isn't science that says that, but rather the history of science. And I don't say that humanity doesn't progress. I say that it is a bad method to pose the problem as: 'How is it that we have progressed?'. The problem is: how do things happen? And what happens now is not necessarily better or more advanced, or better understood, than what happened in the past.

Your researches bear on things that are banal, or which have been made banal because they aren't *seen*. For instance I find it striking that prisons are in cities, and yet *no one sees them*. Or else, if one sees one, one wonders vaguely whether it's a prison, a school, a barracks or a hospital. Your book is an important event because it places before our eyes something that no one was previously able to see. This can in a sense be said as much of certain other very detailed recent studies, such as one made of the peasantry and the fiscal system in the Bas Languedoc during 1880–82, as of your study of a capital phenomenon like the prison which no one had looked at.

In a sense that is how history has always been studied. The making visible of what was previously unseen can sometimes be the effect of using a magnifying instrument. Instead of studying monarchical institutions from the sixteenth to the end of the eighteenth century, one can study exhaustively the institution of the Conseil d'En Haut from the death of Henri IV to the accession of Louis XIII. It's still the same domain of objects, but the object has been magnified. But to make visible the unseen can also mean a change of level, addressing oneself to a layer of material which had hitherto had no pertinence for history and which had not been recognised as having any moral, aesthetic, political or historical value. Today it's self-evident that methods of treating the insane form part of the history of Reason. But this wasn't self-evident fifty years ago when the history of Reason meant Plato, Descartes and Kant, or Archimedes, Galileo and Newton.

> But in your 'history of madness', there was still a sort of mirror-play, a simple antinomy between reason and unreason, which is absent when you now write, 'Histories are written of the congenitally blind, of wolf-children and of hypnosis. But who will write the history of the practice of examination, a history more general, more indefinite, but more determinate as well . . . . For in this simple technique there is involved a whole domain of knowledge and a whole species of power.'

Mechanisms of power in general have never been much studied by history. History has studied those who held power—anecdotal histories of kings and generals; contrasted with this there has been the history of economic processes and infrastructures. Again, distinct from this, we have had histories of institutions, of what has been viewed as a superstructural level in relation to the economy. But power in its strategies, at once general and detailed, and its mechanisms, has never been studied. What has been studied even less is the relation between power and knowledge, the articulation of each on the other. It has been a tradition for humanism to assume that once someone gains power he ceases to know. Power makes men mad, and those who govern are blind; only those who keep their distance from power, who are in no way implicated in tyranny, shut up in their Cartesian *poêle*, their room, their meditations, only they can discover the truth.

Now I have been trying to make visible the constant articulation I think there is of power on knowledge and of knowledge on power. We should not be content to say that power has a need for such-and-such a discovery, such-and-such a form of knowledge, but we should add that the exercise of power itself creates and causes to emerge new objects of knowledge and accumulates new bodies of information. One can understand nothing about economic science if one does not know how power and economic power are exercised in everyday life. The exercise of power perpetually creates knowledge and, conversely, knowledge constantly induces effects of power. The university hierarchy is only the most visible, the most sclerotic and least dangerous form of this phenomenon. One has to be really naive to imagine that the effects of power linked to knowledge have their culmination in university hierarchies. Diffused, entrenched and dangerous, they operate in other places than in the person of the old professor.

Modern humanism is therefore mistaken in drawing this line between knowledge and power. Knowledge and power are integrated with one another, and there is no point in dreaming of a time when knowledge will cease to depend on power; this is just a way of reviving humanism in a utopian guise. It is not possible for power to be exercised without knowledge, it is impossible for knowledge not to engender power. 'Liberate scientific research from the demands of monopoly capitalism': maybe it's a good slogan, but it will never be more than a slogan.

You seem to have kept your distance from Marx and Marxism; this was a reproach that was being addressed to you already about *The Archaeology of Knowledge*.

No doubt. But there is also a sort of game that I play with this. I often quote concepts, texts and phrases from Marx, but without feeling obliged to add the authenticating label of a footnote with a laudatory phrase to accompany the quotation. As long as one does that, one is regarded as someone who knows and reveres Marx, and will be suitably honoured in the so-called Marxist journals. But I quote Marx without saying so, without quotation marks, and because people are incapable of recognising Marx's texts I am thought to be someone who doesn't quote Marx. When a physicist writes a work of physics, does he feel it necessary to quote Newton and Einstein? He uses them, but he doesn't need the quotation marks, the footnote and the eulogistic comment to prove how completely he is being faithful to the master's thought. And because other physicists know what Einstein did, what he discovered and proved, they can recognise him in what the physicist writes. It is impossible at the present time to write history without using a whole range of concepts directly or indirectly linked to Marx's thought and situating oneself within a horizon of thought which has been defined and described by Marx. One might even wonder what difference there could ultimately be between being a historian and being a Marxist.

> So you would regard the term 'Marxist historian' as a pleonasm, as the film critic Astruc said about 'American cinema'?

More or less. And it's within this general horizon of thought defined and coded by Marx that the discussion must take its starting-point with those who call themselves Marxists because they play a game whose rules aren't Marxist but communistological, in other words defined by communist parties who decide how you must use Marx so as to be declared by them to be a Marxist.

> What about Nietzsche? It seems to me that his presence, diffuse but growing, has finally come to figure in contemporary thought over the last ten years or so as an opposition to the hegemony of Marx.

Nowadays I prefer to remain silent about Nietzsche. When I was teaching philosophy I often used to lecture on Nietzsche, but I wouldn't do that any more today. If I wanted to be pretentious, I would use 'the genealogy of morals' as the general title of what I am doing. It was Nietzsche who specified the power relation as the general focus, shall we say, of philosophical discourse — whereas for Marx it was the production relation. Nietzsche is the philosopher of power, a philosopher who managed to think of power without having to confine himself within a political theory in order to do so.
   Nietzsche's contemporary presence is increasingly important. But I am tired of people studying him only to produce the same kind of commentaries that are written on Hegel or Mallarmé. For myself, I prefer to utilise the writers I like. The only valid tribute to thought such as Nietzsche's

is precisely to use it, to deform it, to make it groan and protest. And if commentators then say that I am being faithful or unfaithful to Nietzsche, that is of absolutely no interest.

Notes

1 J. P. Faye, *Theorie du récit* and *Langages totalitaires* (Hermann, Paris, 1972).

2 Mandrin (1725–55), a celebrated bandit in Southern France. Specialised in robbing tax-farmers, noted for his respect for private property, successfully beat off several punitive expeditions.

3 Vidocq, freed from prison on the orders of the Prefect of Police in 1809 and placed in charge of a squad of ex-convict detectives. Dismissed from the police in 1832 on a theft charge. His exploits were fictionalised by Balzac and became celebrated through the publication of his memoirs (in both bogus and authentic versions).

4 Lacenaire's 'tranquil cynicism' at his trial is said to have impressed the 'romantic' Parisian public. His memoirs were published with great success prior to his execution in 1836.

5 M. Foucault (ed.), *I, Pierre Rivière* . . . , (Penguin Books, Harmondsworth, 1978).

3 BODY/POWER

Interviewers: editorial collective of *Quel Corps?*

> You depict in *Discipline and Punish* a political system
> where the King's body plays an essential role . . . .

In a society like that of the seventeenth century, the King's
body wasn't a metaphor, but a political reality. Its physical
presence was necessary for the functioning of the monarchy.

> And what about the Republic, 'one and indivisible'?

That's a formula that was imposed against the Girondins
and the idea of an American-style federalism. But it never
operated in the same manner as the King's body under the
monarchy. On the contrary, it's the body of society which
becomes the new principle in the nineteenth century. It is
this social body which needs to be protected, in a quasi-
medical sense. In place of the rituals that served to restore
the corporal integrity of the monarch, remedies and
therapeutic devices are employed such as the segregation of
the sick, the monitoring of contagions, the exclusion of
delinquents. The elimination of hostile elements by the
supplice (public torture and execution) is thus replaced by
the method of asepsis—criminology, eugenics and the
quarantining of 'degenerates' . . . .

> Is there a fantasy body corresponding to different types
> of institution?

I believe the great fantasy is the idea of a social body
constituted by the universality of wills. Now the phenomenon of the social body is the effect not of a consensus but of
the materiality of power operating on the very bodies of
individuals.

> The eighteenth century is usually seen under the aspect
> of liberation. You describe it as the period when a

network of forms of control (*quadrillage*) is set in place. Is the liberation possible without the *quadrillage*?

As always with relations of power, one is faced with complex phenomena which don't obey the Hegelian form of the dialectic. Mastery and awareness of one's own body can be acquired only through the effect of an investment of power in the body: gymnastics, exercises, muscle-building, nudism, glorification of the body beautiful. All of this belongs to the pathway leading to the desire of one's own body, by way of the insistent, persistent, meticulous work of power on the bodies of children or soldiers, the healthy bodies. But once power produces this effect, there inevitably emerge the responding claims and affirmations, those of one's own body against power, of health against the economic system, of pleasure against the moral norms of sexuality, marriage, decency. Suddenly, what had made power strong becomes used to attack it. Power, after investing itself in the body, finds itself exposed to a counter-attack in that same body. Do you recall the panic of the institutions of the social body, the doctors and politicians, at the idea of non-legalised cohabitation (*l'union libre*) or free abortion? But the impression that power weakens and vacillates here is in fact mistaken; power can retreat here, re-organise its forces, invest itself elsewhere . . . and so the battle continues.

Would this account for the much-discussed 'recuperation' of the body through pornography and advertising?

I don't agree at all with this talk about 'recuperation'. What's taking place is the usual strategic development of a struggle. Let's take a precise example, that of auto-eroticism. The restrictions on masturbation hardly start in Europe until the eighteenth century. Suddenly, a panic-theme appears: an appalling sickness develops in the Western world. Children masturbate. Via the medium of families, though not at their initiative, a system of control of sexuality, an objectivisation of sexuality allied to corporal persecution, is established over the bodies of children. But sexuality, through thus becoming an object of analysis and concern, surveillance and control, engenders at the same time an intensification of each individual's desire, for, in and over his body.

The body thus became the issue of a conflict between parents and children, the child and the instances of control. The revolt of the sexual body is the reverse effect of this encroachment. What is the response on the side of power? An economic (and perhaps also ideological) exploitation of eroticisation, from sun-tan products to pornographic films. Responding precisely to the revolt of the body, we find a new mode of investment which presents itself no longer in the form of control by repression but that of control by stimulation. 'Get undressed—but be slim, good-looking, tanned!' For each move by one adversary, there is an answering one by the other. But this isn't a 'recuperation' in the Leftists' sense. One has to recognise the indefiniteness of the struggle—though this is not to say it won't some day have an end . . . .

> Doesn't a new revolutionary strategy for taking power have to proceed via a new definition of the politics of the body?

The emergence of the problem of the body and its growing urgency have come about through the unfolding of a political struggle. Whether this is a revolutionary struggle, I don't know. One can say that what has happened since 1968, and arguably what made 1968 possible, is something profoundly anti-Marxist. How can European revolutionary movements free themselves from the 'Marx effect', the institutions typical of nineteenth- and twentieth-century Marxism? This was the direction of the questions posed by '68. In this calling in question of the equation: Marxism = the revolutionary process, an equation that constituted a kind of dogma, the importance given to the body is one of the important, if not essential elements.

> What course is the evolution of the bodily relationship between the masses and the State apparatus taking?

First of all one must set aside the widely held thesis that power, in our bourgeois, capitalist, societies has denied the reality of the body in favour of the soul, consciousness, ideality. In fact nothing is more material, physical, corporal than the exercise of power. What mode of investment of the body is necessary and adequate for the functioning of a capitalist society like ours? From the eighteenth to the early twentieth century I think it was believed that the investment of the body by power had to be heavy, ponderous, meticulous and constant. Hence those formidable disciplinary régimes in the schools, hospitals, barracks, factories, cities, lodgings, families. And then, starting in the 1960s, it began to be realised that such a cumbersome form of power was no longer as indispensable as had been thought and that industrial societies could content themselves with a much looser form of power over the body. Then it was discovered that control of sexuality could be attenuated and given new forms. One needs to study what kind of body the current society needs . . . .

> Would you distinguish your interest in the body from that of other contemporary interpretations?

I think I would distinguish myself from both the Marxist and the para-Marxist perspectives. As regards Marxism, I'm not one of those who try to elicit the effects of power at the level of ideology. Indeed I wonder whether, before one poses the question of ideology, it wouldn't be more materialist to study first the question of the body and the effects of power on it. Because what troubles me with these analyses which prioritise ideology is that there is always presupposed a human subject on the lines of the model provided by classical philosophy, endowed with a consciousness which power is then thought to seize on.

> But the Marxist perspective does include an awareness of the effect of power on the body in the working situation.

Certainly. But whereas today political and economic demands are coming to be made more on behalf of the wage-earner's body than of the wage-earning class, one seldom hears the former being discussed as such. It's as though 'revolutionary' discourses were still steeped in the ritualistic themes derived from Marxist analyses. And while there are some very interesting things about the body in Marx's writings, Marxism considered as an historical reality has had a terrible tendency to occlude the question of the body, in favour of consciousness and ideology.

I would also distinguish myself from para-Marxists like Marcuse who give the notion of repression an exaggerated role—because power would be a fragile thing if its only function were to repress, if it worked only through the mode of censorship, exclusion, blockage and repression, in the manner of a great Superego, exercising itself only in a negative way. If, on the contrary, power is strong this is because, as we are beginning to realise, it produces effects at the level of desire—and also at the level of knowledge. Far from preventing knowledge, power produces it. If it has been possible to constitute a knowledge of the body, this has been by way of an ensemble of military and educational disciplines. It was on the basis of power over the body that a physiological, organic knowledge of it became possible.

The fact that power is so deeply rooted and the difficulty of eluding its embrace are effects of all these connections. That is why the notion of repression which mechanisms of power are generally reduced to strikes me as very inadequate and possibly dangerous.

> Your study is concentrated on all those micro-powers that are exercised at the level of daily life. Aren't you neglecting the State apparatus here?

It's true that since the late nineteenth century Marxist and 'Marxised' revolutionary movements have given special importance to the State apparatus as the stake of their struggle. What were the ultimate consequences of this? In order to be able to fight a State which is more than just a government, the revolutionary movement must possess equivalent politico-military forces and hence must constitute itself as a party, organised internally in the same way as a State apparatus with the same mechanisms of hierarchies and organisation of powers. This consequence is heavy with significance. Secondly, there is the question, much discussed within Marxism itself, of the capture of the State apparatus: should this be considered as a straightforward take-over, accompanied by appropriate modifications, or should it be the opportunity for the destruction of that apparatus? You know how the issue was finally settled. The State apparatus must be undermined, but not completely undermined, since the class struggle will not be brought to an immediate end with the establishment of the dictatorship of the proletariat. Hence the State apparatus must be kept sufficiently intact for it to be employed against the class enemy. So we reach a second consequence: during the period of the dictatorship of the proletariat, the State apparatus must to some extent at least be maintained. Finally then, as a third consequence, in order to operate these State apparatuses which have been taken over but not destroyed, it will be necessary to have recourse to technicians and specialists. And in order to do this one has to call upon the old class which is acquainted with the apparatus, namely the bourgeoisie. This clearly is what happened in the USSR. I don't claim at all that the State apparatus is unimportant, but it seems to me that among all the conditions for avoiding a repetition of the Soviet experience and preventing the revolutionary process from running into the ground, one of the first things that has to be understood is that power isn't localised in the State apparatus and that nothing in society will be changed if the mechanisms of power that function outside, below and alongside the State apparatuses, on a much more minute and everyday level, are not also changed.

> Could we now turn then to the human sciences, and psychoanalysis in particular?

The case of psychoanalysis is indeed an interesting one. Psychoanalysis was established in opposition to a certain kind of psychiatry, the psychiatry of degeneracy, eugenics and heredity. This practice and theory, represented in France by Magnan, acted as the great foil to psychoanalysis. Indeed, in relation to that psychiatry—which is still the psychiatry of today's psychiatrists—psychoanalysis played a liberating role. Moreover, in certain countries (I am thinking of Brazil in particular), it has played a political role, denouncing the complicity of psychiatrists with political power. Again, take what is happening in the Eastern countries: the people there who take an interest in psychoanalysis are not the most disciplined among the psychiatrists. But the fact remains that in our societies the career of psychoanalysis has taken other directions and has been the object of different investments. Certain of its activities have effects which fall within the function of control and normalisation. If one can succeed in modifying these relationships of power into which psychoanalysis enters, and rendering unacceptable the effects of power they propagate, this will render the functioning of the State apparatuses much more difficult. Another advantage of conducting a critique of relations existing at a minute level would be to render impossible the reproduction of the form of the State apparatus within revolutionary movements.

> Your studies of madness and the prisons enable us to retrace the constitution of an ever more disciplinary form of society. This historical process seems to follow an almost inexorable logic.

I have attempted to analyse how, at the initial stages of industrial societies, a particular punitive apparatus was set up together with a system for separating the normal and the abnormal. To follow this up, it will be necessary to construct a history of what happens in the nineteenth century and how the present highly-complex relation of forces — the current outline of the battle — has been arrived at through a succession of offensives and counter-offensives, effects and counter-effects. The coherence of such a history does not derive from the revelation of a project but from a logic of opposing strategies. The archaeology of the human sciences has to be established through studying the mechanisms of power which have invested human bodies, acts and forms of behaviour. And this investigation enables us to rediscover one of the conditions of the emergence of the human sciences: the great nineteenth-century effort in discipline and normalisation. Freud was well aware of all this. He was aware of the superior strength of his position on the matter of normalisation. So why this sacralising modesty (*pudeur*) that insists on denying that psychoanalysis has anything to do with normalisation?

> How do you see the intellectual's role in militant practice?

The intellectual no longer has to play the role of an advisor. The project, tactics and goals to be adopted are a matter for those who do the fighting. What the intellectual can do is to provide instruments of analysis, and at present this is the historian's essential role. What's effectively needed is a ramified, penetrative perception of the present, one that makes it possible to locate lines of weakness, strong points, positions where the instances of power have secured and implanted themselves by a system of organisation dating back over 150 years. In other words, a topological and geological survey of the battlefield—that is the intellectual's role. But as for saying, 'Here is what you must do!', certainly not.

> Who or what is it that co-ordinates the activities of agents of the political body?

This is an extremely complex system of relations which leads one finally to wonder how, given that no one person can have conceived it in its entirety, it can be so subtle in its distribution, its mechanisms, reciprocal controls and adjustments. It's a highly intricate mosaic. During certain periods there appear agents of liaison. Take the example of philanthropy in the early nineteenth century: people appear who make it their business to involve themselves in other people's lives, health, nutrition, housing; then, out of this confused set of functions there emerge certain personages, institutions, forms of knowledge: public hygiene, inspectors, social workers, psychologists. And we are now seeing a whole proliferation of different categories of social work.

Naturally it's medicine which has played the basic role as the common denominator. Its discourse circulated from one instance to the next. It was in the name of medicine both that people came to inspect the layout of houses and, equally, that they classified individuals as insane, criminal, or sick. But there also emerged, out of the confused matrix of philanthropy, a highly diverse mosaic comprising all these 'social workers' . . . .

The interesting thing is to ascertain, not what overall project presides over all these developments, but, how, in terms of strategy, the different pieces were set in place.

June 1975

4 QUESTIONS ON GEOGRAPHY

Interviewers: the editors of the journal *Hérodote*.

Your work to a large extent intersects with, and provides material for, our reflections about geography and more generally about ideologies and strategies of space. Our questioning of geography brought us into contact with a certain number of concepts you have used—knowledge (*savoir*), power, science, discursive formation, gaze, *episteme*—and your archaeology has helped give a direction to our reflection. For instance the hypothesis you put forward in *The Archaeology of Knowledge*—that a discursive formation is defined neither in terms of a particular object, nor a style, nor a play of permanent concepts, nor by the persistence of a thematic, but must be grasped in the form of a system of regular dispersion of statements—enabled us to form a clearer outline of geographical discourse. Consequently we were surprised by your silence about geography. (If we are not mistaken, you mention its existence only once in a paper about Cuvier, and then only to number it among the natural sciences.) Yet, paradoxically, we would have been astounded if you had taken account of geography since, despite the example of Kant and Hegel, philosophers know nothing about geography. Should we blame for this the geographers who, ever since Vidal de la Blache, have been careful to shut themselves off under the cover of the human sciences from any contact with Marxism, epistemology or the history of the sciences? Or should we blame the philosophers, put off by a discipline which is unclassifiable, 'displaced', straddling the gulf between the natural and the social sciences? Is there a 'place' for geography in your archaeology of knowledge? Doesn't archaeology here reproduce the division between the sciences of nature (the inquiry and the table) and the human sciences (examination, discipline), and thereby dissolve the site where geography could be located?

First let me give a flatly empirical answer; then we can try and see if beyond that there is more that can be said. If I made a list of all the sciences, knowledges and domains which I should mention and don't, which I border on in one way or another, the list would be practically endless. I don't discuss biochemistry, or archaeology. I haven't even attempted an archaeology of history. To me it doesn't seem a good method to take a particular science to work on just because it's interesting or important or because its history might appear to have some exemplary value. If one wanted to do a correct, clean, conceptually aseptic kind of history, then that would be a good method. But if one is interested in doing historical work that has political meaning, utility and effectiveness, then this is possible only if one has some kind of involvement with the struggles taking place in the area in question. I tried first to do a genealogy of psychiatry because I had had a certain amount of practical experience in psychiatric hospitals and was aware of the combats, the lines of force, tensions and points of collision which existed there. My historical work was undertaken only as a function of those conflicts. The problem and the stake there was the possibility of a discourse which would be both true and strategically effective, the possibility of a historical truth which could have a political effect.

> That point connects up with a hypothesis I would put to you: if there are such points of collision, tensions and lines of force in geography, these remain on a subterranean level because of the very absence of polemic in geography. Whereas what attracts the interest of a philosopher, an epistemologist, an archaeologist is the possibility of either arbitrating or deriving profit from an existing polemic.

It's true that the importance of a polemic can be a factor of attraction. But I am not at all the sort of philosopher who conducts or wants to conduct a discourse of truth on some science or other. Wanting to lay down the law for each and every science is the project of positivism. I'm not sure that one doesn't find a similar temptation at work in certain kinds of 'renovated' Marxism, one which consists in saying, 'Marxism, as the science of sciences, can provide the theory of science and draw the boundary between science and ideology'. Now this role of referee, judge and universal witness is one which I absolutely refuse to adopt, because it seems to me to be tied up with philosophy as a university institution. If I do the analyses I do, it's not because of some polemic I want to arbitrate but because I have been involved in certain conflicts regarding medicine, psychiatry and the penal system. I have never had the intention of doing a general history of the human sciences or a critique of the possibility of the sciences in general. The subtitle to *The Order of Things* is not '*the* archaeology', but '*an* archaeology of the human sciences'.

It's up to you, who are directly involved with what goes on in geography, faced with all the conflicts of power which traverse it, to confront them and construct the instruments which will enable you to fight on that terrain. And what you should basically be saying to me is, 'You haven't occupied yourself with this matter which isn't particularly your affair anyway and which you don't know much about'. And I would say in reply, 'If one or two of these "gadgets" of approach or method that I've tried to employ with psychiatry, the penal system or natural history can be of service to you, then I shall be delighted. If you find the need to transform my tools or use others then show me what they are, because it may be of benefit to me'.

> You often cite historians like Lucien Febvre, Braudel and Le Roy Ladurie, and pay homage to them in various places. As it happens these are historians who have tried to open up a dialogue with geography, in order to found either a geo-history or an anthropo-geography. There might have been occasion for you to make contact with geography through these historians. Again in your studies of political economy and natural history you were verging on the domain of geography. Your work seems to have been constantly bordering on geography without ever taking it explicitly into account.

This isn't a demand for some possible archaeology of geography, nor even really an expression of disappointment, just a certain surprise.

I hesitate to reply only by means of factual arguments, but I think that here again there is a will to essentiality which one should mistrust, which consists in saying, 'If you don't talk about something it must be because you are impeded by some major obstacle which we shall proceed to uncover'. One can perfectly well not talk about something because one doesn't know about it, not because one has a knowledge which is unconscious and therefore inaccessible. You asked if geography has a place in the archaeology of knowledge. The answer is yes, provided one changes the formulation. Finding a place for geography would imply that the archaeology of knowledge embraces a project of global, exhaustive coverage of all domains of knowledge. This is not at all what I had in mind. Archaeology of knowledge only ever means a certain mode of approach.

It is true that Western philosophy, since Descartes at least, has always been involved with the problem of knowledge. This is not something one can escape. If someone wanted to be a philosopher but didn't ask himself the question, 'What is knowledge?', or, 'What is truth?', in what sense could one say he was a philosopher? And for all that I may like to say I'm not a philosopher, nonetheless if my concern is with truth then I am still a philosopher. Since Nietzsche this question of truth has been transformed. It is no longer, 'What is the surest path to Truth?', but, 'What is the hazardous career that Truth has followed?' That was Nietzsche's question, Husserl's as well, in *The Crisis of the European Sciences*. Science, the constraint to truth, the obligation of truth and ritualised procedures for its production have traversed absolutely the whole of Western society for millennia and are now so universalised as to become the general law for all civilisations. What is the history of this 'will to truth'? What are its effects? How is all this interwoven with relations of power? If one takes this line of enquiry then such a method can be applied to geography; indeed, it should be, but just as one could equally do the same with pharmacology, microbiology, demography and who knows what else. Properly speaking there is no 'place' in archaeology for geography, but it should be possible to conduct *an* archaeology of geographical knowledge.

> If geography is invisible or ungrasped in the area of your explorations and excavations, this may be due to the deliberately historical or archaeological approach which privileges the factor of time. Thus, one finds in your work a rigorous concern with periodisation that contrasts with the vagueness and relative indeterminacy of your spatial demarcations. Your domains of reference are alternately Christendom, the Western world, Northern Europe and France, without these spaces of reference ever really being justified or even precisely specified. As you write, 'Each periodisation is the demarcation in history of a certain level of events, and conversely each level of events demands its own specific periodisation, because according to the choice of level different periodisations have to be marked out and, depending on the periodisation one adopts, different levels of events become accessible. This brings us to the complex methodology of discontinuity'. It is possible, essential even, to conceive such a methodology of discontinuity for space and the scales of spatial magnitude. You accord a *de facto* privilege to the factor of time, at the cost of nebulous or nomadic spatial demarcations whose uncertainty is in contrast with your care in marking off sections of time, periods and ages.

We are touching here on a problem of method, but also on a question of material constraint, namely the possibility available to any one individual of covering the whole of this spatio-temporal field. After all, with *Discipline and Punish* I could perfectly well call my subject the history of penal policy in France—alone. That after all is essentially what I did, apart from a certain number of excursions, references and examples taken from elsewhere. If I don't spell that out, but allow the frontier to wander about, sometimes over the whole of the West, that's because the documentation I was using extends in part outside France, and also because in order to grasp a specifically French phenomenon I was often obliged to look at something that happened elsewhere in a more explicit form that antedated or served as a model for what took place in France. This enabled me—allowing for local and regional variations—to situate these French phenomena in the context of Anglo-Saxon, Spanish, Italian and other societies. I don't specify the space of reference more narrowly than that since it would be as warranted to say that I was speaking of France alone as to say I was talking about the whole of Europe. There is indeed a task to be done of making the space in question precise, saying where a certain process stops, what are the limits beyond which something different happens—though this would have to be a collective undertaking.

> This uncertainty about spatialisation contrasts with your profuse use of spatial metaphors—position, displacement, site, field; sometimes geographical metaphors even—territory, domain, soil, horizon, archipelago, geopolitics, region, landscape.

Well, let's take a look at these geographical metaphors. *Territory* is no doubt a geographical notion, but it's first of all a juridico-political one: the area controlled by a certain kind of power. *Field* is an economico-juridical notion. *Displacement*: what displaces itself is an army, a squadron, a population. *Domain* is a juridico-political notion. *Soil* is a historico-geological notion. *Region* is a fiscal, administrative, military notion. *Horizon* is a pictorial, but also a strategic notion.

There is only one notion here that is truly geographical, that of an *archipelago*. I used it only once, and that was to designate, via the title of Solzhenitsyn's work, the carceral archipelago: the way in which a form of punitive system is physically dispersed yet at the same time covers the entirety of a society.

> Certainly these notions are not geographical in a narrow sense. Nonetheless, they are the notions which are basic to every geographical proposition. This pinpoints the fact that geographical discourse produces few concepts of its own, instead picking up notions from

here, there and everywhere. Thus landscape is a
pictorial notion, but also an essential object for traditional geography.

But can you be sure that I am borrowing these terms from
geography rather than from exactly where geography itself
found them?

The point that needs to be emphasised here is that
certain spatial metaphors are equally geographical and
strategic, which is only natural since geography grew up
in the shadow of the military. A circulation of notions
can be observed between geographical and strategic
discourses. The *region* of the geographers is the
military region (from *regere*, to command), a *province*
is a conquered territory (from *vincere*). *Field* evokes
the battlefield . . . .

People have often reproached me for these spatial obsessions, which have indeed been obsessions for me. But I
think through them I did come to what I had basically been
looking for: the relations that are possible between power
and knowledge. Once knowledge can be analysed in terms
of region, domain, implantation, displacement, transposition, one is able to capture the process by which
knowledge functions as a form of power and disseminates
the effects of power. There is an administration of knowledge, a politics of knowledge, relations of power which pass
via knowledge and which, if one tries to transcribe them,
lead one to consider forms of domination designated by such
notions as field, region and territory. And the politico-
strategic term is an indication of how the military and the
administration actually come to inscribe themselves both on
a material soil and within forms of discourse. Anyone
envisaging the analysis of discourses solely in terms of
temporal continuity would inevitably be led to approach and
analyse it like the internal transformation of an individual
consciousness. Which would lead to his erecting a great
collective consciousness as the scene of events.
Metaphorising the transformations of discourse in a vocabulary of time necessarily leads to the utilisation of the model

of individual consciousness with its intrinsic temporality. Endeavouring on the other hand to decipher discourse through the use of spatial, strategic metaphors enables one to grasp precisely the points at which discourses are transformed in, through and on the basis of relations of power.

> In *Reading Capital*, Althusser poses an analogous question: 'The recourse made in this text to spatial metaphors (field, terrain, space, site, situation, position, etc.) poses a theoretical problem: the problem of the validity of its *claim* to existence in a discourse with scientific pretensions. The problem may be formulated as follows: *why* does a certain form of scientific discourse necessarily need the use of metaphors borrowed from scientific disciplines?' Althusser thus presents recourse to spatial metaphors as necessary, but at the same time as regressive, non-rigorous. Everything tends on the contrary to suggest that spatial metaphors, far from being reactionary, technocratic, unwarranted or illegitimate, are rather symptoms of a 'strategic', 'combative' thought, one which poses the space of discourse as a terrain and an issue of political practices.

It is indeed, war, administration, the implantation or management of some form of power which are in question in such expressions. A critique could be carried out of this devaluation of space that has prevailed for generations. Did it start with Bergson, or before? Space was treated as the dead, the fixed, the undialectical, the immobile. Time, on the contrary, was richness, fecundity, life, dialectic.

For all those who confuse history with the old schemas of evolution, living continuity, organic development, the progress of consciousness or the project of existence, the use of spatial terms seems to have the air of an anti-history. If one started to talk in terms of space that meant one was hostile to time. It meant, as the fools say, that one 'denied history', that one was a 'technocrat'. They didn't understand that to trace the forms of implantation, delimitation and demarcation of objects, the modes of tabulation, the organisation of domains meant the throwing into relief of processes— historical ones, needless to say—of power. The spatialising decription of discursive realities gives on to the analysis of related effects of power.

> In *Discipline and Punish*, this strategising method of thought advances a further stage. With the Panoptic system we are no longer dealing with a mere metaphor. What is at issue here is the description of institutions in terms of architecture, of spatial configurations. In the conclusion you even refer to the 'imaginary geopolitics' of the carceral city. Does this figure of the Panopticon offer the basis for a description of the State apparatus in its entirety? In this latest book an implicit model of power emerges: the dissemination of micro-powers, a dispersed network of apparatuses without a single organising system, centre or focus, a transverse co-ordination of disparate institutions and technologies. At the same time, however, you note the installation of State control over schools, hospitals, establishments of correction and education previously in the hands of religious bodies or charitable associations. And parallel with this is the creation of a centralised police, exercising a permanent, exhaustive surveillance which makes all things visible by becoming itself invisible. 'In the eighteenth century the organisation of police ratifies the generalisation of disciplines and attains the dimensions of the State.'

By the term 'Panoptism', I have in mind an ensemble of mechanisms brought into play in all the clusters of procedures used by power. Panoptism was a technological invention in the order of power, comparable with the steam engine in the order of production. This invention had the peculiarity of being utilised first of all on a local level, in schools, barracks and hospitals. This was where the experiment of integral surveillance was carried out. People learned how to establish dossiers, systems of marking and classifying, the integrated accountancy of individual records. Certain of the procedures had of course already been utilised in the economy and taxation. But the permanent surveillance of a group of pupils or patients was a different matter. And, at a certain moment in time, these methods began to become generalised. The police apparatus served as one of the principal vectors of this process of extension, but so too did the Napoleonic administration. I think in the book I quoted a beautiful description of the role of the Attorneys-General under the Empire as the eyes of the Emperor; from the First Attorney-General in Paris to the least Assistant Public Prosecutor in the provinces, one and the same gaze watches for disorder, anticipates the danger of crime, penalising every deviation. And should any part of this universal gaze chance to slacken, the collapse of the State itself would be imminent. The Panoptic system was not so much confiscated by the State apparatuses, rather it was these apparatuses which rested on the basis of small-scale, regional, dispersed Panoptisms. In consequence one cannot confine oneself to analysing the State apparatus alone if one wants to grasp the mechanisms of power in their detail and complexity. There is a sort of schematism that needs to be avoided here—and which incidentally is not to be found in Marx—that consists of locating power in the State apparatus, making this into the major, privileged, capital and almost unique instrument of the power of one class over another. In reality, power in its exercise goes much further, passes through much finer channels, and is much more ambiguous, since each individual has at his disposal a certain power, and for that very reason can also act as the vehicle for transmitting a wider power. The reproduction of the relations of production is not the only function served by power. The systems of domination and the circuits of exploitation certainly interact, intersect and support each other, but they do not coincide.

> Even if the State apparatus isn't the only vector of power, it's still true, especially in France with its Panoptico-prefectoral system, that the State spans the essential sector of disciplinary practices.

The administrative monarchy of Louis XIV and Louis XV, intensely centralised as it was, certainly acted as an initial disciplinary model. As you know, the police was invented in Louis XV's France. I do not mean in any way to minimise the importance and effectiveness of State power. I simply feel that excessive insistence on its playing an exclusive role leads to the risk of overlooking all the mechanisms and effects of power which don't pass directly via the State apparatus, yet often sustain the State more effectively than its own institutions, enlarging and maximising its effectiveness. In Soviet society one has the example of a State apparatus which has changed hands, yet leaves social hierarchies, family life, sexuality and the body more or less as they were in capitalist society. Do you imagine the mechanisms of power that operate between technicians, foremen and workers are that much different here and in the Soviet Union?

> You have shown how psychiatric knowledge presupposed and carried within itself the demand for the closed space of the asylum, how disciplinary knowledge contained within itself the model of the prison, Bichat's clinical medicine the enclave of the hospital and political economy the form of the factory. One might wonder, as a conceit or a hypothesis, whether geographical knowledge doesn't carry within itself the circle of the frontier, whether this be a national, departmental or cantonal frontier; and hence, whether one shouldn't add to the figures of internment you have indicated—that of the madman, the criminal, the patient, the proletarian—the national internment of the citizen-soldier. Wouldn't we have here a space of confinement which is both infinitely vaster and less hermetic?

That's a very appealing notion. And the inmate, in your view, would be national man? Because the geographical discourse which justifies frontiers is that of nationalism?

> Geography being together with history constitutive of this national discourse: this is clearly shown with the establishment of Jules Ferry's universal primary schools which entrust history-geography with the task of implanting and inculcating the civic and patriotic spirit.

Which has as its effect the constitution of a personal identity, because it's my hypothesis that the individual is not a pre-given entity which is seized on by the exercise of power. The individual, with his identity and characteristics, is the product of a relation of power exercised over bodies, multiplicities, movements, desires, forces. There is much that could be said as well on the problems of regional identity and its conflicts with national identity.

> The map as instrument of power/knowledge spans the three successive chronological thresholds you have described: that of measure with the Greeks, that of the inquiry during the Middle Ages, that of the examination in the eighteenth century. The map is linked to each of these forms, being transformed from an instrument of measurement to an instrument of inquiry, becoming finally today an instrument of examination (electoral maps, taxation maps, etc.). All the same the history (and archaeology) of the map doesn't correspond to 'your' chronology.

A map giving numbers of votes cast or choices of parties: this is certainly an instrument of examination. I think there is this historical succession of the three models, but obviously these three techniques didn't remain isolated from each other. Each one directly contaminates the others. The inquiry used the technique of measure, and the examination made use of inquiry. Then examination reacted back on the first two models, and this brings us back to an aspect of your first question: doesn't the distinction between examination and inquiry reproduce the distinction between social science and science of nature? What in fact I would like to see is how inquiry as a model, a fiscal, administrative, political schema, came to serve as a matrix for the great surveys which are made at the end of the eighteenth century where people travel the world gathering information. They don't collect their data raw: literally, they inquire, in terms of schemas which are more or less clear or conscious for them. And I believe the sciences of nature did indeed install themselves within this general form of the inquiry; just as the sciences of man were born at the moment when the procedures of surveillance and record-taking of individuals were established. Although that was only a starting-point.

And because of the effects of intersection that were immediately produced, the forms of inquiry and examination interacted, and as a consequence the sciences of nature and man also overlapped in terms of their concepts, methods and results. I think one could find in geography a good example of a discipline which systematically uses measure, inquiry and examination.

There is a further omnipresent figure in geographical discourse: that of the inventory or catalogue. And this kind of inventory precisely combines the triple register of inquiry, measure and examination. The geographer —and this is perhaps his essential, strategic function— collects information in an inventory which in its raw state does not have much interest and is not in fact usable except by power. What power needs is not science but a mass of information which its strategic position can enable it to exploit.

This give us a better understanding both of the epistemological weakness of geographical studies, and at the same time of their profitability (past more than present) for apparatuses of power. Those seventeenth-century travellers and nineteenth-century geographers were actually intelligence-gatherers, collecting and mapping information which was directly exploitable by colonial powers, strategists, traders and industrialists.

I can cite an anecdote here, for what it's worth. A specialist in documents of the reign of Louis XIV discovered while looking at seventeenth-century diplomatic correspondence that many narratives that were subsequently repeated as travellers' tales of all sorts of marvels, incredible plants and monstrous animals, were actually coded reports. They were precise accounts of the military state of the countries traversed, their economic resources, markets, wealth and possible diplomatic relations. So that what many people ascribe to the persistent naïveté of certain eighteenth-century naturalists and geographers were in reality extraordinarily precise reports whose key has apparently now been deciphered.

Wondering why there have never been polemics within

geography, we immediately thought of the weak influence Marx has had on geographers. There has never
been a Marxist geography nor even a Marxist current in
geography. Those geographers who invoke Marxism
tend in fact to go off into economics or sociology, giving
privileged attention to the planetary or the medium
scale. Marxism and geography are hard to articulate
with one another. Perhaps Marxism, or at any rate
Capital and the economic texts in general, does not lend
itself very readily to a spatialising approach because of
the privilege it gives to the factor of time. Is that what is
at issue in this remark of yours in an interview: 'Whatever the importance of their modification of Ricardo's
analyses, I don't believe Marx's economic analyses
escape from the epistemological space established by
Ricardo'?

As far as I'm concerned, Marx doesn't exist. I mean, the
sort of entity constructed around a proper name, signifying
at once a certain individual, the totality of his writings, and
an immense historical process deriving from him. I believe
Marx's historical analysis, the way he analyses the formation
of capital, is for a large part governed by the concepts he
derives from the framework of Ricardian economics. I take
no credit for that remark, Marx says it himself. However, if
you take his analysis of the Paris Commune or *The
Eighteenth Brumaire of Louis Bonaparte*, there you have a
type of historical analysis which manifestly doesn't rely on
any eighteenth-century model.
    It's always possible to make Marx into an author, localis-
able in terms of a unique discursive physiognomy, subject to
analysis in terms of originality or internal coherence. After
all, people are perfectly entitled to 'academise' Marx. But
that means misconceiving the kind of break he effected.

If one re-reads Marx in terms of the treatment of the
spatial, his work appears heterogenous. There are
whole passages which reveal an astonishing spatial
sensibility.

There are some very remarkable ones. Everything he wrote
on the army and its role in the development of political

power, for instance. There is some very important material there that has been left practically fallow for the sake of endless commentaries on surplus value.

I have enjoyed this discussion with you because I've changed my mind since we started. I must admit I thought you were demanding a place for geography like those teachers who protest when an education reform is proposed, because the number of hours of natural sciences or music is being cut. So I thought, 'It's nice of them to ask me to do their archaeology, but after all, why can't they do it themselves?' I didn't see the point of your objection. Now I can see that the problems you put to me about geography are crucial ones for me. Geography acted as the support, the condition of possibility for the passage between a series of factors I tried to relate. Where geography itself was concerned, I either left the question hanging or established a series of arbitrary connections.

The longer I continue, the more it seems to me that the formation of discourses and the genealogy of knowledge need to be analysed, not in terms of types of consciousness, modes of perception and forms of ideology, but in terms of tactics and strategies of power. Tactics and strategies deployed through implantations, distributions, demarcations, control of territories and organisations of domains which could well make up a sort of geopolitics where my preoccupations would link up with your methods. One theme I would like to study in the next few years is that of the army as a matrix of organisation and knowledge; one would need to study the history of the fortress, the 'campaign', the 'movement', the colony, the territory. Geography must indeed necessarily lie at the heart of my concerns.

5 TWO LECTURES

Lecture One: 7 January 1976

I have wanted to speak to you of my desire to be finished with, and to somehow terminate a series of researches that have been our concern for some four or five years now, in effect, from the date of my arrival here, and which, I am well aware, have met with increasing difficulties, both for you and for myself. Though these researches were very closely related to each other, they have failed to develop into any continuous or coherent whole. They are fragmentary researches, none of which in the last analysis can be said to have proved definitive, nor even to have led anywhere. Diffused and at the same time repetitive, they have continually re-trod the same ground, invoked the same themes, the same concepts etc.

You will recall my work here, such as it has been: some brief notes on the history of penal procedure, a chapter or so on the evolution and institutionalisation of psychiatry in the nineteenth century, some observations on sophistry, on Greek money, on the medieval Inquisition. I have sketched a history of sexuality or at least a history of knowledge of sexuality on the basis of the confessional practice of the seventeenth century or the forms of control of infantile sexuality in the eighteenth to nineteenth century. I have sketched a genealogical history of the origins of a theory and a knowledge of anomaly and of the various techniques that relate to it. None of it does more than mark time. Repetitive and disconnected, it advances nowhere. Since indeed it never ceases to say the same thing, it perhaps says nothing. It is tangled up into an indecipherable, disorganised muddle. In a nutshell, it is inconclusive.

Still, I could claim that after all these were only trails to be followed, it mattered little where they led; indeed, it was important that they did not have a predetermined starting point and destination. They were merely lines laid down for you to pursue or to divert elsewhere, for me to extend upon or re-design as the case might be. They are, in the final analysis, just fragments, and it is up to you or me to see what we can make of them. For my part, it has struck me that I might have seemed a bit like a whale that leaps to the surface of the water disturbing it momentarily with a tiny jet of spray and lets it be believed, or pretends to believe, or wants to believe, or himself does in fact indeed believe, that down in the depths where no one sees him any more, where he is no longer witnessed nor controlled by anyone, he follows a more profound, coherent and reasoned trajectory. Well, anyway, that was more or less how I at least conceived the situation; it could be that you perceived it differently.

After all, the fact that the character of the work I have presented to you has been at the same time fragmentary, repetitive and discontinuous could well be a reflection of something one might describe as a febrile indolence — a typical affliction of those enamoured of libraries, documents, reference works, dusty tomes, texts that are never read, books that are no sooner printed than they are consigned to the shelves of libraries where they thereafter lie dormant to be taken up only some centuries later. It would accord all too well with the busy inertia of those who profess an idle knowledge, a species of luxuriant sagacity, the rich hoard of the *parvenus* whose only outward signs are displayed in footnotes at the bottom of the page. It would accord with all those who feel themselves to be associates of one of the more ancient or more typical secret societies of the West, those oddly indestructible societies unknown it would seem to Antiquity, which came into being with Christianity, most likely at the time of the first monasteries, at the periphery of the invasions, the fires and the forests: I mean to speak of the great warm and tender Freemasonry of useless erudition.

However, it is not simply a taste for such Freemasonry that has inspired my course of action. It seems to me that the work we have done could be justified by the claim that it is adequate to a restricted period, that of the last ten, fifteen, at most twenty years, a period notable for two events which for all they may not be really important are nonetheless to my mind quite interesting.

On the one hand, it has been a period characterised by

what one might term the efficacy of dispersed and discontinuous offensives. There are a number of things I have in mind here. I am thinking, for example, where it was a case of undermining the function of psychiatric institutions, of that curious efficacy of localised anti-psychiatric discourses. These are discourses which you are well aware lacked and still lack any systematic principles of coordination of the kind that would have provided or might today provide a system of reference for them. I am thinking of the original reference towards existential analysis or of certain directions inspired in a general way by Marxism, such as Reichian theory. Again, I have in mind that strange efficacy of the attacks that have been directed against traditional morality and hierarchy, attacks which again have no reference except perhaps in a vague and fairly distant way to Reich and Marcuse. On the other hand there is also the efficacy of the attacks upon the legal and penal system, some of which had a very tenuous connection with the general and in any case pretty dubious notion of class justice, while others had a rather more precisely defined affinity with anarchist themes. Equally, I am thinking of the efficacy of a book such as *L'Anti-Oedipe*, which really has no other source of reference than its own prodigious theoretical inventiveness: a book, or rather a thing, an event, which has managed, even at the most mundane level of psychoanalytic practice, to introduce a note of shrillness into that murmured exchange that has for so long continued uninterrupted between couch and armchair.

I would say, then, that what has emerged in the course of the last ten or fifteen years is a sense of the increasing vulnerability to criticism of things, institutions, practices, discourses. A certain fragility has been discovered in the very bedrock of existence—even, and perhaps above all, in those aspects of it that are most familiar, most solid and most intimately related to our bodies and to our everyday behaviour. But together with this sense of instability and this amazing efficacy of discontinuous, particular and local criticism, one in fact also discovers something that perhaps was not initially foreseen, something one might describe as precisely the inhibiting effect of global, *totalitarian theories*. It is not that these global theories have not provided nor continue to provide in a fairly consistent fashion useful tools for local research: Marxism and psychoanalysis are proofs of this. But I believe these tools have only been provided on the condition that the theoretical unity of these discourses was in some sense put in abeyance, or at least curtailed, divided, overthrown, caricatured, theatricalised, or what you will. In each case, the attempt to think in terms of a totality has in fact proved a hindrance to research.

So, the main point to be gleaned from these events of the last fifteen years, their predominant feature, is the *local* character of criticism. That should not, I believe, be taken to mean that its qualities are those of an obtuse, naive or primitive empiricism; nor is it a soggy eclecticism, an opportunism that laps up any and every kind of theoretical approach; nor does it mean a self-imposed ascetism which taken by itself would reduce to the worst kind of theoretical impoverishment. I believe that what this essentially local character of criticism indicates in reality is an autonomous, non-centralised kind of theoretical production, one that is to say whose validity is not dependent on the approval of the established régimes of thought.

It is here that we touch upon another feature of these events that has been manifest for some time now: it seems to me that this local criticism has proceeded by means of what one might term 'a return of knowledge'. What I mean by that phrase is this: it is a fact that we have repeatedly encountered, at least at a superficial level, in the course of most recent times, an entire thematic to the effect that it is not theory but life that matters, not knowledge but reality, not books but money etc.; but it also seems to me that over and above, and arising out of this thematic, there is something else to which we are witness, and which we might describe as an *insurrection of subjugated knowledges*.

By subjugated knowledges I mean two things: on the one hand, I am referring to the historical contents that have been buried and disguised in a functionalist coherence or formal systemisation. Concretely, it is not a semiology of the life of the asylum, it is not even a sociology of delinquency, that has made it possible to produce an effective criticism of the asylum and likewise of the prison, but rather the immediate emergence of historical contents. And this is simply because only the historical contents allow us to rediscover the ruptural effects of conflict and struggle that the order imposed by functionalist or systematising thought is designed to mask. Subjugated knowledges are thus those blocs of historical knowledge which were present but disguised within the body of functionalist and systematising theory and which criticism — which obviously draws upon scholarship — has been able to reveal.

On the other hand, I believe that by subjugated knowledges one should understand something else, something which in a sense is altogether different, namely, a whole set of knowledges that have been disqualified as inadequate to their task or insufficiently elaborated: naive knowledges, located low down on the hierarchy, beneath the required level of cognition or scientificity. I also believe that it is through the re-emergence of these low-ranking knowledges, these unqualified, even directly disqualified knowledges (such as that of the psychiatric patient, of the ill person, of the nurse, of the doctor — parallel and marginal as they are to the knowledge of medicine — that of the delinquent etc.), and which involve what I would call a popular knowledge (*le savoir des gens*) though it is far from being a general commonsense knowledge, but is on the contrary a particular, local, regional knowledge, a differential knowledge incapable of unanimity and which owes its force only to the harshness with which it is opposed by everything surrounding it — that it is through the re-appearance of this knowledge, of these local popular knowledges, these disqualified knowledges, that criticism performs its work.

However, there is a strange kind of paradox in the desire to assign to this same category of subjugated knowledges what are on the one hand the products of meticulous, erudite, exact historical knowledge, and on the other hand local and specific knowledges which have no common meaning and which are in some fashion allowed to fall into disuse whenever they are not effectively and explicitly maintained in themselves. Well, it seems to me that our critical discourses of the last fifteen years have in effect discovered their essential force in this association between the buried knowledges of erudition and those disqualified from the hierarchy of knowledges and sciences.

In the two cases—in the case of the erudite as in that of the disqualified knowledges—with what in fact were these buried, subjugated knowledges really concerned? They were concerned with a *historical knowledge of struggles*. In the specialised areas of erudition as in the disqualified, popular knowledge there lay the memory of hostile encounters which even up to this day have been confined to the margins of knowledge.

What emerges out of this is something one might call a genealogy, or rather a multiplicity of genealogical researches, a painstaking rediscovery of struggles together with the rude memory of their conflicts. And these genealogies, that are the combined product of an erudite knowledge and a popular knowledge, were not possible and could not even have been attempted except on one condition, namely that the tyranny of globalising discourses with their hierarchy and all their privileges of a theoretical *avant-garde* was eliminated.

Let us give the term *genealogy* to the union of erudite knowledge and local memories which allows us to establish a historical knowledge of struggles and to make use of this knowledge tactically today. This then will be a provisional definition of the genealogies which I have attempted to compile with you over the last few years.

You are well aware that this research activity, which one can thus call genealogical, has nothing at all to do with an opposition between the abstract unity of theory and the concrete multiplicity of facts. It has nothing at all to do with a disqualification of the speculative dimension which opposes to it, in the name of some kind of scientism, the rigour of well established knowledges. It is not therefore via an empiricism that the genealogical project unfolds, nor even via a positivism in the ordinary sense of that term. What it really does is to entertain the claims to attention of local, discontinuous, disqualified, illegitimate knowledges against the claims of a unitary body of theory which would filter, hierarchise and order them in the name of some true knowledge and some arbitrary idea of what constitutes a science and its objects. Genealogies are therefore not positivistic returns to a more careful or exact form of science. They are precisely anti-sciences. Not that they vindicate a lyrical right to ignorance or non-knowledge: it is not that they are concerned to deny knowledge or that they esteem the virtues of direct cognition and base their practice upon an immediate experience that escapes encapsulation in knowledge. It is not that with which we are concerned. We are concerned, rather, with the insurrection of knowledges that are opposed primarily not to the contents, methods or concepts of a science, but to the effects of the centralising powers which are linked to the institution and functioning of an organised scientific discourse within a society such as ours. Nor does it basically matter all that much that this institutionalisation of scientific discourse is embodied in a university, or, more generally, in an educational apparatus, in a theoretical-commercial institution such as psycho-analysis or within the framework of reference that is pro-vided by a political system such as Marxism; for it is really against the effects of the power of a discourse that is considered to be scientific that the genealogy must wage its struggle.

To be more precise, I would remind you how numerous have been those who for many years now, probably for more than half a century, have questioned whether Marxism was, or was not, a science. One might say that the same issue has been posed, and continues to be posed, in the case of psychoanalysis, or even worse, in that of the semiology of literary texts. But to all these demands of: 'Is it or is it not a science?', the genealogies or the genealogists would reply: 'If you really want to know, the fault lies in your very determination to make a science out of Marxism or psycho-analysis or this or that study'. If we have any objection against Marxism, it lies in the fact that it could effectively be a science. In more detailed terms, I would say that even before we can know the extent to which something such as Marxism or psychoanalysis can be compared to a scientific practice in its everyday functioning, its rules of construction, its working concepts, that even before we can pose the question of a formal and structural analogy between Marxist or psychoanalytic discourse, it is surely necessary to question ourselves about our aspirations to the kind of power that is presumed to accompany such a science. It is surely the following kinds of question that would need to be posed:

What types of knowledge do you want to disqualify in the very instant of your demand: 'Is it a science'? Which speaking, discoursing subjects—which subjects of experience and knowledge—do you then want to 'diminish' when you say: 'I who conduct this discourse am conducting a scientific discourse, and I am a scientist'? Which theoretical-political *avant garde* do you want to enthrone in order to isolate it from all the discontinuous forms of knowledge that circulate about it? When I see you straining to establish the scientificity of Marxism I do not really think that you are demonstrating once and for all that Marxism has a rational structure and that therefore its propositions are the outcome of verifiable procedures; for me you are doing something altogether different, you are investing Marxist discourses and those who uphold them with the effects of a power which the West since Medieval times has attributed to science and has reserved for those engaged in scientific discourse.

By comparison, then, and in contrast to the various projects which aim to inscribe knowledges in the hierarchical order of power associated with science, a genealogy should be seen as a kind of attempt to emancipate historical knowledges from that subjection, to render them, that is, capable of opposition and of struggle against the coercion of a theoretical, unitary, formal and scientific discourse. It is based on a reactivation of local knowledges—of minor knowledges, as Deleuze might call them—in opposition to the scientific hierarchisation of knowledges and the effects intrinsic to their power: this, then, is the project of these disordered and fragmentary genealogies. If we were to characterise it in two terms, then 'archaeology' would be the appropriate methodology of this analysis of local discursivities, and 'genealogy' would be the tactics whereby, on the basis of the descriptions of these local discursivities, the subjected knowledges which were thus released would be brought into play.

So much can be said by way of establishing the nature of the project as a whole. I would have you consider all these fragments of research, all these discourses, which are simultaneously both superimposed and discontinuous, which I have continued obstinately to pursue for some four or five years now, as elements of these genealogies which have been composed—and by no means by myself alone—in the course of the last fifteen years. At this point, however, a problem arises, and a question: why not continue to pursue a theory which in its discontinuity is so attractive and plausible, albeit so little verifiable? Why not continue to settle upon some aspect of psychiatry or of the theory of sexuality etc.? It is true, one could continue (and in a certain sense I shall try to do so) if it were not for a certain number of changes in the current situation. By this I mean that it could be that in the course of the last five, ten or even fifteen years, things have assumed a different complexion—the contest could be said to present a different physiognomy. Is the relation of forces today still such as to allow these disinterred knowledges some kind of autonomous life? Can they be isolated by these means from every subjugating relationship? What force do they have taken in themselves? And, after all, is it not perhaps the case that these fragments of genealogies are no sooner brought to light, that the particular elements of the knowledge that one seeks to disinter are no sooner accredited and put into circulation, than they run the risk of re-codification, re-colonisation? In fact, those unitary discourses, which first disqualified and then ignored them when they made their appearance, are, it seems, quite ready now to annex them, to take them back within the fold of their own discourse and to invest them with everything this implies in terms of their effects of knowledge and power. And if we want to protect these only lately liberated fragments are we not in danger of ourselves constructing, with our own hands, that unitary discourse to which we are invited, perhaps to lure us into a trap, by those who say to us: 'All this is fine, but where are you heading? What kind of unity are you after?' The temptation, up to a certain point, is to reply: 'Well, we just go on, in a cumulative fashion; after all, the moment at which we risk colonisation has not yet arrived'. One could even attempt to throw out a challenge: 'Just try to colonize us then!' Or one might say, for example, 'Has there been, from the time when anti-psychiatry or the genealogy of psychiatric institutions were launched—and it is now a good fifteen years ago—a single Marxist, or a single psychiatrist, who has gone over the same ground in his own terms and shown that these genealogies that we produced were false, inadequately elaborated, poorly articulated and ill-founded?' In fact, as things stand in reality, these collected fragments of a genealogy remain as they have always been, surrounded by a prudent silence. At most, the only arguments that we have heard against them have been of the kind I believe were voiced by Monsieur Juquin:[1] 'All this is all very well, but Soviet psychiatry nonetheless remains the foremost in the world'. To which I would reply: 'How right you are; Soviet psychiatry is indeed the foremost in the world and it is precisely that which one would hold against it'.

The silence, or rather the prudence, with which the unitary theories avoid the genealogy of knowledges might therefore be a good reason to continue to pursue it. Then at least one could proceed to multiply the genealogical fragments in the form of so many traps, demands, challenges, what you will. But in the long run, it is probably over-optimistic, if we are thinking in terms of a contest— that of knowledge against the effects of the power of scientific discourse—to regard the silence of one's adversaries as indicative of a fear we have inspired in them. For perhaps the silence of the enemy—and here at the very least we have a methodological or tactical principle that it is always useful to bear in mind—can also be the index of our failure to produce any such fear at all. At all events, we must proceed just as if we had not alarmed them at all, in which case it will be no part of our concern to provide a solid and homogeneous theoretical terrain for all these dispersed genealogies, nor to descend upon them from on high with some kind of halo of theory that would unite them. Our task, on the contrary, will be to expose and specify the issue at stake in this opposition, this struggle, this insurrection of knowledges against the institutions and against effects of the knowledge and power that invests scientific discourse.

What is at stake in all these genealogies is the nature of this power which has surged into view in all its violence, aggression and absurdity in the course of the last forty years, contemporaneously, that is, with the collapse of Fascism and the decline of Stalinism. What, we must ask, is this power—or rather, since that is to give a formulation to the

question that invites the kind of theoretical coronation of
the whole which I am so keen to avoid—what are these
various contrivances of power, whose operations extend to
such differing levels and sectors of society and are possessed
of such manifold ramifications? What are their mechanisms,
their effects and their relations? The issue here can, I
believe, be crystallised essentially in the following question:
is the analysis of power or of powers to be deduced in one way
or another from the economy? Let me make this question
and my reasons for posing it somewhat clearer. It is not at
all my intention to abstract from what are innumerable and
enormous differences; yet despite, and even because of
these differences, I consider there to be a certain point in
common between the juridical, and let us call it, liberal,
conception of political power (found in the *philosophes* of
the eighteenth century) and the Marxist conception, or at
any rate a certain conception currently held to be Marxist. I
would call this common point an economism in the theory of
power. By that I mean that in the case of the classic,
juridical theory, power is taken to be a right, which one is
able to possess like a commodity, and which one can in
consequence transfer or alienate, either wholly or partially,
through a legal act or through some act that establishes a
right, such as takes place through cession or contract. Power
is that concrete power which every individual holds, and
whose partial or total cession enables political power or
sovereignty to be established. This theoretical construction
is essentially based on the idea that the constitution of
political power obeys the model of a legal transaction
involving a contractual type of exchange (hence the clear
analogy that runs through all these theories between power
and commodities, power and wealth). In the other case—I
am thinking here of the general Marxist conception of
power—one finds none of all that. Nonetheless, there is
something else inherent in this latter conception, something
which one might term an economic functionality of power.
This economic functionality is present to the extent that
power is conceived primarily in terms of the role it plays in
the maintenance simultaneously of the relations of production and of a class domination which the development
and specific forms of the forces of production have rendered

possible. On this view, then, the historical *raison d'être* of political power is to be found in the economy. Broadly speaking, in the first case we have a political power whose formal model is discoverable in the process of exchange, the economic circulation of commodities; in the second case, the historical *raison d'être* of political power and the principle of its concrete forms and actual functioning, is located in the economy. Well then, the problem involved in the researches to which I refer can, I believe, be broken down in the following manner: in the first place, is power always in a subordinate position relative to the economy? Is it always in the service of, and ultimately answerable to, the economy? Is its essential end and purpose to serve the economy? Is it destined to realise, consolidate, maintain and reproduce the relations appropriate to the economy and essential to its functioning? In the second place, is power modelled upon the commodity? Is it something that one possesses, acquires, cedes through force or contract, that one alienates or recovers, that circulates, that voids this or that region? Or, on the contrary, do we need to employ varying tools in its analysis—even, that is, when we allow that it effectively remains the case that the relations of power do indeed remain profoundly enmeshed in and with economic relations and participate with them in a common circuit? If that is the case, it is not the models of functional subordination or formal isomorphism that will characterise the interconnection between politics and the economy. Their indissolubility will be of a different order, one that it will be our task to determine.

What means are available to us today if we seek to conduct a non-economic analysis of power? Very few, I believe. We have in the first place the assertion that power is neither given, nor exchanged, nor recovered, but rather exercised, and that it only exists in action. Again, we have at our disposal another assertion to the effect that power is not primarily the maintenance and reproduction of economic relations, but is above all a relation of force. The questions to be posed would then be these: if power is exercised, what sort of exercise does it involve? In what does it consist? What is its mechanism? There is an immediate answer that many contemporary analyses would appear to offer: power is essentially that which represses. Power represses nature, the instincts, a class, individuals. Though one finds this definition of power as repression endlessly repeated in present day discourse, it is not that discourse which invented it—Hegel first spoke of it, then Freud and later Reich. In any case, it has become almost automatic in the parlance of the times to define power as an organ of repression. So should not the analysis of power be first and foremost an analysis of the mechanisms of repression?

Then again, there is a second reply we might make: if power is properly speaking the way in which relations of forces are deployed and given concrete expression, rather than analysing it in terms of cession, contract or alienation, or functionally in terms of its maintenance of the relations of production, should we not analyse it primarily in terms of *struggle*, *conflict* and *war*? One would then confront the original hypothesis, according to which power is essentially repression, with a second hypothesis to the effect that power is war, a war continued by other means. This reversal of Clausewitz's assertion that war is politics continued by other means has a triple significance: in the first place, it implies that the relations of power that function in a society such as ours essentially rest upon a definite relation of forces that is established at a determinate, historically specifiable moment, in war and by war. Furthermore, if it is true that political power puts an end to war, that it installs, or tries to install, the reign of peace in civil society, this by no means implies that it suspends the effects of war or neutralises the disequilibrium revealed in the final battle. The role of political power, on this hypothesis, is perpetually to re-inscribe this relation through a form of unspoken warfare; to re-inscribe it in social institutions, in economic inequalities, in language, in the bodies themselves of each and everyone of us.

So this would be the first meaning to assign to the inversion of Clausewitz's aphorism that war is politics continued by other means. It consists in seeing politics as sanctioning and upholding the disequilibrium of forces that was displayed in war. But there is also something else that the inversion signifies, namely, that none of the political struggles, the conflicts waged over power, with power, for power, the alterations in the relations of forces, the favouring of certain tendencies, the reinforcements etc., etc., that come about within this 'civil peace'–that none of these phenomena in a political system should be interpreted except as the continuation of war. They should, that is to say, be understood as episodes, factions and displacements in that same war. Even when one writes the history of peace and its institutions, it is always the history of this war that one is writing. The third, and final, meaning to be assigned to the inversion of Clausewitz's aphorism, is that the end result can only be the outcome of war, that is, of a contest of strength, to be decided in the last analyses by recourse to arms. The political battle would cease with this final battle. Only a final battle of that kind would put an end, once and for all, to the exercise of power as continual war.

So, no sooner do we attempt to liberate ourselves from economistic analyses of power, than two solid hypotheses offer themselves: the one argues that the mechanisms of power are those of repression. For convenience sake, I shall term this Reich's hypothesis. The other argues that the basis of the relationship of power lies in the hostile engagement of forces. Again for convenience, I shall call this Nietzsche's hypothesis.

These two hypotheses are not irreconcilable; they even seem to be linked in a fairly convincing manner. After all, repression could be seen as the political consequence of war, somewhat as oppression, in the classic theory of political right, was seen as the abuse of sovereignty in the juridical order.

One might thus contrast two major systems of approach to the analysis of power: in the first place, there is the old system as found in the *philosophes* of the eighteenth century. The conception of power as an original right that is given up in the establishment of sovereignty, and the contract, as matrix of political power, provide its points of articulation. A power so constituted risks becoming oppression whenever it over-extends itself, whenever—that is—it goes beyond the terms of the contract. Thus we have contract-power, with oppression as its limit, or rather as the transgression of this limit. In contrast, the other system of approach no longer tries to analyse political power according to the schema of contract-oppression, but in accordance with that of war-repression, and, at this point, repression no longer occupies the place that oppression occupies in relation to the contract, that is, it is not abuse, but is, on the contrary, the mere effect and continuation of a relation of domination. On this view, repression is none other than the realisation, within the continual warfare of this pseudo-peace, of a perpetual relationship of force.

Thus we have two schemes for the analysis of power. The contract–oppression schema, which is the juridical one, and the domination–repression or war–repression schema for which the pertinent opposition is not between the legitimate and illegitimate, as in the first schema, but between struggle and submission.

It is obvious that all my work in recent years has been couched in the schema of struggle–repression, and it is this — which I have hitherto been attempting to apply — which I have now been forced to reconsider, both because it is still insufficiently elaborated at a whole number of points, and because I believe that these two notions of repression and war must themselves be considerably modified if not ultimately abandoned. In any case, I believe that they must be submitted to closer scrutiny.

I have always been especially diffident of this notion of repression: it is precisely with reference to those genealogies of which I was speaking just now — of the history of penal right, of psychiatric power, of the control of infantile sexuality etc. — that I have tried to demonstrate to you the extent to which the mechanisms that were brought into operation in these power formations were something quite other, or in any case something much more, than repression. The need to investigate this notion of repression more thoroughly springs therefore from the impression I have that it is wholly inadequate to the analysis of the mechanisms and effects of power that it is so pervasively used to characterise today.

Lecture Two: 14 January 1976
The course of study that I have been following until now — roughly since 1970/71 — has been concerned with the *how* of power. I have tried, that is, to relate its mechanisms to two

points of reference, two limits: on the one hand, to the rules of right that provide a formal delimitation of power; on the other, to the effects of truth that this power produces and transmits, and which in their turn reproduce this power. Hence we have a triangle: power, right, truth.

Schematically, we can formulate the traditional question of political philosophy in the following terms: how is the discourse of truth, or quite simply, philosophy as that discourse which *par excellence* is concerned with truth, able to fix limits to the rights of power? That is the traditional question. The one I would prefer to pose is rather different. Compared to the traditional, noble and philosophic question it is much more down to earth and concrete. My problem is rather this: what rules of right are implemented by the relations of power in the production of discourses of truth? Or alternatively, what type of power is susceptible of producing discourses of truth that in a society such as ours are endowed with such potent effects? What I mean is this: in a society such as ours, but basically in any society, there are manifold relations of power which permeate, characterise and constitute the social body, and these relations of power cannot themselves be established, consolidated nor implemented without the production, accumulation, circulation and functioning of a discourse. There can be no possible exercise of power without a certain economy of discourses of truth which operates through and on the basis of this association. We are subjected to the production of truth through power and we cannot exercise power except through the production of truth. This is the case for every society, but I believe that in ours the relationship between power, right and truth is organised in a highly specific fashion. If I were to characterise, not its mechanism itself, but its intensity and constancy, I would say that we are forced to produce the truth of power that our society demands, of which it has need, in order to function: we *must* speak the truth; we are constrained or condemned to confess or to discover the truth. Power never ceases its interrogation, its inquisition, its registration of truth: it institutionalises, professionalises and rewards its pursuit. In the last analysis, we must produce truth as we must produce wealth, indeed we must produce truth in order to produce wealth in the first place. In another way, we are also subjected to truth in the sense in which it is truth that makes the laws, that produces the true discourse which, at least partially, decides, transmits and itself extends upon the effects of power. In the end, we are judged, condemned, classified, determined in our undertakings, destined to a certain mode of living or dying, as a function of the true discourses which are the bearers of the specific effects of power.

So, it is the rules of right, the mechanisms of power, the effects of truth or if you like, the rules of power and the powers of true discourses, that can be said more or less to have formed the general terrain of my concern, even if, as I know full well, I have traversed it only partially and in a very zig-zag fashion. I should like to speak briefly about this course of research, about what I have considered as being its guiding principle and about the methodological imperatives and precautions which I have sought to adopt. As regards the general principle involved in a study of the relations between right and power, it seems to me that in Western societies since Medieval times it has been royal power that has provided the essential focus around which legal thought has been elaborated. It is in reponse to the demands of royal power, for its profit and to serve as its instrument or justification, that the juridical edifice of our own society has been developed. Right in the West is the King's right. Naturally everyone is familiar with the famous, celebrated, repeatedly emphasised role of the jurists in the organisation of royal power. We must not forget that the re-vitalisation of Roman Law in the twelfth century was the major event around which, and on whose basis, the juridical edifice which had collapsed after the fall of the Roman Empire was reconstructed. This resurrection of Roman Law had in effect a technical and constitutive role to play in the establishment of the authoritarian, administrative, and, in the final analysis, absolute power of the monarchy. And when this legal edifice escapes in later centuries from the control of the monarch, when, more accurately, it is turned against that control, it is always the limits of this sovereign power that are put in question, its prerogatives that are challenged. In other words, I believe that the King remains the central personage in the whole legal edifice of the West.

When it comes to the general organisation of the legal system in the West, it is essentially with the King, his rights, his power and its eventual limitations, that one is dealing. Whether the jurists were the King's henchmen or his adversaries, it is of royal power that we are speaking in every case when we speak of these grandiose edifices of legal thought and knowledge.

There are two ways in which we do so speak. Either we do so in order to show the nature of the juridical armoury that invested royal power, to reveal the monarch as the effective embodiment of sovereignty, to demonstrate that his power, for all that it was absolute, was exactly that which befitted his fundamental right. Or, by contrast, we do so in order to show the necessity of imposing limits upon this sovereign power, of submitting it to certain rules of right, within whose confines it had to be exercised in order for it to remain legitimate. The essential role of the theory of right, from medieval times onwards, was to fix the legitimacy of power; that is the major problem around which the whole theory of right and sovereignty is organised.

When we say that sovereignty is the central problem of right in Western societies, what we mean basically is that the essential function of the discourse and techniques of right has been to efface the domination intrinsic to power in order to present the latter at the level of appearance under two different aspects: on the one hand, as the legitimate rights of sovereignty, and on the other, as the legal obligation to obey it. The system of right is centred entirely upon the King, and it is therefore designed to eliminate the fact of domination and its consequences.

My general project over the past few years has been, in essence, to reverse the mode of analysis followed by the entire discourse of right from the time of the Middle Ages. My aim, therefore, was to invert it, to give due weight, that is, to the fact of domination, to expose both its latent nature and its brutality. I then wanted to show not only how right is, in a general way, the instrument of this domination—which scarcely needs saying—but also to show the extent to which, and the forms in which, right (not simply the laws but the whole complex of apparatuses, institutions and regulations responsible for their application) transmits and puts in motion relations that are not relations of sovereignty, but of domination. Moreover, in speaking of domination I do not have in mind that solid and global kind of domination that one person exercises over others, or one group over another, but the manifold forms of domination that can be exercised within society. Not the domination of the King in his central position, therefore, but that of his subjects in their mutual relations: not the uniform edifice of sovereignty, but the multiple forms of subjugation that have a place and function within the social organism.

The system of right, the domain of the law, are permanent agents of these relations of domination, these polymorphous techniques of subjugation. Right should be viewed, I believe, not in terms of a legitimacy to be established, but in terms of the methods of subjugation that it instigates.

The problem for me is how to avoid this question, central to the theme of right, regarding sovereignty and the obedience of individual subjects in order that I may substitute the problem of domination and subjugation for that of sovereignty and obedience. Given that this was to be the general line of my analysis, there were a certain number of methodological precautions that seemed requisite to its pursuit. In the very first place, it seemed important to accept that the analysis in question should not concern itself with the regulated and legitimate forms of power in their central locations, with the general mechanisms through which they operate, and the continual effects of these. On the contrary, it should be concerned with power at its extremities, in its ultimate destinations, with those points where it becomes capillary, that is, in its more regional and local forms and institutions. Its paramount concern, in fact, should be with the point where power surmounts the rules of right which organise and delimit it and extends itself beyond them, invests itself in institutions, becomes embodied in techniques, and equips itself with instruments and eventually even violent means of material intervention. To give an example: rather than try to discover where and how the right of punishment is founded on sovereignty, how it is presented in the theory of monarchical right or in that of democratic right, I have tried to see in what ways punishment and the power of punishment are effectively embodied in a certain number of local, regional, material institutions, which are concerned with torture or imprisonment, and to place these in the climate—at once institutional and physical, regulated and violent—of the effective apparatuses of punishment. In other words, one should try to locate power at the extreme points of its exercise, where it is always less legal in character.

A second methodological precaution urged that the analysis should not concern itself with power at the level of conscious intention or decision; that it should not attempt to consider power from its internal point of view and that it should refrain from posing the labyrinthine and unanswerable question: 'Who then has power and what has he in mind? What is the aim of someone who possesses power?' Instead, it is a case of studying power at the point where its intention, if it has one, is completely invested in its real and effective practices. What is needed is a study of power in its external visage, at the point where it is in direct and immediate relationship with that which we can provisionally call its object, its target, its field of application, there—that is to say—where it installs itself and produces its real effects.

Let us not, therefore, ask why certain people want to dominate, what they seek, what is their overall strategy. Let us ask, instead, how things work at the level of on-going subjugation, at the level of those continuous and un-interrupted processes which subject our bodies, govern our gestures, dictate our behaviours etc. In other words, rather than ask ourselves how the sovereign appears to us in his lofty isolation, we should try to discover how it is that subjects are gradually, progressively, really and materially constituted through a multiplicity of organisms, forces, energies, materials, desires, thoughts etc. We should try to grasp subjection in its material instance as a constitution of subjects. This would be the exact opposite of Hobbes' project in *Leviathan*, and of that, I believe, of all jurists for whom the problem is the distillation of a single will—or rather, the constitution of a unitary, singular body animated by the spirit of sovereignty—from the particular wills of a multiplicity of individuals. Think of the scheme of Leviathan: insofar as he is a fabricated man, Leviathan is no other than the amalgamation of a certain number of separate individualities, who find themselves reunited by the complex of elements that go to compose the State; but at the heart of the State, or rather, at its head, there exists something which constitutes it as such, and this is sovereignty, which Hobbes says is precisely the spirit of Leviathan. Well, rather than worry about the problem of the central spirit, I believe that we must attempt to study the myriad of bodies which are constituted as peripheral *subjects* as a result of the effects of power.

A third methodological precaution relates to the fact that power is not to be taken to be a phenomenon of one individual's consolidated and homogeneous domination over others, or that of one group or class over others. What, by contrast, should always be kept in mind is that power, if we do not take too distant a view of it, is not that which makes the difference between those who exclusively possess and retain it, and those who do not have it and submit to it. Power must by analysed as something which circulates, or rather as something which only functions in the form of a chain. It is never localised here or there, never in anybody's hands, never appropriated as a commodity or piece of wealth. Power is employed and exercised through a net-like organisation. And not only do individuals circulate between its threads; they are always in the position of simultaneously undergoing and exercising this power. They are not only its inert or consenting target; they are always also the elements of its articulation. In other words, individuals are the vehicles of power, not its points of application.

The individual is not to be conceived as a sort of elementary nucleus, a primitive atom, a multiple and inert material on which power comes to fasten or against which it happens to strike, and in so doing subdues or crushes individuals. In fact, it is already one of the prime effects of power that certain bodies, certain gestures, certain discourses, certain desires, come to be identified and constituted as individuals. The individual, that is, is not the *vis-à-vis* of power; it is, I believe, one of its prime effects. The individual is an effect of power, and at the same time, or precisely to the extent to which it is that effect, it is the element of its articulation. The individual which power has constituted is at the same time its vehicle.

There is a fourth methodological precaution that follows from this: when I say that power establishes a network through which it freely circulates, this is true only up to a certain point. In much the same fashion we could say that therefore we all have a fascism in our heads, or, more profoundly, that we all have a power in our bodies. But I do not believe that one should conclude from that that power is the best distributed thing in the world, although in some sense that is indeed so. We are not dealing with a sort of democratic or anarchic distribution of power through bodies. That is to say, it seems to me — and this then would be the fourth methodological precaution — that the important thing is not to attempt some kind of deduction of power starting from its centre and aimed at the discovery of the extent to which it permeates into the base, of the degree to which it reproduces itself down to and including the most molecular elements of society. One must rather conduct an *ascending* analysis of power, starting, that is, from its infinitesimal mechanisms, which each have their own history, their own trajectory, their own techniques and tactics, and then see how these mechanisms of power have been — and continue to be — invested, colonised, utilised, involuted, transformed, displaced, extended etc., by ever more general mechanisms and by forms of global domination. It is not that this global domination extends itself right to the base in a plurality of repercussions: I believe that the manner in which the phenomena, the techniques and the procedures of power enter into play at the most basic levels must be analysed, that the way in which these procedures are displaced, extended and altered must certainly be demonstrated; but above all what must be shown is the manner in which they are invested and annexed by more global phenomena and the subtle fashion in which more general powers or economic interests are able to engage with these technologies that are at once both relatively autonomous of power and act as its infinitesimal elements. In order to make this clearer, one might cite the example of madness. The descending type of analysis, the one of which I believe one ought to be wary, will say that the bourgeoisie has, since the sixteenth or seventeenth century, been the dominant class; from this premise, it will then set out to deduce the internment of the insane. One can always make this deduction, it is always easily done and that is precisely what I would hold against it. It is in fact a simple matter to show that since lunatics are precisely those persons who are useless to industrial production, one is obliged to dispense with them. One could argue similarly in regard to infantile sexuality—and several thinkers, including Wilhelm Reich have indeed sought to do so up to a certain point. Given the domination of the bourgeois class, how can one understand the repression of infantile sexuality? Well, very simply—given that the human body had become essentially a force of production from the time of the seventeenth and eighteenth century, all the forms of its expenditure which did not lend themselves to the constitution of the productive forces—and were therefore exposed as redundant—were banned, excluded and repressed. These kinds of deduction are always possible. They are simultaneously correct and false. Above all they are too glib, because one can always do exactly the opposite and show, precisely by appeal to the principle of the dominance of the bourgeois class, that the forms of control of infantile sexuality could in no way have been predicted. On the contrary, it is equally plausible to suggest that what was needed was sexual training, the encouragement of a sexual precociousness, given that what was fundamentally at stake was the constitution of a labour force whose optimal state, as we well know, at least at the beginning of the nineteenth century, was to be infinite: the greater the labour force, the better able would the system of capitalist production have been to fulfil and improve its functions.

I believe that anything can be deduced from the general phenomenon of the domination of the bourgeois class. What needs to be done is something quite different. One needs to investigate historically, and beginning from the lowest level, how mechanisms of power have been able to function. In regard to the confinement of the insane, for example, or the repression and interdiction of sexuality, we need to see the manner in which, at the effective level of the family, of the immediate environment, of the cells and most basic units of society, these phenomena of repression or exclusion possessed their instruments and their logic, in response to a certain number of needs. We need to identify the agents responsible for them, their real agents (those which constituted the immediate social *entourage*, the family, parents, doctors etc.), and not be content to lump them under the formula of a generalised bourgeoisie. We need to see how these mechanisms of power, at a given moment, in a precise conjuncture and by means of a certain number of transformations, have begun to become economically advantageous and politically useful. I think that in this way one could easily manage to demonstrate that what the bourgeoisie needed, or that in which its system discovered its real interests, was not the exclusion of the mad or the surveillance and prohibition of infantile masturbation (for, to repeat, such a system can perfectly well tolerate quite opposite practices), but rather, the techniques and procedures themselves of such an exclusion. It is the mechanisms of that exclusion that are necessary, the apparatuses of surveillance, the medicalisation of sexuality, of madness, of delinquency, all the micro-mechanisms of power, that came, from a certain moment in time, to represent the interests of the bourgeoisie. Or even better, we could say that to the extent to which this view of the bourgeoisie and of its interests appears to lack content, at least in regard to the problems with which we are here concerned, it reflects the fact that it was not the bourgeoisie itself which thought that madness had to be excluded or infantile sexuality repressed. What in fact happened instead was that the mechanisms of the exclusion of madness, and of the surveillance of infantile sexuality, began from a particular point in time, and for reasons which need to be studied, to reveal their political usefulness and to lend themselves to economic profit, and that as a natural consequence, all of a sudden, they came to be colonised and maintained by global mechanisms and the entire State system. It is only if we grasp these techniques of power and demonstrate the economic advantages or political utility that derives from them in a given context for specific reasons, that we can understand how these mechanisms come to be effectively incorporated into the social whole.

To put this somewhat differently: the bourgeoisie has never had any use for the insane; but the procedures it has employed to exclude them have revealed and realised—from the nineteenth century onwards, and again on the basis of certain transformations—a political advantage, on occasion even a certain economic utility, which have consolidated the system and contributed to its overall functioning. The bourgeoisie is interested in power, not in madness, in the system of control of infantile sexuality, not in that phenomenon itself. The bourgeoisie could not care less about delinquents, about their punishment and rehabilitation, which economically have little importance, but it is concerned about the complex of mechanisms with which delinquency is controlled, pursued, punished and reformed etc.

As for our fifth methodological precaution: it is quite possible that the major mechanisms of power have been accompanied by ideological productions. There has, for example, probably been an ideology of education, an ideology of the monarchy, an ideology of parliamentary democracy etc.; but basically I do not believe that what has taken place can be said to be ideological. It is both much more and much less than ideology. It is the production of effective instruments for the formation and accumulation of knowledge—methods of observation, techniques of registration, procedures for investigation and research, apparatuses of control. All this means that power, when it is exercised through these subtle mechanisms, cannot but evolve, organise and put into circulation a knowledge, or rather apparatuses of knowledge, which are not ideological constructs.

By way of summarising these five methodological precautions, I would say that we should direct our researches on the nature of power not towards the juridical edifice of sovereignty, the State apparatuses and the ideologies which accompany them, but towards domination and the material operators of power, towards forms of subjection and the inflections and utilisations of their localised systems, and towards strategic apparatuses. We must eschew the model of Leviathan in the study of power. We must escape from the limited field of juridical sovereignty and State institutions, and instead base our analysis of power on the study of the techniques and tactics of domination.

This, in its general outline, is the methodological course that I believe must be followed, and which I have tried to pursue in the various researches that we have conducted over recent years on psychiatric power, on infantile sexuality, on political systems, etc. Now as one explores these fields of investigation, observing the methodological precautions I have mentioned, I believe that what then comes into view is a solid body of historical fact, which will ultimately bring us into confrontation with the problems of which I want to speak this year.

This solid, historical body of fact is the juridical-political theory of sovereignty of which I spoke a moment ago, a theory which has had four roles to play. In the first place, it has been used to refer to a mechanism of power that was effective under the feudal monarchy. In the second place, it has served as instrument and even as justification for the construction of the large scale administrative monarchies. Again, from the time of the sixteenth century and more than ever from the seventeenth century onwards, but already at the time of the wars of religion, the theory of sovereignty has been a weapon which has circulated from one camp to another, which has been utilised in one sense or another, either to limit or else to re-inforce royal power: we find it among Catholic monarchists and Protestant anti-monarchists, among Protestant and more-or-less liberal monarchists, but also among Catholic partisans of regicide or dynastic transformation. It functions both in the hands of aristocrats and in the hands of parliamentarians. It is found among the representatives of royal power and among the last feudatories. In short, it was the major instrument of political and theoretical struggle around systems of power of the sixteenth and seventeenth centuries. Finally, in the eighteenth century, it is again this same theory of sovereignty, re-activated through the doctrine of Roman Law, that we find in its essentials in Rousseau and his contemporaries, but now with a fourth role to play: now it is concerned with the construction, in opposition to the administrative, authoritarian and absolutist monarchies, of an alternative model, that of parliamentary democracy. And it is still this role that it plays at the moment of the Revolution.

Well, it seems to me that if we investigate these four roles there is a definite conclusion to be drawn: as long as a feudal type of society survived, the problems to which the theory of sovereignty was addressed were in effect confined to the general mechanisms of power, to the way in which its forms of existence at the higher level of society influenced its exercise at the lowest levels. In other words, the relationship of sovereignty, whether interpreted in a wider or a narrower sense, encompasses the totality of the social body. In effect, the mode in which power was exercised could be defined in its essentials in terms of the relationship sovereign–subject. But in the seventeenth and eighteenth centuries, we have the production of an important phenomenon, the emergence, or rather the invention, of a new mechanism of power possessed of highly specific procedural techniques, completely novel instruments, quite different apparatuses, and which is also, I believe, absolutely incompatible with the relations of sovereignty.

This new mechanism of power is more dependent upon bodies and what they do than upon the Earth and its products. It is a mechanism of power which permits time and labour, rather than wealth and commodities, to be extracted from bodies. It is a type of power which is constantly exercised by means of surveillance rather than in a discontinuous manner by means of a system of levies or obligations distributed over time. It presupposes a tightly knit grid of material coercions rather than the physical existence of a sovereign. It is ultimately dependent upon the principle, which introduces a genuinely new economy of power, that one must be able simultaneously both to increase the subjected forces and to improve the force and efficacy of that which subjects them.

This type of power is in every aspect the antithesis of that mechanism of power which the theory of sovereignty described or sought to transcribe. The latter is linked to a form of power that is exercised over the Earth and its products, much more than over human bodies and their operations. The theory of sovereignty is something which refers to the displacement and appropriation on the part of power, not of time and labour, but of goods and wealth. It allows discontinuous obligations distributed over time to be given legal expression but it does not allow for the codification of a continuous surveillance. It enables power to be founded in the physical existence of the sovereign, but not in continuous and permanent systems of surveillance. The theory of sovereignty permits the foundation of an absolute power in the absolute expenditure of power. It does not allow for a calculation of power in terms of the minimum expenditure for the maximum return.

This new type of power, which can no longer be formulated in terms of sovereignty, is, I believe, one of the great inventions of bourgeois society. It has been a fundamental instrument in the constitution of industrial capitalism and of the type of society that is its accompaniment. This non-sovereign power, which lies outside the form of sovereignty, is disciplinary power. Impossible to describe in the terminology of the theory of sovereignty from which it differs so radically, this disciplinary power ought by rights to have led to the disappearance of the grand juridical edifice created by that theory. But in reality, the theory of sovereignty has continued not only to exist as an ideology of right, but also to provide the organising principle of the legal codes which Europe acquired in the nineteenth century, beginning with the Napoleonic Code.

Why has the theory of sovereignty persisted in this fashion as an ideology and an organising principle of these major legal codes? For two reasons, I believe. On the one hand, it has been, in the eighteenth and again in the nineteenth century, a permanent instrument of criticism of the monarchy and of all the obstacles that can thwart the development of disciplinary society. But at the same time, the theory of sovereignty, and the organisation of a legal code centred upon it, have allowed a system of right to be superimposed upon the mechanisms of discipline in such a way as to conceal its actual procedures, the element of domination inherent in its techniques, and to guarantee to everyone, by virtue of the sovereignty of the State, the exercise of his proper sovereign rights. The juridical systems — and this applies both to their codification and to their theorisation — have enabled sovereignty to be democratised through the constitution of a public right articulated upon collective sovereignty, while at the same time this democratisation of sovereignty was fundamentally determined by and grounded in mechanisms of disciplinary coercion.

To put this in more rigorous terms, one might say that

once it became necessary for disciplinary constraints to be exercised through mechanisms of domination and yet at the same time for their effective exercise of power to be disguised, a theory of sovereignty was required to make an appearance at the level of the legal apparatus, and to re-emerge in its codes. Modern society, then, from the nineteenth century up to our own day, has been characterised on the one hand, by a legislation, a discourse, an organisation based on public right, whose principle of articulation is the social body and the delegative status of each citizen; and, on the other hand, by a closely linked grid of disciplinary coercions whose purpose is in fact to assure the cohesion of this same social body. Though a theory of right is a necessary companion to this grid, it cannot in any event provide the terms of its endorsement. Hence these two limits, a right of sovereignty and a mechanism of discipline, which define, I believe, the arena in which power is exercised. But these two limits are so heterogeneous that they cannot possibly be reduced to each other. The powers of modern society are exercised through, on the basis of, and by virtue of, this very heterogeneity between a public right of sovereignty and a polymorphous disciplinary mechanism. This is not to suggest that there is on the one hand an explicit and scholarly system of right which is that of sovereignty, and, on the other hand, obscure and unspoken disciplines which carry out their shadowy operations in the depths, and thus constitute the bedrock of the great mechanism of power. In reality, the disciplines have their own discourse. They engender, for the reasons of which we spoke earlier, apparatuses of knowledge (*savoir*) and a multiplicity of new domains of understanding. They are extraordinarily inventive participants in the order of these knowledge-producing apparatuses. Disciplines are the bearers of a discourse, but this cannot be the discourse of right. The discourse of discipline has nothing in common with that of law, rule, or sovereign will. The disciplines may well be the carriers of a discourse that speaks of a rule, but this is not the juridical rule deriving from sovereignty, but a natural rule, a norm. The code they come to define is not that of law but that of normalisation. Their reference is to a theoretical horizon which of necessity has nothing in common with the edifice of right. It is human science which constitutes their domain, and clinical knowledge their juris-prudence.

In short, what I have wanted to demonstrate in the course of the last few years is not the manner in which at the advance front of the exact sciences the uncertain, recal-citrant, confused dominion of human behaviour has little by little been annexed to science: it is not through some advancement in the rationality of the exact sciences that the human sciences are gradually constituted. I believe that the process which has really rendered the discourse of the human sciences possible is the juxtaposition, the encounter between two lines of approach, two mechanisms, two absolutely heterogeneous types of discourse: on the one hand there is the re-organisation of right that invests sovereignty, and on the other, the mechanics of the coercive forces whose exercise takes a disciplinary form. And I believe that in our own times power is exercised simul-taneously through this right and these techniques and that these techniques and these discourses, to which the disci-plines give rise invade the area of right so that the pro-cedures of normalisation come to be ever more constantly engaged in the colonisation of those of law. I believe that all this can explain the global functioning of what I would call a *society of normalisation*. I mean, more precisely, that disciplinary normalisations come into ever greater conflict with the juridical systems of sovereignty: their incom-patibility with each other is ever more acutely felt and apparent; some kind of arbitrating discourse is made ever more necessary, a type of power and of knowledge that the sanctity of science would render neutral. It is precisely in the extension of medicine that we see, in some sense, not so much the linking as the perpetual exchange or encounter of mechanisms of discipline with the principle of right. The developments of medicine, the general medicalisation of behaviours, conducts, discourses, desires etc., take place at the point of intersection between the two heterogeneous levels of discipline and sovereignty. For this reason, against these usurpations by the disciplinary mechanisms, against this ascent of a power that is tied to scientific knowledge, we find that there is no solid recourse available to us today, such being our situation, except that which lies precisely in the return to a theory of right organised around sovereignty and articulated upon its ancient principle. When today one wants to object in some way to the disciplines and all the effects of power and knowledge that are linked to them, what is it that one does, concretely, in real life, what do the Magistrates Union[2] or other similar institutions do, if not precisely appeal to this canon of right, this famous, formal right, that is said to be bourgeois, and which in reality is the right of sovereignty? But I believe that we find ourselves here in a kind of blind alley: it is not through recourse to sovereignty against discipline that the effects of disciplinary power can be limited, because sovereignty and disciplinary mechanisms are two absolutely integral constituents of the general mechanism of power in our society.

If one wants to look for a non-disciplinary form of power, or rather, to struggle against disciplines and disciplinary power, it is not towards the ancient right of sovereignty that one should turn, but towards the possibility of a new form of right, one which must indeed be anti-disciplinarian, but at the same time liberated from the principle of sovereignty. It is at this point that we once more come up against the notion of repression, whose use in this context I believe to be doubly unfortunate. On the one hand, it contains an obscure reference to a certain theory of sovereignty, the sovereignty of the sovereign rights of the individual, and on the other hand, its usage introduces a system of psychological reference points borrowed from the human sciences, that is to say, from discourses and practices that belong to the disciplinary realm. I believe that the notion of repression remains a juridical-disciplinary notion whatever the critical use one would make of it. To this extent the critical application of the notion of repression is found to be vitiated and nullified from the outset by the two-fold juridical and disciplinary reference it contains to sovereignty on the one hand and to normalisation on the other.

Notes

1 A deputy of the French Communist Party.
2 This Union, established after 1968, has adopted a radical line on civil rights, the law and the prisons.

6 TRUTH AND POWER

Interviewers: Alessandro Fontana, Pasquale Pasquino.

Could you briefly outline the route which led you from your work on madness in the Classical age to the study of criminality and delinquency?

When I was studying during the early 1950s, one of the great problems that arose was that of the political status of science and the ideological functions which it could serve. It wasn't exactly the Lysenko business which dominated everything, but I believe that around that sordid affair—which had long remained buried and carefully hidden—a whole number of interesting questions were provoked. These can all be summed up in two words: power and knowledge. I believe I wrote *Madness and Civilisation* to some extent within the horizon of these questions. For me, it was a matter of saying this: if, concerning a science like theoretical physics or organic chemistry, one poses the problem of its relations with the political and economic structures of society, isn't one posing an excessively complicated question? Doesn't this set the threshold of possible explanations impossibly high? But on the other hand, if one takes a form of knowledge (*savoir*) like psychiatry, won't the question be much easier to resolve, since the epistemological profile of psychiatry is a low one and psychiatric practice is linked with a whole range of institutions, economic requirements and political issues of social regulation? Couldn't the interweaving of effects of power and knowledge be grasped with greater certainty in the case of a science as 'dubious' as psychiatry? It was this same question which I wanted to pose concerning medicine in *The Birth of the Clinic*: medicine certainly has a much more solid scientific armature than psychiatry, but it too is profoundly enmeshed in social structures. What rather threw me at the time was the fact that the question I was posing totally failed to interest those to whom I addressed it. They regarded it as a problem which was politically unimportant and epistemologically vulgar.

I think there were three reasons for this. The first is that for Marxist intellectuals in France (and there they were playing the role prescribed for them by the PCF) the problem consisted in gaining for themselves the recognition of the university institutions and establishment. Consequently they found it necessary to pose the same theoretical questions as the academic establishment, to deal with the same problems and topics: 'We may be Marxists, but for all that we are not strangers to your preoccupations, rather we are the only ones able to provide new solutions for your old concerns'. Marxism sought to win acceptance as a renewal of the liberal university tradition—just as, more broadly, during the same period the Communists presented themselves as the only people capable of taking over and reinvigorating the nationalist tradition. Hence, in the field we are concerned with here, it followed that they wanted to take up the 'noblest', most academic problems in the history of the sciences: mathematics and physics, in short the themes valorised by Duhem, Husserl and Koyré. Medicine and psychiatry didn't seem to them to be very noble or serious matters, nor to stand on the same level as the great forms of classical rationalism.

The second reason is that post-Stalinist Stalinism, by excluding from Marxist discourse everything that wasn't a frightened repetition of the already said, would not permit the broaching of uncharted domains. There were no ready-made concepts, no approved terms of vocabulary available for questions like the power-effects of psychiatry or the political function of medicine, whereas on the contrary innumerable exchanges between Marxists and academics, from Marx via Engels and Lenin down to the present, had nourished a whole tradition of discourse on 'science', in the nineteenth-century sense of that term. The price Marxists paid for their fidelity to the old positivism was a radical deafness to a whole series of questions posed by science.

Finally, there is perhaps a third reason, but I can't be absolutely sure that it played a part. I wonder nevertheless whether among intellectuals in or close to the PCF there wasn't a refusal to pose the problem of internment, of the political use of psychiatry and, in a more general sense, of the disciplinary grid of society. No doubt little was then known in 1955–60 of the real extent of the Gulag, but I believe that many sensed it, in any case many had a feeling that it was better not to talk about those things: it was a danger zone, marked by warning signs. Of course it's difficult in retrospect to judge people's degree of awareness. But in any case, you well know how easily the Party leadership—which knew everything of course—could circulate instructions preventing people from speaking about this or that, or precluding this or that line of research. At any rate, if the question of Pavlovian psychiatry did get discussed among a few doctors close to the PCF, psychiatric politics and psychiatry as politics were hardly considered to be respectable topics.

What I myself tried to do in this domain was met with a great silence among the French intellectual Left. And it was only around 1968, and in spite of the Marxist tradition and the PCF, that all these questions came to assume their political significance, with a sharpness that I had never envisaged, showing how timid and hesitant those early books of mine had still been. Without the political opening created during those years, I would surely never have had the courage to take up these problems again and pursue my research in the direction of penal theory, prisons and disciplines.

> So there is a certain 'discontinuity' in your theoretical trajectory. Incidentally, what do you think today about this concept of discontinuity, on the basis of which you have been all too rapidly and readily labelled as a 'structuralist' historian?

This business about discontinuity has always rather bewildered me. In the new edition of the *Petit Larousse* it says: 'Foucault: a philosopher who founds his theory of history on discontinuity'. That leaves me flabbergasted. No doubt I didn't make myself sufficiently clear in *The Order of Things*, though I said a good deal there about this question. It seemed to me that in certain empirical forms of knowledge like biology, political economy, psychiatry, medicine etc., the rhythm of transformation doesn't follow the smooth, continuist schemas of development which are normally accepted. The great biological image of a progressive maturation of science still underpins a good many historical analyses; it does not seem to me to be pertinent to history. In a science like medicine, for example, up to the end of the eighteenth century one has a certain type of discourse whose gradual transformation, within a period of twenty-five or thirty years, broke not only with the 'true' propositions which it had hitherto been possible to formulate but also, more profoundly, with the ways of speaking and seeing, the whole ensemble of practices which served as supports for medical knowledge. These are not simply new discoveries, there is a whole new 'régime' in discourse and forms of knowledge. And all this happens in the space of a few years. This is something which is undeniable, once one has looked at the texts with sufficient attention. My problem was not at all to say, '*Voilà*, long live discontinuity, we are in the discontinuous and a good thing too', but to pose the question, 'How is it that at certain moments and in certain orders of knowledge, there are these sudden take-offs, these hastenings of evolution, these transformations which fail to correspond to the calm, continuist image that is normally accredited?' But the important thing here is not that such changes can be rapid and extensive, or rather it is that this extent and rapidity are only the sign of something else: a modification in the rules of formation of statements which are accepted as scientifically true. Thus it is not a change of content (refutation of old errors, recovery of old truths), nor is it a change of theoretical form (renewal of a paradigm, modification of systematic ensembles). It is a question of what *governs* statements, and the way in which they *govern* each other so as to constitute a set of propositions which are scientifically acceptable, and hence capable of being verified or falsified by scientific procedures. In short, there is a problem of the régime, the politics of the scientific statement. At this level it's not so much a matter of knowing what external power imposes itself on science, as of what effects of power circulate among scientific statements, what constitutes, as it were, their internal régime of power, and how and why at certain moments that régime undergoes a global modification.

It was these different régimes that I tried to identify and describe in *The Order of Things*, all the while making it clear that I wasn't trying for the moment to explain them, and that it would be necessary to try and do this in a subsequent work. But what was lacking here was this problem of the 'discursive régime', of the effects of power peculiar to the play of statements. I confused this too much with systematicity, theoretical form, or something like a paradigm. This same central problem of power, which at that time I had not yet properly isolated, emerges in two very different aspects at the point of junction of *Madness and Civilisation* and *The Order of Things*.

> We need, then, to locate the notion of discontinuity in its proper context. And perhaps there is another concept which is both more difficult and more central to your thought, the concept of an event. For in relation to the event a whole generation was long trapped in an *impasse*, in that following the works of ethnologists, some of them great ethnologists, a dichotomy was established between structures (the *thinkable*) and the event considered as the site of the irrational, the unthinkable, that which doesn't and cannot enter into the mechanism and play of analysis, at least in the form which this took in structuralism. In a recent discussion published in the journal '*L'Homme*', three eminent anthropologists posed this question once again about the concept of event, and said: the event is what always escapes our rational grasp, the domain of 'absolute contingency'; we are thinkers who analyse structures, history is no concern of ours, what could we be expected to have to say about it, and so forth. This opposition then between event and structure is the site and the product of a certain anthropology. I would say this has had devastating effects among historians who have finally reached the point of trying to dismiss the event and the '*évènementiel*' as an inferior order of history dealing with trivial facts, chance occurrences and so on. Whereas it is a fact that there are nodal

problems in history which are neither a matter of trivial circumstances nor of those beautiful structures that are so orderly, intelligible and transparent to analysis. For instance, the 'great internment' which you described in *Madness and Civilisation* perhaps represents one of these nodes which elude the dichotomy of structure and event. Could you elaborate from our present standpoint on this renewal and reformulation of the concept of event?

One can agree that structuralism formed the most systematic effort to evacuate the concept of the event, not only from ethnology but from a whole series of other sciences and in the extreme case from history. In that sense, I don't see who could be more of an anti-structuralist than myself. But the important thing is to avoid trying to do for the event what was previously done with the concept of structure. It's not a matter of locating everything on one level, that of the event, but of realising that there are actually a whole order of levels of different types of events differing in amplitude, chronological breadth, and capacity to produce effects.

The problem is at once to distinguish among events, to differentiate the networks and levels to which they belong, and to reconstitute the lines along which they are connected and engender one another. From this follows a refusal of analyses couched in terms of the symbolic field or the domain of signifying structures, and a recourse to analyses in terms of the genealogy of relations of force, strategic developments, and tactics. Here I believe one's point of reference should not be to the great model of language (*langue*) and signs, but to that of war and battle. The history which bears and determines us has the form of a war rather than that of a language: relations of power, not relations of meaning. History has no 'meaning', though this is not to say that it is absurd or incoherent. On the contrary, it is intelligible and should be susceptible of analysis down to the smallest detail—but this in accordance with the intelligibility of struggles, of strategies and tactics. Neither the dialectic, as logic of contradictions, nor semiotics, as the structure of communication, can account for the intrinsic intelligibility of conflicts. 'Dialectic' is a way of evading the

always open and hazardous reality of conflict by reducing it
to a Hegelian skeleton, and 'semiology' is a way of avoiding
its violent, bloody and lethal character by reducing it to the
calm Platonic form of language and dialogue.

> In the context of this problem of discursivity, I think
> one can be confident in saying that you were the first
> person to pose the question of power regarding dis-
> course, and that at a time when analyses in terms of the
> concept or object of the 'text', along with the accom-
> panying methodology of semiology, structuralism, etc.,
> were the prevailing fashion. Posing for discourse the
> question of power means basically to ask whom does
> discourse serve? It isn't so much a matter of analysing
> discourse into its unsaid, its implicit meaning, because
> (as you have often repeated) discourses are transparent,
> they need no interpretation, no one to assign them a
> meaning. If one reads 'texts' in a certain way, one
> perceives that they speak clearly to us and require no
> further supplementary sense or interpretation. This
> question of power that you have addressed to discourse
> naturally has particular effects and implications in
> relation to methodology and contemporary historical
> researches. Could you briefly situate within your work
> this question you have posed—if indeed it's true that
> you have posed it?

I don't think I was the first to pose the question. On the
contrary, I'm struck by the difficulty I had in formulating it.
When I think back now, I ask myself what else it was that I
was talking about, in *Madness and Civilisation* or *The Birth
of the Clinic*, but power? Yet I'm perfectly aware that I
scarcely ever used the word and never had such a field of
analyses at my disposal. I can say that this was an incapacity
linked undoubtedly with the political situation we found
ourselves in. It is hard to see where, either on the Right or
the Left, this problem of power could then have been posed.
On the Right, it was posed only in terms of constitution,
sovereignty, etc., that is, in juridical terms; on the Marxist
side, it was posed only in terms of the State apparatus. The
way power was exercised—concretely and in detail—with

its specificity, its techniques and tactics, was something that no one attempted to ascertain; they contented themselves with denouncing it in a polemical and global fashion as it existed among the 'others', in the adversary camp. Where Soviet socialist power was in question, its opponents called it totalitarianism; power in Western capitalism was denounced by the Marxists as class domination; but the mechanics of power in themselves were never analysed. This task could only begin after 1968, that is to say on the basis of daily struggles at grass roots level, among those whose fight was located in the fine meshes of the web of power. This was where the concrete nature of power became visible, along with the prospect that these analyses of power would prove fruitful in accounting for all that had hitherto remained outside the field of political analysis. To put it very simply, psychiatric internment, the mental normalisation of individuals, and penal institutions have no doubt a fairly limited importance if one is only looking for their economic significance. On the other hand, they are undoubtedly essential to the general functioning of the wheels of power. So long as the posing of the question of power was kept subordinate to the economic instance and the system of interests which this served, there was a tendency to regard these problems as of small importance.

> So a certain kind of Marxism and a certain kind of phenomenology constituted an objective obstacle to the formulation of this problematic?

Yes, if you like, to the extent that it's true that, in our student days, people of my generation were brought up on these two forms of analysis, one in terms of the constituent subject, the other in terms of the economic in the last instance, ideology and the play of superstructures and infrastructures.

> Still within this methodological context, how would you situate the genealogical approach? As a questioning of the conditions of possibility, modalities and constitution of the 'objects' and domains you have successively analysed, what makes it necessary?

I wanted to see how these problems of constitution could be resolved within a historical framework, instead of referring them back to a constituent object (madness, criminality or whatever). But this historical contextualisation needed to be something more than the simple relativisation of the phenomenological subject. I don't believe the problem can be solved by historicising the subject as posited by the phenomenologists, fabricating a subject that evolves through the course of history. One has to dispense with the constituent subject, to get rid of the subject itself, that's to say, to arrive at an analysis which can account for the constitution of the subject within a historical framework. And this is what I would call genealogy, that is, a form of history which can account for the constitution of knowledges, discourses, domains of objects etc., without having to make reference to a subject which is either transcendental in relation to the field of events or runs in its empty sameness throughout the course of history.

Marxist phenomenology and a certain kind of Marxism have clearly acted as a screen and an obstacle; there are two further concepts which continue today to act as a screen and an obstacle, ideology on the one hand and repression on the other.

All history comes to be thought of within these categories which serve to assign a meaning to such diverse phenomena as normalisation, sexuality and power. And regardless of whether these two concepts are explicitly utilised, in the end one always comes back, on the one hand to ideology—where it is easy to make the reference back to Marx—and on the other to repression, which is a concept often and readily employed by Freud throughout the course of his career. Hence I would like to put forward the following suggestion. Behind these concepts and among those who (properly or improperly) employ them, there is a kind of nostalgia; behind the concept of ideology, the nostalgia for a quasi-transparent form of knowledge, free from all error and illusion, and behind the concept of repression, the longing for a form of power innocent of all coercion, discipline and normalisation. On the one hand, a power without a bludgeon, and on the other hand knowledge without deception. You have called these two concepts, ideology and repression, negative, 'psychological', insufficiently analytical. This is particularly the case in *Discipline and Punish* where, even if there isn't an extended discussion of these concepts, there is nevertheless a kind of analysis that allows one to go beyond the traditional forms of explanation and intelligibility which, in the last (and not only the last) instance rest on the concepts of ideology and repression. Could you perhaps use this occasion to specify more explicitly your thoughts on these matters? With *Discipline and Punish*, a kind of positive history seems to be emerging which is free of all the negativity and psychologism implicit in those two universal skeleton-keys.

The notion of ideology appears to me to be difficult to make use of, for three reasons. The first is that, like it or not, it always stands in virtual opposition to something else which is supposed to count as truth. Now I believe that the problem does not consist in drawing the line between that in a discourse which falls under the category of scientificity or truth, and that which comes under some other category, but in seeing historically how effects of truth are produced within discourses which in themselves are neither true nor false. The second drawback is that the concept of ideology refers, I think necessarily, to something of the order of a subject. Thirdly, ideology stands in a secondary position relative to something which functions as its infrastructure, as its material, economic determinant, etc. For these three reasons, I think that this is a notion that cannot be used without circumspection.

The notion of repression is a more insidious one, or at all events I myself have had much more trouble in freeing myself of it, in so far as it does indeed appear to correspond so well with a whole range of phenomena which belong among the effects of power. When I wrote *Madness and Civilisation*, I made at least an implicit use of this notion of repression. I think indeed that I was positing the existence of a sort of living, voluble and anxious madness which the mechanisms of power and psychiatry were supposed to have come to repress and reduce to silence. But it seems to me now that the notion of repression is quite inadequate for capturing what is precisely the productive aspect of power. In defining the effects of power as repression, one adopts a purely juridical conception of such power, one identifies power with a law which says no, power is taken above all as carrying the force of a prohibition. Now I believe that this is a wholly negative, narrow, skeletal conception of power, one which has been curiously widespread. If power were never anything but repressive, if it never did anything but to say no, do you really think one would be brought to obey it? What makes power hold good, what makes it accepted, is simply the fact that it doesn't only weigh on us as a force that says no, but that it traverses and produces things, it induces pleasure, forms knowledge, produces discourse. It needs to be considered as a productive network which runs through the whole social body, much more than as a negative instance whose function is repression. In *Discipline and Punish* what I wanted to show was how, from the seventeenth and eighteenth centuries onwards, there was a veritable technological take-off in the productivity of power. Not only did the monarchies of the Classical period develop great state apparatuses (the army, the police and fiscal administration), but above all there was established at this period what one might call a new 'economy' of power, that is to say procedures which allowed the effects of power to circulate in a manner at once continuous, uninterrupted, adapted and 'individualised' throughout the entire social body. These new techniques are both much more efficient and much less wasteful (less costly economically, less risky in their results, less open to loopholes and resistances) than the techniques previously employed which were based on a mixture of more or less forced tolerances (from recognised privileges to endemic criminality) and costly ostentation (spectacular and discontinuous interventions of power, the most violent form of which was the 'exemplary', because exceptional, punishment).

Repression is a concept used above all in relation to sexuality. It was held that bourgeois society represses sexuality, stifles sexual desire, and so forth. And when one considers for example the campaign launched against masturbation in the eighteenth century, or the medical discourse on homosexuality in the second half of the nineteenth century, or discourse on sexuality in general, one does seem to be faced with a discourse of repression. In reality however this discourse serves to make possible a whole series of interventions, tactical and positive interventions of surveillance, circulation, control and so forth, which seem to have been intimately linked with techniques that give the appearance of repression, or are at least liable to be interpreted as such. I believe the crusade against masturbation is a typical example of this.

Certainly. It is customary to say that bourgeois society repressed infantile sexuality to the point where it refused even to speak of it or acknowledge its existence. It was necessary to wait until Freud for the discovery at last to be made that children have a sexuality. Now if you read all the books on pedagogy and child medicine— all the manuals for parents that were published in the eighteenth century— you find that children's sex is spoken of constantly and in every possible context. One might argue that the purpose of these discourses was precisely to prevent children from having a sexuality. But their *effect* was to din it into parents' heads that their children's sex constituted a fundamental problem in terms of their parental educational responsibilities, and to din it into children's heads that their relationship with their own body and their own sex was to be a fundamental problem as far as *they* were concerned; and this had the consequence of sexually exciting the bodies of children while at the same time fixing the parental gaze and vigilance on the peril of infantile sexuality. The result was a sexualising of the infantile body, a sexualising of the bodily relationship between parent and child, a sexualising of the familial domain. 'Sexuality' is far more of a positive product of power than power was ever repression of sexuality. I believe that it is precisely these positive mechanisms that need to be investigated, and here one must free oneself of the juridical schematism of all previous characterisations of the nature of power. Hence a historical problem arises, namely that of discovering why the West has insisted for so long on seeing the power it exercises as juridical and negative rather than as technical and positive.

> Perhaps this is because it has always been thought that power is mediated through the forms prescribed in the great juridical and philosophical theories, and that there is a fundamental, immutable gulf between those who exercise power and those who undergo it.

I wonder if this isn't bound up with the institution of monarchy. This developed during the Middle Ages against the backdrop of the previously endemic struggles between feudal power agencies. The monarchy presented itself as a referee, a power capable of putting an end to war, violence and pillage and saying no to these struggles and private feuds. It made itself acceptable by allocating itself a juridical and negative function, albeit one whose limits it naturally began at once to overstep. Sovereign, law and prohibition formed a system of representation of power which was extended during the subsequent era by the theories of right: political theory has never ceased to be obsessed with the person of the sovereign. Such theories still continue today to busy themselves with the problem of sovereignty. What we need, however, is a political philosophy that isn't erected around the problem of sovereignty, nor therefore around the problems of law and prohibition. We need to cut off the King's head: in political theory that has still to be done.

> The King's head still hasn't been cut off, yet already people are trying to replace it by discipline, that vast system instituted in the seventeenth century comprising the functions of surveillance, normalisation and control and, a little later, those of punishment, correction, education and so on. One wonders where this system comes from, why it emerges and what its use is. And today there is rather a tendency to attribute a subject to it, a great, molar, totalitarian subject, namely the modern State, constituted in the sixteenth and seven-

teenth centuries and bringing with it (according to the classical theories) the professional army, the police and the administrative bureaucracy.

To pose the problem in terms of the State means to continue posing it in terms of sovereign and sovereignty, that is to say in terms of law. If one describes all these phenomena of power as dependant on the State apparatus, this means grasping them as essentially repressive: the Army as a power of death, police and justice as punitive instances, etc. I don't want to say that the State isn't important; what I want to say is that relations of power, and hence the analysis that must be made of them, necessarily extend beyond the limits of the State. In two senses: first of all because the State, for all the omnipotence of its apparatuses, is far from being able to occupy the whole field of actual power relations, and further because the State can only operate on the basis of other, already existing power relations. The State is superstructural in relation to a whole series of power networks that invest the body, sexuality, the family, kinship, knowledge, technology and so forth. True, these networks stand in a conditioning–conditioned relationship to a kind of 'meta-power' which is structured essentially round a certain number of great prohibition functions; but this meta-power with its prohibitions can only take hold and secure its footing where it is rooted in a whole series of multiple and indefinite power relations that supply the necessary basis for the great negative forms of power. That is just what I was trying to make apparent in my book.

> Doesn't this open up the possibility of overcoming the dualism of political struggles that eternally feed on the opposition between the State on the one hand and Revolution on the other? Doesn't it indicate a wider field of conflicts than that of those where the adversary is the State?

I would say that the State consists in the codification of a whole number of power relations which render its functioning possible, and that Revolution is a different type of codification of the same relations. This implies that there are many different kinds of revolution, roughly speaking as many kinds as there are possible subversive recodifications of power relations, and further that one can perfectly well conceive of revolutions which leave essentially untouched the power relations which form the basis for the functioning of the State.

> You have said about power as an object of research that one has to invert Clausewitz's formula so as to arrive at the idea that politics is the continuation of war by other means. Does the military model seem to you on the basis of your most recent researches to be the best one for describing power; is war here simply a metaphorical model, or is it the literal, regular, everyday mode of operation of power?

This is the problem I now find myself confronting. As soon as one endeavours to detach power with its techniques and procedures from the form of law within which it has been theoretically confined up until now, one is driven to ask this basic question: isn't power simply a form of warlike domination? Shouldn't one therefore conceive all problems of power in terms of relations of war? Isn't power a sort of generalised war which assumes at particular moments the forms of peace and the State? Peace would then be a form of war, and the State a means of waging it.

A whole range of problems emerge here. Who wages war against whom? Is it between two classes, or more? Is it a war of all against all? What is the role of the army and military institutions in this civil society where permanent war is waged? What is the relevance of concepts of tactics and strategy for analysing structures and political processes? What is the essence and mode of transformation of power relations? All these questions need to be explored. In any case it's astonishing to see how easily and self-evidently people talk of war-like relations of power or of class struggle without ever making it clear whether some form of war is meant, and if so what form.

> We have already talked about this disciplinary power whose effects, rules and mode of constitution you

describe in *Discipline and Punish*. One might ask here, why surveillance? What is the use of surveillance? Now there is a phenomenon that emerges during the eighteenth century, namely the discovery of population as an object of scientific investigation; people begin to inquire into birth-rates, death-rates and changes in population and to say for the first time that it is impossible to govern a State without knowing its population. Moheau for example, who was one of the first to organise this kind of research on an administrative basis, seems to see its goal as lying in the problems of political control of a population. Does this disciplinary power then act alone and of itself, or doesn't it rather draw support from something more general, namely this fixed conception of a population that reproduces itself in the proper way, composed of people who marry in the proper way and behave in the proper way, according to precisely determined norms? One would then have on the one hand a sort of global, molar body, the body of the population, together with a whole series of discourses concerning it, and then on the other hand and down below, the small bodies, the docile, individual bodies, the micro-bodies of discipline. Even if you are only perhaps at the beginning of your researches here, could you say how you see the nature of the relationships (if any) which are engendered between these different bodies: the molar body of the population and the micro-bodies of individuals?

Your question is exactly on target. I find it difficult to reply because I am working on this problem right now. I believe one must keep in view the fact that along with all the fundamental technical inventions and discoveries of the seventeenth and eighteenth centuries, a new technology of the exercise of power also emerged which was probably even more important than the constitutional reforms and new forms of government established at the end of the eighteenth century. In the camp of the Left, one often hears people saying that power is that which abstracts, which negates the body, represses, suppresses, and so forth. I would say instead that what I find most striking about these new technologies of power introduced since the seventeenth and eighteenth centuries is their concrete and precise character, their grasp of a multiple and differentiated reality. In feudal societies power functioned essentially through signs and levies. Signs of loyalty to the feudal lords, rituals, ceremonies and so forth, and levies in the form of taxes, pillage, hunting, war etc. In the seventeenth and eighteenth centuries a form of power comes into being that begins to exercise itself through social production and social service. It becomes a matter of obtaining productive service from individuals in their concrete lives. And in consequence, a real and effective 'incorporation' of power was necessary, in the sense that power had to be able to gain access to the bodies of individuals, to their acts, attitudes and modes of everyday behaviour. Hence the significance of methods like school discipline, which succeeded in making children's bodies the object of highly complex systems of manipulation and conditioning. But at the same time, these new techniques of power needed to grapple with the phenomena of population, in short to undertake the administration, control and direction of the accumulation of men (the economic system that promotes the accumulation of capital and the system of power that ordains the accumulation of men are, from the seventeenth century on, correlated and inseparable phenomena): hence there arise the problems of demography, public health, hygiene, housing conditions, longevity and fertility. And I believe that the political significance of the problem of sex is due to the fact that sex is located at the point of intersection of the discipline of the body and the control of the population.

Finally, a question you have been asked before: the work you do, these preoccupations of yours, the results you arrive at, what use can one finally make of all this in everyday political struggles? You have spoken previously of local struggles as the specific site of confrontation with power, outside and beyond all such global, general instances as parties or classes. What does this imply about the role of intellectuals? If one isn't an 'organic' intellectual acting as the spokesman for a global organisation, if one doesn't purport to function as the bringer, the master of truth, what position is the intellectual to assume?

For a long period, the 'left' intellectual spoke and was acknowledged the right of speaking in the capacity of master of truth and justice.[1] He was heard, or purported to make himself heard, as the spokesman of the universal. To be an intellectual meant something like being the consciousness/conscience of us all. I think we have here an idea transposed from Marxism, from a faded Marxism indeed. Just as the proletariat, by the necessity of its historical situation, is the bearer of the universal (but its immediate, unreflected bearer, barely conscious of itself as such), so the intellectual, through his moral, theoretical and political choice, aspires to be the bearer of this universality in its conscious, elaborated form. The intellectual is thus taken as the clear, individual figure of a universality whose obscure, collective form is embodied in the proletariat.

Some years have now passed since the intellectual was called upon to play this role. A new mode of the 'connection between theory and practice' has been established. Intellectuals have got used to working, not in the modality of the 'universal', the 'exemplary', the 'just-and-true-for-all', but within specific sectors, at the precise points where their own conditions of life or work situate them (housing, the hospital, the asylum, the laboratory, the university, family and sexual relations). This has undoubtedly given them a much more immediate and concrete awareness of struggles. And they have met here with problems which are specific, 'non-universal', and often different from those of the proletariat or the masses. And yet I believe intellectuals have actually been drawn closer to the proletariat and the masses, for two reasons. Firstly, because it has been a question of real, material, everyday struggles, and secondly because they have often been confronted, albeit in a different form, by the same adversary as the proletariat, namely the multinational corporations, the judicial and police apparatuses, the property speculators, etc. This is what I would call the 'specific' intellectual as opposed to the 'universal' intellectual.

This new configuration has a further political significance. It makes it possible, if not to integrate, at least to re-articulate categories which were previously kept separate. The intellectual *par excellence* used to be the writer: as a universal consciousness, a free subject, he was counter-posed to those intellectuals who were merely *competent instances* in the service of the State or Capital—technicians, magistrates, teachers. Since the time when each individual's specific activity began to serve as the basis for politicisation, the threshold of *writing*, as the sacralising mark of the intellectual, has disappeared. And it has become possible to develop lateral connections across different forms of knowledge and from one focus of politicisation to another. Magistrates and psychiatrists, doctors and social workers, laboratory technicians and sociologists have become able to participate, both within their own fields and through mutual exchange and support, in a global process of politicisation of intellectuals. This process explains how, even as the writer tends to disappear as a figurehead, the university and the academic emerge, if not as principal elements, at least as 'exchangers', privileged points of intersection. If the universities and education have become politically ultrasensitive areas, this is no doubt the reason why. And what is called the crisis of the universities should not be interpreted as a loss of power, but on the contrary as a multiplication and re-inforcement of their power-effects as centres in a polymorphous ensemble of intellectuals who virtually all pass through and relate themselves to the academic system. The whole relentless theorisation of writing which we saw in the 1960s was doubtless only a swansong. Through it, the writer was fighting for the preservation of his political privilege; but the fact that it was precisely a matter of theory, that he needed scientific credentials, founded in linguistics, semiology, psychoanalysis, that this theory took its references from the direction of Saussure, or Chomsky, etc., and that it gave rise to such mediocre literary products, all this proves that the activity of the writer was no longer at the focus of things.

It seems to me that this figure of the 'specific' intellectual has emerged since the Second World War. Perhaps it was the atomic scientist (in a word, or rather a name: Oppenheimer) who acted as the point of transition between the universal and the specific intellectual. It's because he had a direct and localised relation to scientific knowledge and institutions that the atomic scientist could make his intervention; but, since the nuclear threat affected the whole human race and the fate of the world, his discourse could at the same time be the discourse of the universal. Under the rubric of this protest, which concerned the entire world, the atomic expert brought into play his specific position in the order of knowledge. And for the first time, I think, the intellectual was hounded by political powers, no longer on account of a general discourse which he conducted, but because of the knowledge at his disposal: it was at this level that he constituted a political threat. I am only speaking here of Western intellectuals. What happened in the Soviet Union is analogous with this on a number of points, but different on many others. There is certainly a whole study that needs to be made of scientific dissidence in the West and the socialist countries since 1945.

It is possible to suppose that the 'universal' intellectual, as he functioned in the nineteenth and early twentieth centuries was in fact derived from a quite specific historical figure: the man of justice, the man of law, who counterposes to power, despotism and the abuses and arrogance of wealth the universality of justice and the equity of an ideal law. The great political struggles of the eighteenth century were fought over law, right, the constitution, the just in reason and law, that which can and must apply universally. What we call today 'the intellectual' (I mean the intellectual in the political, not the sociological sense of the word, in other words the person who utilises his knowledge, his competence and his relation to truth in the field of political struggles) was, I think, an offspring of the jurist, or at any rate of the man who invoked the universality of a just law, if necessary against the legal professions themselves (Voltaire, in France, is the prototype of such intellectuals). The 'universal' intellectual derives from the jurist or notable, and finds his fullest manifestation in the writer, the bearer of values and significations in which all can recognise themselves. The 'specific' intellectual derives from quite another figure, not the jurist or notable, but the savant or expert. I said just now that it's with the atomic scientists that this

latter figure comes to the forefront. In fact, it was preparing
in the wings for some time before, and was even present on
at least a corner of the stage from about the end of the
nineteenth century. No doubt it's with Darwin or rather
with the post-Darwinian evolutionists that this figure begins
to appear clearly. The stormy relationship between evolutionism and the socialists, as well as the highly ambiguous
effects of evolutionism (on sociology, criminology, psychiatry and eugenics, for example) mark the important
moment when the savant begins to intervene in contemporary political struggles in the name of a 'local' scientific truth
—however important the latter may be. Historically,
Darwin represents this point of inflection in the history of
the Western intellectual. (Zola is very significant from this
point of view: he is the type of the 'universal' intellectual,
bearer of law and militant of equity, but he ballasts his
discourse with a whole invocation of nosology and evolutionism, which he believes to be scientific, grasps very
poorly in any case, and whose political effects on his own
discourse are very equivocal.) If one were to study this
closely, one would have to follow how the physicists, at the
turn of the century, re-entered the field of political debate.
The debates between the theorists of socialism and the
theorists of relativity are of capital importance in this
history.

   At all events, biology and physics were to a privileged
degree the zones of formation of this new personage, the
specific intellectual. The extension of technico-scientific
structures in the economic and strategic domain was what
gave him his real importance. The figure in which the
functions and prestige of this new intellectual are concentrated is no longer that of the 'writer of genius', but that of
the 'absolute savant', no longer he who bears the values of
all, opposes the unjust sovereign or his ministers and makes
his cry resound even beyond the grave. It is rather he who,
along with a handful of others, has at his disposal, whether
in the service of the State or against it, powers which can
either benefit or irrevocably destroy life. He is no longer the
rhapsodist of the eternal, but the strategist of life and death.
Meanwhile we are at present experiencing the disappearance of the figure of the 'great writer'.

Now let's come back to more precise details. We accept, alongside the development of technico-scientific structures in contemporary society, the importance gained by the specific intellectual in recent decades, as well as the acceleration of this process since around 1960. Now the specific intellectual encounters certain obstacles and faces certain dangers. The danger of remaining at the level of conjunctural struggles, pressing demands restricted to particular sectors. The risk of letting himself be manipulated by the political parties or trade union apparatuses which control these local struggles. Above all, the risk of being unable to develop these struggles for lack of a global strategy or outside support; the risk too of not being followed, or only by very limited groups. In France we can see at the moment an example of this. The struggle around the prisons, the penal system and the police-judicial system, because it has developed 'in solitary', among social workers and ex-prisoners, has tended increasingly to separate itself from the forces which would have enabled it to grow. It has allowed itself to be penetrated by a whole naive, archaic ideology which makes the criminal at once into the innocent victim and the pure rebel—society's scapegoat—and the young wolf of future revolutions. This return to anarchist themes of the late nineteenth century was possible only because of a failure of integration of current strategies. And the result has been a deep split between this campaign with its monotonous, lyrical little chant, heard only among a few small groups, and the masses who have good reason not to accept it as valid political currency, but who also—thanks to the studiously cultivated fear of criminals—tolerate the maintenance, or rather the reinforcement, of the judicial and police apparatuses.

It seems to me that we are now at a point where the function of the specific intellectual needs to be reconsidered. Reconsidered but not abandoned, despite the nostalgia of some for the great 'universal' intellectuals and the desire for a new philosophy, a new world-view. Suffice it to consider the important results which have been achieved in psychiatry: they prove that these local, specific struggles haven't been a mistake and haven't led to a dead end. One may even say that the role of the specific intellectual must become more and more important in proportion to the political responsibilities which he is obliged willy-nilly to accept, as a nuclear scientist, computer expert, pharmacologist, etc. It would be a dangerous error to discount him politically in his specific relation to a local form of power, either on the grounds that this is a specialist matter which doesn't concern the masses (which is doubly wrong: they are already aware of it, and in any case implicated in it), or that the specific intellectual serves the interests of State or Capital (which is true, but at the same time shows the strategic position he occupies), or, again, on the grounds that he propagates a scientific ideology (which isn't always true, and is anyway certainly a secondary matter compared with the fundamental point: the effects proper to true discourses).

The important thing here, I believe, is that truth isn't outside power, or lacking in power: contrary to a myth whose history and functions would repay further study, truth isn't the reward of free spirits, the child of protracted solitude, nor the privilege of those who have succeeded in liberating themselves. Truth is a thing of this world: it is produced only by virtue of multiple forms of constraint. And it induces regular effects of power. Each society has its régime of truth, its 'general politics' of truth: that is, the types of discourse which it accepts and makes function as true; the mechanisms and instances which enable one to distinguish true and false statements, the means by which each is sanctioned; the techniques and procedures accorded value in the acquisition of truth; the status of those who are charged with saying what counts as true.

In societies like ours, the 'political economy' of truth is characterised by five important traits. 'Truth' is centred on the form of scientific discourse and the institutions which produce it; it is subject to constant economic and political incitement (the demand for truth, as much for economic production as for political power); it is the object, under diverse forms, of immense diffusion and consumption (circulating through apparatuses of education and information whose extent is relatively broad in the social body, not withstanding certain strict limitations); it is produced and transmitted under the control, dominant if not exclusive, of a few great political and economic apparatuses (university, army, writing, media); lastly, it is the issue of a whole political debate and social confrontation ('ideological' struggles).

It seems to me that what must now be taken into account in the intellectual is not the 'bearer of universal values'. Rather, it's the person occupying a specific position — but whose specificity is linked, in a society like ours, to the general functioning of an apparatus of truth. In other words, the intellectual has a three-fold specificity: that of his class position (whether as petty-bourgeois in the service of capitalism or 'organic' intellectual of the proletariat); that of his conditions of life and work, linked to his condition as an intellectual (his field of research, his place in a laboratory, the political and economic demands to which he submits or against which he rebels, in the university, the hospital, etc.); lastly, the specificity of the politics of truth in our societies. And it's with this last factor that his position can take on a general significance and that his local, specific struggle can have effects and implications which are not simply professional or sectoral. The intellectual can operate and struggle at the general level of that régime of truth which is so essential to the structure and functioning of our society. There is a battle 'for truth', or at least 'around truth' — it being understood once again that by truth I do not mean 'the ensemble of truths which are to be discovered and accepted', but rather 'the ensemble of rules according to which the true and the false are separated and specific effects of power attached to the true', it being understood also that it's not a matter of a battle 'on behalf' of the truth, but of a battle about the status of truth and the economic and political role it plays. It is necessary to think of the political problems of intellectuals not in terms of 'science' and 'ideology', but in terms of 'truth' and 'power'. And thus the question of the professionalisation of intellectuals and the division between intellectual and manual labour can be envisaged in a new way.

All this must seem very confused and uncertain. Uncertain indeed, and what I am saying here is above all to be taken as a hypothesis. In order for it to be a little less confused, however, I would like to put forward a few 'propositions'—not firm assertions, but simply suggestions to be further tested and evaluated.

'Truth' is to be understood as a system of ordered procedures for the production, regulation, distribution, circulation and operation of statements.

'Truth' is linked in a circular relation with systems of power which produce and sustain it, and to effects of power which it induces and which extend it. A 'régime' of truth.

This régime is not merely ideological or superstructural; it was a condition of the formation and development of capitalism. And it's this same régime which, subject to certain modifications, operates in the socialist countries (I leave open here the question of China, about which I know little).

The essential political problem for the intellectual is not to criticise the ideological contents supposedly linked to science, or to ensure that his own scientific practice is accompanied by a correct ideology, but that of ascertaining the possibility of constituting a new politics of truth. The problem is not changing people's consciousnesses—or what's in their heads—but the political, economic, institutional régime of the production of truth.

It's not a matter of emancipating truth from every system of power (which would be a chimera, for truth is already power) but of detaching the power of truth from the forms of hegemony, social, economic and cultural, within which it operates at the present time.

The political question, to sum up, is not error, illusion, alienated consciousness or ideology; it is truth itself. Hence the importance of Nietzsche.

Note

1 Foucault's response to this final question was given in writing.

7 POWERS AND STRATEGIES

Interviewers: editorial collective of *Les révoltes logiques*—
Jean Borreil, Geneviève Fraisse, Jacques Rancière, Pierre
Saint-Germain, Michel Souletie, Patrick Vauday, Patrice
Vermeren.

Your book *Madness and Civilisation* concludes by
exposing the illusory nature of Pinel's 'liberation' of the
insane. *The Birth of the Clinic* starts by pouring scorn
on medical humanisms and 'acephalous phenomen-
ologies of understanding'. Yet prevailing Leftist and
post-Leftist opinion has been happy to regard 'internment' as encapsulating the efficacy and the oppressive
nature of power, and turned Michel Foucault into a sort
of new Pinel announcing the joyous liberation of desire
and the marginal.

This same theme of internment is used to reduce the
analysis of mechanisms of domination to the schema of
a purely external relation between power and the plebs,
positing the equation: Classical Reason/Internment =
Marxism/the Gulag.

Isn't it an inversion of your arguments to make the
critique of 'internment' serve as a neo-liberal or neo-
populist slogan?

I am indeed worried by a certain use that is made of the
Gulag–Internment parallel. A certain use which consists in
saying, 'Everyone has their own Gulag, the Gulag is here at
our door, in our cities, our hospitals, our prisons, it's here in
our heads'. I fear that under the pretext of 'systematic
denunciation' a sort of open-ended eclecticism will be
installed which will serve as a cover for all sorts of ma-
noeuvres. With immense indignation, with a great philanthropic sigh, we embrace the whole world's political
persecutions, and so make it possible for the PCF to take

part in a meeting where Plioutch is speaking. Which enables the said communist party to produce three parallel lines of argument: (i) From the wings: 'Here we all are together, all terribly concerned. The USSR has the same problems as every country in the world, neither better nor worse, and vice versa. So let's share our struggle, that is divide it up between us'. (ii) To the partners in the electoral alliance: 'Look what an independent line we too are taking towards the USSR. We are denouncing the Gulag just as you are, so leave us in peace'. (iii) Inside the Party: 'Look how skilful we are at evading the problem of the Soviet Gulag by dissolving it in the troubled waters of political imprisonment in general'.

It seems to me that one must make a distinction between the *Gulag institution* and the *Gulag question*. Like all political technologies, the Gulag institution has its history, its transformations and transpositions, its functions and effects. The internment practiced in the Classical age forms in all likelihood a part of its archaeology. The Gulag question, on the other hand, involves a political choice. There are those who pose it and those who don't. To pose it means four things:

(a) Refusing to question the Gulag on the basis of the texts of Marx or Lenin or to ask oneself how, through what error, deviation, misunderstanding or distortion of speculation or practice, their theory could have been betrayed to such a degree. On the contrary, it means questioning all these theoretical texts, however old, from the standpoint of the reality of the Gulag. Rather than of searching in those texts for a condemnation in advance of the Gulag, it is a matter of asking what in those texts could have made the Gulag possible, what might even now continue to justify it, and what makes it intolerable truth still accepted today. The Gulag question must be posed not in terms of error (reduction of the problem to one of theory), but in terms of reality.

(b) Refusing to restrict one's questioning to the level of causes. If one begins by asking for the 'cause' of the Gulag (Russia's retarded development, the transformation of the party into a bureaucracy, the specific economic difficulties of the USSR), one makes the Gulag appear as a sort of disease or abscess, an infection, degeneration or involution. This is to think of the Gulag only negatively, as an obstacle to be removed, a dysfunctioning to be rectified—a maternity illness of the country which is painfully giving birth to socialism. The Gulag question has to be posed in positive terms. The problem of causes must not be dissociated from that of function: what use is the Gulag, what functions does it assure, in what strategies is it integrated? The Gulag should be analysed as a politico-economic operator in a socialist state. We must avoid all historicist reductionism. The Gulag is not a residue or a sequel of the past: it is a positive present.

(c) Refusing to adopt for the critique of the Gulag a law or principle of selection internal to our own discourse or dream. By this I mean giving up the politics of inverted commas, not attempting to evade the problem by putting inverted commas, whether damning or ironic, round Soviet socialism in order to protect the good, true socialism—with no inverted commas—which alone can provide a legitimate standpoint for a politically valid critique of the Gulag. Actually the only socialism which deserves these scornful scare-quotes is the one which leads the dreamy life of ideality in our heads. We must open our eyes on the contrary to what enables people there, on the spot, to resist the Gulag, what makes it intolerable for them, and what can give the people of the anti-Gulag the courage to stand up and die in order to be able to utter a word or a poem. We must discover what makes Mikhail Stern say 'I will not give in'. We must find out too how those 'almost illiterate' men and women gathered together (under what threats?) to accuse him found the strength to publicly exonerate him. We should listen to these people, not to our century-old little love song for 'socialism'. What is it that sustains them, what gives them their energy, what is the force at work in their resistance, what makes them stand and fight? And above all let us not ask them if they are really, still and despite everything, 'communists', as if that were the condition for our consenting to listen to them.[1] The leverage against the Gulag is not in our heads, but in their bodies, their energy, what they say, think and do.

(d) Rejecting the universalising dissolution of the problem

into the 'denunciation' of every possible form of internment. The Gulag is not a question to be posed for any and every country. It has to be posed for every *socialist* country, insofar as none of these since 1917 has managed to function without a more-or-less developed Gulag system.

To sum up, it seems to me that we must insist on the specificity of the Gulag question against all theoretical reductionisms (which make the Gulag an error already to be read in the texts), against all historicist reductionisms (which make the Gulag a conjunctural effect which can be isolated in terms of its causes), against all utopian dissociations (which would set it, with 'pseudo-socialism', in opposition to socialism 'itself'), against all universalising dissolutions into the general form of internment. These operations all serve the same role (and they are none too many for the accomplishment of so difficult a task): to preserve the currency among us of a Leftist discourse whose organising principles remain unchanged. It seems to me that Glucksmann's analysis escapes all these so readily practiced forms of reduction.[2]

This much having been said regarding the specificity of the Gulag question, two problems remain: (i) How to relate concretely, both in analysis and in practice, the critique of the technologies of normalisation which derive historically from Classical internment with the struggle against the historically growing threat posed by the Soviet Gulag? What should the priorities be? What organic links ought we to establish between the two tasks? (ii) The other problem, which is linked with the preceding one (the answer to the second conditioning in part that to the first), concerns the existence of a 'plebs', the permanent, ever silent target for apparatuses of power.

To the former question it seems to me impossible at present to offer any categorical, individual response. We have to try and elaborate one via the political conjunctures which we are now traversing. To the second question however it seems to me that one can at least give the outline of an answer. No doubt it would be mistaken to conceive the plebs as the permanent ground of history, the final objective of all subjections, the ever smouldering centre of all revolts. The plebs is no doubt not a real sociological entity. But there is indeed always something in the social body, in classes, groups and individuals themselves which in some sense escapes relations of power, something which is by no means a more or less docile or reactive primal matter, but rather a centrifugal movement, an inverse energy, a discharge. There is certainly no such thing as 'the' plebs; rather there is, as it were, a certain plebeian quality or aspect ('*de la*' *plèbe*). There is plebs in bodies, in souls, in individuals, in the proletariat, in the bourgeoisie, but everywhere in a diversity of forms and extensions, of energies and irreducibilities. This measure of plebs is not so much what stands outside relations of power as their limit, their underside, their counter-stroke, that which responds to every advance of power by a movement of disengagement. Hence it forms the motivation for every new development of networks of power. The reduction of the plebs can be achieved in three ways, either by its effective subjection, or by its utilisation as a plebs (as in the example of criminality in the nineteenth century), or alternatively by its stabilising itself through a strategy of resistance. This point of view of the plebs, the point of view of the underside and limit of power, is thus indispensable for an analysis of its apparatuses (*dispositifs*); this is the starting point for understanding its functioning and developments. I don't think this can be confused in any way with a neo-populism that substantialises the plebs as an entity, or a neo-liberalism that sanctifies its basic rights.

The question of the exercise of power tends to be conceptualised today in terms of love (of the master) or desire (of the masses for fascism). Is it possible to establish the genealogy of this form of subjectivisation? And is it possible to establish the forms of consent, the 'reasons for obedience' whose functioning it serves to travesty? For some, the domain of sex is where the ineluctability of the master is established; for others, it is the source of the most radical of all subversions. Power is thus represented as interdict, with law as its form and sex as its content. Is this device for legitimating two contradictory discourses tied to the historical 'accident' of the Freudian discovery, or does it denote a specific function of sexuality in the economy of power?

It doesn't seem to me that one can deal with both of these questions—love of the master and desire of the masses for fascism—in the same way. It is true that in each case one finds a certain 'subjectivisation' of power relations, but this is not produced in the same way in the two cases.

In the affirmation of the desire of the masses for fascism, what is troubling is that an *affirmation* covers up for the lack of any precise historical analysis. In this I see above all the effect of a general complicity in the refusal to decipher what fascism really was (a refusal that manifests itself either in generalisation—fascism is everywhere, above all in our heads—or in Marxist schematisation). The non-analysis of fascism is one of the important political facts of the past thirty years. It enables fascism to be used as a floating signifier, whose function is essentially that of denunciation. The procedures of every form of power are suspected of being fascist, just as the masses are in their desires. There lies beneath the affirmation of the desire of the masses for fascism a historical problem which we have yet to secure the means of resolving.

The notion of 'love of the master' poses other problems, I think. It is a certain way of not posing the problem of power, or rather of posing it in such a way that it cannot be analysed. This is due to the insubstantiality of the notion of the master, an empty form haunted only by the various phantoms of the master and his slave, the master and his disciple, the master and his workman, the master who pronounces law and speaks the truth, the master who censors and forbids. The key point is that to this reduction of power to the figure of the master there is linked another reduction, that of procedures of power to the law of prohibition. This reduction of power to law has three main roles: (i) It underwrites a schema of power which is homogeneous for every level and domain—family or State, relations of education or production. (ii) It enables power never to be thought of in other than negative terms: refusal, limitation, obstruction, censorship. Power is what says no. And the challenging of power as thus conceived can appear only as transgression. (iii) It allows the fundamental operation of power to be thought of as that of a speech-act: enunciation of law, discourse of prohibition. The manifestation of power takes on the pure form of 'Thou shalt not'.

Such a conception has a certain number of epistemological advantages because of the possibility of linking it with an ethnology centred on the analysis of the great kinship-prohibitions and with a psychoanalysis centred on the mechanisms of repression. Thus one single and identical 'formula' of power (the interdict) comes to be applied to all forms of society and all levels of subjection. And so through treating power as the instance of negation one is led to a double 'subjectivisation'. In the aspect of its exercise, power is conceived as a sort of great absolute Subject which pronounces the interdict (no matter whether this Subject is taken as real, imaginary, or purely juridical): the Sovereignty of the Father, the Monarch or the general will. In the aspect of subjection to power, there is an equal tendency to 'subjectivise' it by specifying the point at which the interdict is accepted, the point where one says yes or no to power. This is how, in order to account for the exercise of Sovereignty, there is assumed either a renunciation of natural rights, a Social Contract, or a love of the master. It seems to me that the problem is always posed in the same terms, from the edifice constructed by the classical jurists down to current conceptions: an essentially negative power, presupposing on the one hand a sovereign whose role is to forbid and on the other a subject who must somehow effectively say yes to this prohibition. The contemporary analysis of power in terms of libido is still articulated by this old juridical conception.

Why has this kind of analysis enjoyed a centuries-old privilege? Why is power so invariably interpreted in the purely negative terms of law and prohibition? Why is power immediately represented as a system of law? It will be said no doubt that law (*droit*) in Western societies has always served as a mask for power. This explanation does not seem wholly adequate. Law was an effective instrument for the constitution of monarchical forms of power in Europe, and political thought was ordered for centuries around the problem of Sovereignty and its rights. Moreover, law, particularly in the eighteenth century, was a weapon of the struggle against the same monarchical power which had initially made use of it to impose itself. Finally, law was the principal mode of representation of power (and representation should not be understood here as a screen or an illusion, but as a real mode of action).

Law is neither the truth of power nor its alibi. It is an instrument of power which is at once complex and partial. The form of law with its effects of prohibition needs to be resituated among a number of other, non-juridical mechanisms. Thus the penal system should not be analysed purely and simply as an apparatus of prohibition and repression of one class by another, nor as an alibi for the lawless violence of the ruling class. The penal system makes possible a mode of political and economic management which exploits the difference between legality and illegalities. The same holds true for sexuality: prohibition is certainly not the principal form of the investment of sexuality by power.

> Your analysis of the techniques of power opposes itself to discourses about love of the master or desire for fascism. But doesn't it also allow room for them by absolutising power, assuming it as always already there, an enduring entity which confronts the equally enduring guerilla warfare of the masses — and thus letting slip the question: whom and what does power serve? Isn't there an underlying duplicity between this political anatomy and Marxism: the class struggle is rejected as the *ratio* for the exercise of power, yet preserved in the last analysis as that which guarantees the intelligibility of techniques for the dressage of body and mind (the production of a labour force suitable for the tasks assigned to it by capitalist exploitation, and so forth)?

It seems to me that power *is* 'always already there', that one is never 'outside' it, that there are no 'margins' for those who break with the system to gambol in. But this does not entail the necessity of accepting an inescapable form of domination or an absolute privilege on the side of the law. To say that one can never be 'outside' power does not mean that one is trapped and condemned to defeat no matter what.

I would suggest rather (but these are hypotheses which will need exploring): (i) that power is co-extensive with the social body; there are no spaces of primal liberty between the meshes of its network; (ii) that relations of power are interwoven with other kinds of relations (production, kinship, family, sexuality) for which they play at once a conditioning and a conditioned role; (iii) that these relations don't take the sole form of prohibition and punishment, but are of multiple forms; (iv) that their interconnections delineate general conditions of domination, and this domination is organised into a more-or-less coherent and unitary strategic form; that dispersed, heteromorphous, localised procedures of power are adapated, re-inforced and transformed by these global strategies, all this being accompanied by numerous phenomena of inertia, displacement and resistance; hence one should not assume a massive and primal condition of domination, a binary structure with 'dominators' on one side and 'dominated' on the other, but rather a multiform production of relations of domination which are partially susceptible of integration into overall strategies; (v) that power relations do indeed 'serve', but not at all because they are 'in the service of' an economic interest taken as primary, rather because they are capable of being utilised in strategies; (vi) that there are no relations of power without resistances; the latter are all the more real and effective because they are formed right at the point where relations of power are exercised; resistance to power does not have to come from elsewhere to be real, nor is it inexorably frustrated through being the compatriot of power. It exists all the more by being in the same place as power; hence, like power, resistance is multiple and can be integrated in global strategies.

Thus it is possible for class struggle not to be the '*ratio* for the exercise of power', yet still be the 'guarantee of intelligibility' for certain grand strategies.

Can the analysis of the guerilla struggle between the masses and power avoid the reformist thought which turns revolt into the signal that prompts a new policy of adaptation from above, or the trap leading to some new form of domination? Can the act of refusal be thought outside the dilemma of reformism or 'angelism'?[3] Your discussion with Deleuze[4] assigned to theory the function of a tool-kit for the use of new political subjects, basing this idea on experiments like the Prisons Information Group (GIP). Now that the traditional political parties have reestablished their hegemony over the Left, can one use the toolkit as something other than an instrument for research into the past?

It is necessary to make a distinction between critique of reformism as a political practice and the critique of a political practice on the grounds that it may give rise to a reform. This latter form of critique is frequent in left-wing groups and its employment is part of the mechanisms of micro-terrorism by which they have often operated. It amounts to saying, 'Beware: however ideally radical your intentions may be, your action is so localised and your objectives so isolated that at this particular spot the adversary will be able to handle the situation, to yield if necessary without in any way compromising his global position; even better, this will allow him to locate the sites of necessary transformation; and so you will have been recuperated'. The anathema is pronounced. Now it seems to me that this critique rests on two errors:

First, there is a misunderstanding of the strategic form that processes of struggle take. If one accepts that the form — both general and concrete — of struggle is contradiction, then clearly everything which allows the contradiction to be localised or narrowed down will be seen as a brake or a blockage. But the problem is precisely as to whether the logic of contradiction can actually serve as a principle of intelligibility and rule of action in political struggle. This touches on a momentous political question: how is it that since the nineteenth century the specific problems of struggle and the strategy of struggle have tended so constantly to be dissolved into the meagre logic of contradiction? There are a whole series of reasons for this that will need to be analysed some day. In any case, one must try to think struggle and its forms, objectives, means and processes in terms of a logic free of the sterilising constraints of the dialectic. In order to think the social bond, 'bourgeois' political thought of the eighteenth century adopted the *juridical form of the contract*. In order to think struggle, the 'revolutionary' thought of the nineteenth century adopted the *logical form of contradiction*. The latter, no doubt, is no more valid than the former. In contrast, the great States of the nineteenth century adopted a strategic mode of thought, while the revolutionary struggles conceived their strategy only in a very conjunctural manner, endeavouring at the same time always to inscribe it within the horizon of contradiction.

The phobia of the adversary's reformist riposte is also linked with second error. This is the privilege accorded to what is solemnly termed the 'theory' of the weakest link. A local attack is considered to have sense and legitimacy only when directed at the element which, if broken, will allow the total breach of the chain. That is, it must be a local action but one which, through the choice of its site, will act radically on the whole. Here again we should ask why this thesis has had such success in the twentieth century, and why it has been erected into a theory. Certainly it rendered thinkable the event that Marxism had failed to foresee: the revolution in Russia. But in general it must be recognised that we are dealing here not with a dialectical, but a strategic proposition—and a very elementary one at that. It provided the acceptable minimum of strategy for a mode of thinking ruled by the dialectic, and has remained closely linked to dialectic because it expressed the possibility for a local situation to count as the contradiction of the whole. Hence the solemnity with which this 'Leninist' thesis was erected into a 'theory'—one which is barely on a level with the preliminary training given to a sub-lieutenant in the reserves. And it's in the name of this thesis that every local action is terrorised with the following dilemma: either you attack on a local level, but you must be sure that it's at the weakest link, the one whose breakage will demolish the whole structure; or else, since the whole structure fails to collapse, the link wasn't the weakest one, the adversary needed only to re-organise his front, and a reform has reabsorbed your attack.

It seems to me that this whole intimidation with the bogy of reform is linked to the lack of a strategic analysis appropriate to political struggle, to struggles in the field of political power. The role for theory today seems to me to be just this: not to formulate the global systematic theory which holds everything in place, but to analyse the specificity of mechanisms of power, to locate the connections and extensions, to build little by little a strategic knowledge (*savoir*). If 'the traditional parties have re-established their hegemony over the Left', and over the diverse forms of struggle which had not originally been under their control, one reason among many for this was that only a profoundly inadequate logic was available to these struggles for the analysis of their unfolding and their effects.

The notion of theory as a tookit means: (i) The theory to be constructed is not a system but an instrument, a *logic* of the specificity of power relations and the struggles around them; (ii) That this investigation can only be carried out step by step on the basis of reflection (which will necessarily be historical in some of its aspects) on given situations.

These questions were put to me in writing. The replies were also given in writing, but in an improvised fashion, with hardly any alteration of the first draft. This was not through any faith in the virtues of spontaneity, but so as to leave the propositions put forward their problematic, intentionally uncertain character. What I have said here is not 'what I think', but often rather what I wonder whether one couldn't think. [M.F.]

Notes

1 It should be noted that one doesn't find in France as in other countries the regular publication of the writings of the Soviet counter-culture. It's these rather than the texts of Marx which should serve here as the material for our reflection.
2 A. Glucksmann, *La Cuisinière et le Mangeur d'Hommes* (Editions du Seuil, Paris, 1975).
3 G. Lardreau and C. Jambet, *L'Ange* ('The Angel') (Grasset, Paris, 1976), one of the texts of the '*nouveaux philosophes*' circle; it advocates a form of sublime pessimism in political matters.
4 'Les intellectuels et le pouvoir', *L'Arc* 49 (1972), translated in *Telos* 16 (1973) and in D. F. Bouchard (ed), *Language, Counter-Memory, Practice* (Cornell University Press, 1976).

8 THE EYE OF POWER

A conversation with Jean-Pierre Barou and Michelle Perrot

BAROU: Jeremy Bentham's *Panopticon*[1] is a work published at the end of the eighteenth century and since then fallen into oblivion. Yet in *Discipline and Punish* you cite such astonishing phrases having been applied to it as 'an event in the history of the human mind', 'a sort of Columbus's egg in the order of politics'. And you have presented its author as 'the Fourier of a police society'. For us this is baffling. But tell us first how you came upon the *Panopticon*.

FOUCAULT: It was while I was studying the origins of clinical medicine. I had been planning a study of hospital architecture in the second half of the eighteenth century, when the great movement for the reform of medical institutions was getting under way. I wanted to find out how the medical gaze was institutionalised, how it was effectively inscribed in social space, how the new form of the hospital was at once the effect and the support of a new type of gaze. In examining the series of different architectural projects which followed the second fire at the Hotel-Dieu in 1772, I noticed how the whole problem of the visibility of bodies, individuals and things, under a system of centralised observation, was one of their most constant directing principles. In the case of the hospitals this general problem involves a further difficulty: it was necessary to avoid undue contact, contagion, physical proximity and overcrowding, while at the same time ensuring ventilation and circulation of air, at once dividing space up and keeping it open, ensuring a surveillance which would be both global and individualising while at the same time carefully separating the individuals under observation. For some time I thought all these problems were specific to eighteenth-century medicine and its beliefs.

Then while studying the problems of the penal system, I noticed that all the great projects for re-organising the prisons (which date, incidentally, from a slightly later period, the first half of the nineteenth century) take up this same theme, but accompanied this time by the almost invariable reference to Bentham. There was scarcely a text or a proposal about the prisons which didn't mention Bentham's 'device'—the 'Panopticon'.

The principle was this. A perimeter building in the form of a ring. At the centre of this, a tower, pierced by large windows opening on to the inner face of the ring. The outer building is divided into cells each of which traverses the whole thickness of the building. These cells have two windows, one opening on to the inside, facing the windows of the central tower, the other, outer one allowing daylight to pass through the whole cell. All that is then needed is to put an overseer in the tower and place in each of the cells a lunatic, a patient, a convict, a worker or a schoolboy. The back lighting enables one to pick out from the central tower the little captive silhouettes in the ring of cells. In short, the principle of the dungeon is reversed; daylight and the overseer's gaze capture the inmate more effectively than darkness, which afforded after all a sort of protection.

It's striking to note that already, well before Bentham, this same concern was manifested. It seems that one of the first models of this system of isolating visibility was put into practice in 1751 in the dormitories of the Military School in Paris. Each pupil there was assigned a glassed-in cell where he could be observed throughout the night without being able to have the slightest contact with his fellows or even with the domestics. There existed moreover a complicated contraption whose sole purpose was to ensure that the barber could cut each cadet's hair without physically touching him. The boy's head was passed through a sort of hatch, while his body remained behind a glass partition through which everything that occurred could be observed. Bentham relates that it was his brother who had the idea of the Panopticon while visiting the Military School. At all events the theme was in the air at the time. The installations built by Claude-Nicolas Ledoux, notably the salt plant which he constructed at Arc-et-Senans, serve to give the same effect of visibility but with an additional feature: there was a central observation-point which served as the focus of the exercise of power and, simultaneously, for the registration of knowledge. Anyway, even if the idea of the Panopticon antedates Bentham, it was he who truly formulated it—and baptised it. The very word 'Panopticon' seems crucial here, as designating the principle of a system. Thus Bentham didn't merely imagine an architectural design calculated to solve a specific problem, such as that of a prison, a school or a hospital. He proclaimed it as a veritable discovery, saying of it himself that it was 'Christopher Columbus's egg'. And indeed what Bentham proposed to the doctors, penologists, industrialists and educators was just what they had been looking for. He invented a technology of power designed to solve the problems of surveillance. One important point should be noted: Bentham thought and said that his optical system was *the* great innovation needed for the easy and effective exercise of power. It has in fact been widely employed since the end of the eighteenth century. But the procedures of power that are at work in modern societies are much more numerous, diverse and rich. It would be wrong to say that the principle of visibility governs all technologies of power used since the nineteenth century.

PERROT: So the key was architecture! Indeed, what of architecture as a mode of political organisation? For after all, in this eighteenth-century current of thought everything is spatial, on the material as well as the mental level.

FOUCAULT: The point, it seems to me, is that architecture begins at the end of the eighteenth century to become involved in problems of population, health and the urban question. Previously, the art of building corresponded to the need to make power, divinity and might manifest. The palace and the church were the great architectural forms, along with the stronghold. Architecture manifested might, the Sovereign, God. Its development was for long centred on these requirements. Then, late in the eighteenth century, new problems emerge: it becomes a question of using the disposition of space for economico-political ends.

A specific type of architecture takes shape. Philippe Ariès has written some things which seem important to me, regarding the fact that the house remains until the eighteenth century an undifferentiated space. There are rooms: one sleeps, eats, receives visitors in them, it doesn't matter which. Then gradually space becomes specified and functional. We see this illustrated with the building of the *cités ouvrières*, between the 1830s and 1870s. The working-class family is to be fixed; by assigning it a living space with a room that serves as kitchen and dining-room, a room for the parents which is the place of procreation, and a room for the children, one prescribes a form of morality for the family. Sometimes, in the more favourable cases, you have a boys' and a girls' room. A whole history remains to be written of *spaces*—which would at the same time be the history of *powers* (both these terms in the plural)—from the great strategies of geo-politics to the little tactics of the habitat, institutional architecture from the classroom to the design of hospitals, passing via economic and political installations. It is surprising how long the problem of space took to emerge as a historico-political problem. Space used to be either dismissed as belonging to 'nature'—that is, the given, the basic conditions, 'physical geography', in other words a sort of 'prehistoric' stratum; or else it was conceived as the residential site or field of expansion of peoples, of a culture, a language or a State. It took Marc Bloch and Fernand Braudel to develop a history of rural and maritime spaces. The development must be extended, by no longer just saying that space predetermines a history which in turn reworks and sediments itself in it. Anchorage in a space is an economico-political form which needs to be studied in detail.

   Among all the reasons which led to spaces suffering for so long a certain neglect, I will mention just one, which has to do with the discourse of philosophers. At the moment when a considered politics of spaces was starting to develop, at the end of the eighteenth century, the new achievements in theoretical and experimental physics dislodged philosophy from its ancient right to speak of the world, the cosmos, finite or infinite space. This double investment of space by political technology and scientific practice reduced philosophy to the field of a problematic of time. Since Kant, what is to be thought by the philosopher is time. Hegel, Bergson, Heidegger. Along with this goes a correlative devaluation of space, which stands on the side of the understanding, the analytical, the conceptual, the dead, the fixed, the inert. I remember ten years or so ago discussing these problems of the politics of space, and being told that it was reactionary to go on so much about space, and that time and the 'project' were what life and progress are about. I should say that this reproach came from a psychologist— psychology, the truth and the shame of nineteenth-century philosophy.

PERROTT: By the way, it seems to me that the notion of sexuality is very important in this regard. You remarked on this in the context of surveillance among the military, and it appears again in relation to the working-class family. No doubt this is a fundamental relationship.

FOUCAULT: Absolutely. With these themes of surveillance, and especially in the schools, it seems that control over sexuality becomes inscribed in architecture. In the Military Schools, the very walls speak the struggle against homo-sexuality and masturbation.

PERROT: Still on the question of architecture, doesn't it strike you that people like the doctors, with their consider-able involvement in social policy at the end of the eighteenth century, acted in some sense as agents of the disposition of space? This is when social hygiene is born. In the name of health and cleanliness, all sorts of spatial arrangements are subjected to control. And with the renaissance of Hip-pocratic medicine, doctors are among those who are most sensitised to the problem of the environment, the facts of place and temperature, data which we encounter again in Howard's investigation of the prisons.[2]

FOUCAULT: Doctors at that time were among other things the specialists of space. They posed four fundamental problems. That of local conditions (regional climates, soil, humidity and dryness: under the term 'constitution', they studied these combinations of local determinants and seasonal variations which at a given moment favour a par-ticular sort of disease); that of co-existences (either between men, questions of density and proximity, or between men and things, the question of water, sewage, ventilation, or between men and animals, the question of stables and abattoirs, or between men and the dead, the question of cemeteries); that of residences (the environment, urban problems); that of displacements (the migration of men, the propagation of diseases). Doctors were, along with the military, the first managers of collective space. But the military were chiefly concerned to think the space of 'campaigns' (and thus of 'passages') and that of fortresses, whereas the doctors were concerned to think the space of habitations and towns. Countless people have sought the origins of sociology in Montesquieu and Comte. That is a very ignorant enterprise. Sociological knowledge (*savoir*) is formed rather in practices like those of the doctors. For instance, at the start of the nineteenth century Guépin wrote a marvellous study of the city of Nantes.

In fact if the intervention of the doctors was of capital importance at this period, this was because it was demanded by a whole new range of political and economic problems, highlighting the importance of the *facts* of population.

PERROT: What is striking moreover in Bentham's thinking is the question of the number of people. He repeatedly makes the claim to have solved the problems of discipline posed by a great number of persons in the hands of a very few.

FOUCAULT: Like his contemporaries, he faced the problem of the accumulation of men. But whereas the economists posed the problem in terms of wealth (population being in itself both wealth as labour force, source of economic activity and consumption, and cause of poverty, when excessive or idle), Bentham poses the question in terms of power—population as object of relations of domination. I think one can say that the mechanisms of power at work even in such a highly developed administration as the French monarchy were full of loopholes. It was a discontinuous, rambling, global system with little hold on detail, either exercised over consolidated social groups or else imposing itself only by means of exemplary interventions (as can be readily seen in its fiscal system and its criminal justice). Power had only a weak capacity for 'resolution', as one might say in photographic terms; it was incapable of an individualising, exhaustive analysis of the social body. But the economic changes of the eighteenth century made it necessary to ensure the circulation of effects of power through progressively finer channels, gaining access to individuals themselves, to their bodies, their gestures and all their daily actions. By such means power, even when faced with ruling a multiplicity of men, could be as efficacious as if it were being exercised over a single one.

PERROT: The demographic upswings of the eighteenth century certainly contributed towards the development of such a form of power.

BAROU: Isn't it astonishing then to find the French Revolution, through people like Lafayette, welcoming the project of the Panopticon? We know that he helped to have Bentham made a 'French citizen' in 1791.

FOUCAULT: I would say Bentham was the complement to Rousseau. What in fact was the Rousseauist dream that motivated many of the revolutionaries? It was the dream of a transparent society, visible and legible in each of its parts, the dream of there no longer existing any zones of darkness, zones established by the privileges of royal power or the prerogatives of some corporation, zones of disorder. It was the dream that each individual, whatever position he occupied, might be able to see the whole of society, that men's hearts should communicate, their vision be unobstructed by obstacles, and that opinion of all reign over each. Starobinski has written some most interesting pages about this in *La Transparence et l'Obstacle* and *L'Invention de la liberté*.

Bentham is both that and the opposite. He poses the problem of visibility, but thinks of a visibility organised entirely around a dominating, overseeing gaze. He effects the project of a universal visibility which exists to serve a rigorous, meticulous power. Thus Bentham's obsession, the technical idea of the exercise of an 'all-seeing' power, is grafted on to the great Rousseauist theme which is in some sense the lyrical note of the Revolution. The two things combine into a working whole, Rousseau's lyricism and Bentham's obsession.

PERROT: There is a phrase in the *Panopticon*: 'Each comrade becomes an overseer'.

FOUCAULT: Rousseau no doubt would have said the reverse: each overseer should become a comrade. Take *Émile*: Émile's tutor is an overseer, he must also be a comrade.

BAROU: Not only does the French Revolution not read Bentham as we do today, it even finds a humanitarian intention in his project.

FOUCAULT: Exactly. When the Revolution poses the question of a new justice, what does it envisage as its principle? Opinion. The new aspect of the problem of justice, for the Revolution, was not so much to punish wrongdoers as to prevent even the possibility of wrong-doing, by immersing people in a field of total visibility where the opinion, observation and discourse of others would restrain them from harmful acts. This idea is constantly present in the texts of the Revolution.

PERROT: The immediate context also had a part to play in the adoption of the Panopticon by the Revolution. The problem of prisons was on the order of the day. Beginning in the 1770s, in England as well as in France, there was much preoccupation with this subject; this can be seen in Howard's investigation into the prisons, translated into French in 1788. Hospitals and prisons were two great themes of enlightened circles of discussion in Parisian salons. It became a matter of scandal that prisons should be as they were, a school of vice and crime, places so devoid of hygiene that people died in them. The doctors began saying how the body is wrecked in such conditions. The French Revolution in its turn undertook an investigation on a European scale. One Duquesnoy was commissioned to make a report on the so-called 'establishments of humanity', a term embracing both hospitals and prisons.

FOUCAULT: A fear haunted the latter half of the eighteenth century: the fear of darkened spaces, of the pall of gloom which prevents the full visibility of things, men and truths. It sought to break up the patches of darkness that blocked the light, eliminate the shadowy areas of society, demolish the unlit chambers where arbitrary political acts, monarchical caprice, religious superstitions, tyrannical and priestly plots, epidemics and the illusions of ignorance were fomented. The chateaux, lazarets, bastilles and convents inspired even in the pre-Revolutionary period a suspicion and hatred exacerbated by a certain political overdetermination. The new political and moral order could not be established until these places were eradicated. During the Revolutionary period the

Gothic novels develop a whole fantasy-world of stone walls, darkness, hideouts and dungeons which harbour, in significant complicity, brigands and aristocrats, monks and traitors. The landscapes of Ann Radcliffe's novels are composed of mountains and forests, caves, ruined castles and terrifyingly dark and silent convents. Now these imaginary spaces are like the negative of the transparency and visibility which it is aimed to establish. This reign of 'opinion', so often invoked at this time, represents a mode of operation through which power will be exercised by virtue of the mere fact of things being known and people seen in a sort of immediate, collective and anonymous gaze. A form of power whose main instance is that of opinion will refuse to tolerate areas of darkness. If Bentham's project aroused interest, this was because it provided a formula applicable to many domains, the formula of 'power through transparency', subjection by 'illumination'. In the Panopticon, there is used a form close to that of the castle—a keep surrounded by walls—to paradoxically create a space of exact legibility.

BAROU: It's also the areas of darkness in man that the century of Enlightenment wants to make disappear.

FOUCAULT: Absolutely.

PERROT: At the same time one is very struck by the techniques of power used within the Panopticon. Essentially it's the gaze; but also speech, because he has those famous 'tin tubes', that extraordinary invention, connecting the chief inspector with each of the cells, in which Bentham tells us that not just a single prisoner, but small groups of prisoners are confined. Finally, it's the importance of dissuasion that's very marked in Bentham's text. 'It is necessary', he writes, 'for the inmate to be ceaselessly under the eyes of an inspector; this is to lose the power and even almost the idea of wrong-doing'. Here we are at the heart of the preoccupations of the Revolution: preventing people from wrong-doing, taking away their wish to commit wrong. In a word, to make people unable and unwilling.

FOUCAULT: We are talking about two things here: the gaze, and interiorisation. And isn't it basically the problem of the cost of power? In reality power is only exercised at a cost. Obviously, there is an economic cost, and Bentham talks about this. How many overseers will the Panopticon need?

How much will the machine then cost to run? But there is also a specifically political cost. If you are too violent, you risk provoking revolts. Again, if you intervene in too discontinuous a manner, you risk allowing politically costly phenomena of resistance and disobedience to develop in the interstices. This was how monarchical power operated. For instance, the judiciary only arrested a derisory proportion of criminals; this was made into the argument that punishment must be spectacular so as to frighten the others. Hence there was a violent form of power which tried to attain a continuous mode of operation through the virtue of examples. The new theorists of the eighteenth century objected to this: such a form of power was too costly in proportion to its results. A great expenditure of violence is made which ultimately only had the force of an example. It even becomes necessary to multiply violence, but precisely by doing so one multiplies revolts.

PERROT: Which is what happened in the gallows riots.

FOUCAULT: In contrast to that you have the system of surveillance, which on the contrary involves very little expense. There is no need for arms, physical violence, material constraints. Just a gaze. An inspecting gaze, a gaze which each individual under its weight will end by interiorising to the point that he is his own overseer, each individual thus exercising this surveillance over, and against, himself. A superb formula: power exercised continuously and for what turns out to be a minimal cost. When Bentham realises what he has discovered, he calls it the Colombus's egg of political thought, a formula exactly the opposite of monarchical power. It is indeed the case that the gaze has had great importance among the techniques of power developed in the modern era, but, as I have said, it is far from being the only or even the principal system employed.

PERROT: It seems that Bentham is mainly concerned here with the problem of power over small groups of individuals. Why is this? Is it because he considers the part as already the whole—if one can succeed at the level of the small group, one can extend the procedure to take in the whole of society? Or is it rather that the ensemble of society, the question of power on the scale of the social whole were tasks that had not as yet been properly conceived? And in that case, why not?

FOUCAULT: It's the whole problem of eliminating blockages and obstacles, such as the obstacles placed in the way of decisions of power by constituted bodies and the privileges of particular groups, the clergy, the magistrature, the corporations. The bourgeoisie is perfectly well aware that a new constitution or legislature will not suffice to assure its hegemony; it realises that it has to invent a new technology ensuring the irrigation by effects of power of the whole social body down to its smallest particles. And it was by such means that the bourgeoisie not only made a revolution but succeeded in establishing a social hegemony which it has never relinquished. This is why all these inventions were so important, and why no doubt Bentham is one of the most exemplary inventors of technologies of power.

BAROU: Yet it is hard to discern who it is who stands to profit from the organised space that Bentham conceived. This seems uncertain even regarding those who occupy or visit the central tower. One has the feeling of confronting an infernal model that no one, either the watcher or the watched, can escape.

FOUCAULT: This indeed is the diabolical aspect of the idea and all the applications of it. One doesn't have here a power which is wholly in the hands of one person who can exercise it alone and totally over the others. It's a machine in which everyone is caught, those who exercise power just as much as those over whom it is exercised. This seems to me to be the characteristic of the societies installed in the nineteenth century. Power is no longer substantially identified with an individual who possesses or exercises it by right of birth; it becomes a machinery that no one owns. Certainly everyone doesn't occupy the same position; certain positions preponderate and permit an effect of supremacy to be produced. This is so much the case that class domination can be exercised just to the extent that power is dissociated from individual might.

PERROT: The working of the Panopticon is somewhat contradictory from this point of view. There is the chief inspector who watches over the prisoners from the central tower; but he watches his subordinates as well, the personnel in the hierarchy. This chief inspector has little faith in his overseers. He even speaks rather slightingly of them, though they are supposed to be his auxiliaries. Bentham's thinking sounds rather aristocratic here!

At the same time, I would say that the subject of administrative personnel was a problem for industrial society. Finding the foremen and technicians to regiment and oversee the factories can't have been easy for the bosses.

FOUCAULT: This is a considerable problem that begins to be posed in the eighteenth century. It can clearly be seen in the army, when it becomes necessary to create a corps of NCO's sufficiently competent to marshal troops effectively in tactical manouvres which were often difficult, especially with the perfecting of the rifle. Military movements, shifts, lines and marches required a disciplinary personnel of this kind. The industrial workshops posed this same problem in their own way; so did the school with its masters, ushers and monitors. The Church was one of the few social bodies where these lower cadres already existed. The monk, neither particularly literate nor wholly ignorant, the vicar and the curé were indispensable when it became necessary to school hundreds of thousands of children. The State only acquired comparable cadres much later on; as for the hospitals, it's not long since the majority of their staff were nuns.

PERROT: Nuns also had a significant role in women's work: there were the well known residential establishments of the nineteenth century which housed a female work-force under the control of nuns specially trained in maintaining factory discipline.

The Panopticon is by no means foreign to such preoccupations, if one takes account of the chief inspector's surveillance of his staff and the constant watch kept over everyone through the windows of the tower, an unbroken succession of observations recalling the motto: each comrade becomes an overseer. So much so that one has the vertiginous sense of being in the presence of an invention that even its inventor is incapable of controlling. Yet it's Bentham who begins by relying on a single power, that of the central tower. As one reads him one wonders who he is putting in the tower. Is it the eye of God? But God is hardly present in the text; religion only plays a role of utility. Then who is it? In the last analysis one is forced to conclude that Bentham himself has no clear idea to whom power is to be entrusted.

FOUCAULT: He can't entrust it to any one person since no one can or may occupy the role that the King had in the old system, that is as the source of power and justice. It was implicit in the theory of monarchy that trust in the King was a necessity. His very existence, founded in God's will, he was the source of justice, law and power. Power, in his person, could only be good; a bad King was either an accident of history or a punishment by God, the absolutely good sovereign. On the other hand, if power is arranged as a machine working by a complex system of cogs and gears, where it's the place of a person which is determining, not his nature, no reliance can be placed on a single individual. If the machine were such that someone could stand outside it and assume sole responsibility for managing it, power would be identified with that one man and we would be back with a monarchical type of power. In the Panopticon each person, depending on his place, is watched by all or certain of the others. You have an apparatus of total and circulating mistrust, because there is no absolute point. The perfected form of surveillance consists in a summation of *malveillance*.

BAROU: As you say, it's a diabolical piece of machinery, sparing no one. The image, perhaps, of power today. How do you see this as having been brought about? By whose, or what will?

FOUCAULT: One impoverishes the question of power if one poses it solely in terms of legislation and constitution, in terms solely of the state and the state apparatus. Power is quite different from and more complicated, dense and pervasive than a set of laws or a state apparatus. It's impossible to get the development of productive forces characteristic of capitalism if you don't at the same time have apparatuses of power. Take the example of the division of labour in the great workshops of the eighteenth century: how could this separation of tasks have been attained without a new distribution of power on the plane of the management of the forces of production? Similarly with the modern army. New types of armament, new forms of recruitment were not sufficient: it was necessary to have at the same time this new distribution of power known as discipline, with its structures and hierarchies, its inspections, exercises and methods of training and conditioning. Without this the army as it functioned from the eighteenth century on could not have existed.

BAROU: All the same, does someone initiate the whole business, or not?

FOUCAULT: A distinction needs to be made here. It's obvious that in an apparatus like an army or a factory, or some other such type of institution, the system of power takes a pyramidical form. Hence there is an apex. But even so, even in such a simple case, this summit doesn't form the 'source' or 'principle' from which all power derives as though from a luminous focus (the image by which the monarchy represents itself). The summit and the lower elements of the hierarchy stand in a relationship of mutual support and conditioning, a mutual 'hold' (power as a mutual and indefinite 'blackmail'). But if you ask me, 'Does this new technology of power take its historical origin from an identifiable individual or group of individuals who decide to implement it so as to further their interests or facilitate their utilisation of the social body?' then I would say 'No'. These tactics were invented and organised from the starting points of local conditions and particular needs. They took shape in piecemeal fashion, prior to any class strategy designed to weld them into vast, coherent ensembles. It should also be noted that these ensembles don't consist in a homogenisation, but rather of a complex play of supports in mutual engagement, different mechanisms of power which retain all their specific character. Thus where children are concerned at the present time, the interplay of the family, medicine, psychiatry, psychoanalysis, the school and justice doesn't have the effect of homogenising these different instances but of establishing connections, cross-references, complementarities and demarcations between them which assume that each instance retains to some extent its own special modalities.

PERROT: You are opposed to the idea of power as a super-structure, but not to the idea that power is in some sense consubstantial with the development of forces of production, that it forms part of them.

FOUCAULT: Absolutely. And power is constantly being transformed along with them. The Panopticon was at once a programme and a utopia. But the theme of a spatialising, observing, immobilising, in a word disciplinary power was in fact already in Bentham's day being transcended by other and much more subtle mechanisms for the regulation of phenomena of population, controlling their fluctuations and compensating their irregularities. The tendency of Bentham's thought is archaic in the importance it gives to the gaze; but it is very modern in the general importance it assigns to techniques of power.

PERROT: There is no global State in Bentham: there is the installation of micro-societies, microcosms.

BAROU: Does the deployment of the Panoptic system pertain to the whole of industrial society? Is it the work of capitalist society?

FOUCAULT: Industrial society, capitalist society? I have no answer, except to say that these forms of power recur in socialist societies; their transposition was immediate. But on this point I would rather have the historian speak.

PERROT: It's true that capital accumulation was the work of industrial technology and of the installation of a whole apparatus of power. But it is no less true that a similar process is repeated in Soviet socialist society. In certain respects Stalinism corresponds to the period both of capital accumulation and of the installation of a strong form of power.

BAROU: This returns us to the notion of profit—how Bentham's inhuman machine proves a precious acquisition, for some at least.

FOUCAULT: Of course! It takes the rather naive optimism of the nineteenth century 'dandies' to imagine that the bourgeoisie is stupid. On the contrary, one has to reckon with its strokes of genius, and among these is precisely the fact of its managing to construct machines of power allowing circuits of profit, which in turn re-inforced and modified the power apparatuses in a mobile and circular manner. Feudal power, operating primarily through exaction and expenditure, ended by undermining itself. The power of the bourgeoisie is self-amplifying, in a mode not of conservation but of successive transformations. Hence the fact that its form isn't given in a definitive historical figure as is that of feudalism. Hence both its precariousness and its supple inventiveness. Hence the fact, the possibility, of its fall and of the revolution has been integral to its history almost from the beginning.

PERROT: One can note that Bentham gives a great deal of space to the question of labour; he returns to it again and again.

FOUCAULT: That accords with the fact that techniques of power are invented to meet the demands of production. I mean production here in the broad sense—it can be a matter of the 'production' of destruction, as with the army.

BAROU: When you use the term 'labour' in your books, it's seldom in relation to productive labour.

FOUCAULT: That's because I happened to be dealing with people situated outside the circuits of productive labour: the insane, prisoners, and now children. For them labour, insofar as they have to perform it, has a value which is chiefly disciplinary.

BAROU: Labour as a form of *dressage*? Isn't it always that?

FOUCAULT: Certainly! There is always present this triple function of labour: the productive function, the symbolic function and the function of *dressage*, or discipline. The productive function equals practically zero for the categories of individuals I am concerned with, whereas the symbolic and disciplinary functions are very important. But most often the three components go together.

PERROT: In any case Bentham seems to me very sure of himself, very confident in the penetrative power of the gaze. One feels he has a very inadequate awareness of the degree of opacity and resistance of the material to be corrected and integrated into society—the prisoners. And isn't Bentham's Panopticon at the same time something of an illusion of power?

FOUCAULT: It's the illusion of almost all of the eighteenth-century reformers who credited opinion with considerable potential force. Since opinion could only be good, being the immediate consciousness of the whole social body, they thought people would become virtuous by the simple fact of being observed. For them, opinion was like a spontaneous re-actualisation of the social contract. They overlooked the real conditions of possibility of opinion, the 'media' of opinion, a materiality caught up in the mechanisms of the economy and power in its forms of the press, publishing, and later the cinema and television.

PERROT: When you say they overlooked the media, you mean that they failed to see the necessity of working through the media?

FOUCAULT: And failed to see that these media would necessarily be under the command of economico-political interests. They failed to perceive the material and economic components of opinion. They believed opinion would be inherently just, that it would spread of its own accord, that it would be a sort of democratic surveillance. Basically it was journalism, that capital invention of the nineteenth century, which made evident all the utopian character of this politics of the gaze.

PERROT: These thinkers generally misunderstood the difficulty they would have in making their system take effect. They didn't realise that there would always be ways of slipping through their net, or that resistances would have a role to play. In the domain of prisons, the convicts weren't passive beings. It's Bentham who gives us to suppose that they were. The discourse of the penitentiary unfolds as though there were no people confronting it, nothing except a *tabula rasa* of subjects to be reformed and returned to the circuit of production. In reality it had to work with a material—the prisoners—which put up formidable resistance. The same could be said about Taylorism. The system of Taylorism was an extraordinary invention by an engineer who wants to combat laziness and everything that slows down production. But one can still ask: did Taylorism ever really work?

FOUCAULT: This indeed is another of the factors which shift Bentham into the domain of the unreal: the effective resistance of people. This is something you have studied, Michelle Perrot. How did people in the workshops and the *cités ouvrières* resist the system of surveillance and constant record-taking? Were they aware of the constraining, subjecting, unbearable character of that surveillance? In a word, were there revolts against the gaze?

PERROT: There were indeed revolts against the gaze. The workers' repugnance for living in the *cités ouvrières* is patent. The *cités ouvrières* were failures for a long time. So too was the system of units of time which is so evident in the Panopticon. The factory with its time-schedules long aroused passive resistance manifested by the fact of people simply not turning up for work. Such is the epic of the Saint-Lundi, 'Holy Monday', the day workers invented as a weekly break. There were many forms of resistance to the industrial system, to the extent that for an initial period the bosses had to beat a retreat. And to take another point, the system of micro-powers wasn't installed at a stroke. This type of surveillance and hierarchy was developed first in the mechanised sectors occupied by mainly female and child labour, that is by those already accustomed to obey. But in, shall we say, the virile sectors such as engineering, one finds quite a different situation. The management isn't successful all at once in installing its surveillance; it has therefore, for the first half of the nineteenth century, to delegate its powers. It contracts with a team of labourers through the person of their chief, often the oldest or most skilled worker. One sees a veritable counter-power being exercised by the craftsmen, one which sometimes has two facets: one directed at the bosses, in defence of the workers' community; the other sometimes turned against the workers themselves, since the petty chief oppresses his apprentices or his fellows. In fact these forms of working-class counter-power continued to exist up to the time when management were able to mechanise those functions which had escaped their control until then. It was able thereby to abolish the power of the skilled worker. There were countless examples of this: in the rolling-mills the chief of a shop had the capacity to resist a boss up until the time when semi-automatic machines were installed. In a flash the thermal control mechanism replaced the expert mill-hand, able to judge—at a glance, once again—the instant the material was ready. Reading a thermometer was sufficient.

FOUCAULT: That being so, resistances to the Panopticon will have to be analysed in tactical and strategic terms, positing that each offensive from the one side serves as leverage for a counter-offensive from the other. The analysis of power-mechanisms has no built-in tendency to show power as being at once anonymous and always victorious. It is a matter rather of establishing the positions occupied and modes of actions used by each of the forces at work, the possibilities of resistance and counter-attack on either side.

BAROU: Battles, actions and reactions, offensives and counter-offensives: you talk like a strategist. Are resistances to power then essentially physical in character? What about the content of struggles, the aspirations that manifest themselves in them?

FOUCAULT: This is indeed an important question of theory and method. One thing strikes me about this. Certain political discourses make a lot of use of the language of relations of forces: 'struggle' is the word used most often. Yet it seems to me that people sometimes hesitate to follow through the consequences of this, or even to pose the problem implicit in this vocabulary—namely, whether these 'struggles' are, or are not, to be analysed as episodes in a war, whether the grid for deciphering them should be that of strategy and tactics? Is the relation between forces in the order of politics a warlike one? I don't personally feel prepared to answer this with a definite yes or no. It just seems to me that the affirmation, pure and simple, of a 'struggle' can't act as the beginning and end of all explanations in the analysis of power-relations. This theme of struggle only really becomes operative if one establishes concretely—in each particular case—who is engaged in struggle, what the struggle is about, and how, where, by what means and according to what rationality it evolves. In other words, if one wants to take seriously the assertion that struggle is the core of relations of power, one must take into account the fact that the good old 'logic' of contradiction is no longer sufficient, far from it, for the unravelling of actual processes.

PERROT: In other words, coming back to the Panopticon, Bentham doesn't merely formulate the project of a utopian society, he also describes a society that actually exists.

FOUCAULT: He describes, in the utopian form of a general system, particular mechanisms which really exist.

PERROT: And there's no point for the prisoners in taking over the central tower?

FOUCAULT: Oh yes, provided that isn't the final purpose of the operation. Do you think it would be much better to have the prisoners operating the Panoptic apparatus and sitting in the central tower, instead of the guards?

Notes

1 Cf. the note on Translations and Sources in this volume.
2 John Howard, *The State of the Prisons in England and Wales, with Preliminary Observations and an Account of some Foreign Prisons and Hospitals* (1777).

9 THE POLITICS OF HEALTH IN THE EIGHTEENTH CENTURY

First of all, two preliminary remarks:

(1) No doubt it is scarcely fruitful to look for a relation of anteriority or dependence between the two terms of a private, 'liberal' medicine subject to the mechanisms of individual initiative and laws of the market, and a medical politics drawing support from structures of power and concerning itself with the health of a collectivity. It is somewhat mythical to suppose that Western medicine originated as a collective practice, endowed by magico-religious institutions with its social character and gradually dismantled through the subsequent organisation of private clienteles.[1] But it is equally inadequate to posit the existence at the historical threshold of modern medicine of a singular, private, individual medical relation, 'clinical' in its economic functioning and epistemological form, and to imagine that a series of corrections, adjustments and constraints gradually came to socialise this relation, causing it to be to some degree taken charge of by the collectivity.

What the eighteenth century shows, in any case, is a double-sided process. The development of a medical market in the form of private clienteles, the extension of a network of personnel offering qualified medical attention, the growth of individual and family demand for health care, the emergence of a clinical medicine strongly centred on individual examination, diagnosis and therapy, the explicitly moral and scientific—and secretly economic—exaltation of 'private consultation', in short the progressive emplacement of what was to become the great medical edifice of the nineteenth century, cannot be divorced from the concurrent organisation of a politics of health, the consideration of disease as a political and economic problem for social collectivities which they must seek to resolve as a matter of overall policy. 'Private' and 'socialised' medicine, in their reciprocal support and opposition, both derive from a common global strategy. No doubt there is no society which does not practice some kind of 'noso-politics': the eighteenth century didn't invent this. But it prescribed new rules, and above all transposed the practice on to an explicit, concerted level of analysis such as had been previously unknown. At this point the age is entered not so much of social medicine as of a considered noso-politics.

(2) The centre of initiative, organisation and control for this politics should not be located only in the apparatuses of the State. In fact there were a number of distinct health policies, and various different methods for taking charge of medical problems: those of religious groups (the considerable importance, for example, of the Quakers and the various dissenting movements in England); those of charitable and benevolent associations, ranging from the parish *bureaux* to the philanthropic societies, which operated somewhat like organs of the surveillance of one class over those others which, precisely because they are less able to defend themselves, are sources of collective danger; those of the learned societies, the eighteenth-century Academies and the early nineteenth-century statistics societies which endeavour to organise a global, quantifiable knowledge of morbid phenomena. Health and sickness, as characteristics of a group, a population, are problematised in the eighteenth century through the initiatives of multiple social instances, in relation to which the State itself plays various different roles. On occasion, it intervenes directly: a policy of free distributions of medicines is pursued in France on a varying scale from Louis XIV to Louis XVI. From time to time it also establishes bodies for purposes of consultation and information (the Prussian Sanitary Collegium dates from 1685; the Royal Society of Medicine is founded in France in 1776). Sometimes the State's projects for authoritarian medical organisation are thwarted: the Code of Health elaborated by Mai and accepted by the Elector Palatine in 1800 was never put into effect. Occasionally the State is also the object of solicitations which it resists.

Thus the eighteenth-century problematisation of noso-politics does not correlate with a uniform trend of State intervention in the practice of medicine, but rather with the emergence at a multitude of sites in the social body of health and disease as problems requiring some form or other of collective control measures. Rather than being the product of a vertical initiative coming from above, noso-politics in the eighteenth century figures as a problem with a number of different origins and orientations, being the problem of the health of all as a priority for all, the state of health of a population as a general objective of policy.

The most striking trait of this noso-politics, concern with which extends throughout French, and indeed European society in the eighteenth century, no doubt consists in the displacement of health problems relative to problems of assistance. Schematically, one can say that up to the end of the seventeenth century institutions for assistance to the poor serve as the collective means of dealing with disease. Certainly there are exceptions to this: the regulations for times of epidemic, measures taken in plague-towns, and the quarantines enforced in certain large ports all constituted forms of authoritarian medicalisation not organically linked to techniques of assistance. But outside these limit-cases, medicine understood and practiced as a 'service' operated simply as one of the components of 'assistance'. It was addressed to the category, so important despite the vagueness of its boundaries, of the 'sick poor'. In economic terms, this medical service was provided mainly thanks to charitable foundations. Institutionally it was exercised within the framework of lay and religious organisations devoted to a number of ends: distribution of food and clothing, care of abandoned children, projects of elementary education and moral proselytism, provision of workshops and workrooms, and in some cases the surveillance of 'unstable' or 'troublesome' elements (in the cities, the hospital *bureaux* had a jurisdiction over vagabonds and beggars, and the parish *bureaux* and charitable societies also very explicitly adopted the role of denouncing 'bad subjects'). From a technical point of view, the role of therapeutics in the working of the hospitals in the Classical age was limited in extent in comparison with the scale of provision of material assistance, and with the administrative structure. Sickness is only one among a range of factors, including infirmity, old age, inability to find work and destitution, which compose the figure of the 'necessitous pauper' who deserves hospitalisation.

The first phenomenon during the eighteenth century which should be noted is the progressive dislocation of these mixed and polyvalent procedures of assistance. This dismantling is carried out, or rather is called for (since it only begins to become effective late in the century) as the upshot of a general re-examination of modes of investment and capitalisation. The system of 'foundations', which immobilise substantial sums of money and whose revenues serve to support the idle and thus allow them to remain outside the circuits of production, is criticised by economists and administrators. The process of dismemberment is also carried out as a result of a finer grid of observation of the population and the distinctions which this observation aims to draw between the different categories of unfortunates to which charity confusedly addresses itself. In this process of the gradual attenuation of traditional social statuses, the 'pauper' is one of the first to be effaced, giving way to a whole series of functional discriminations (the good poor and the bad poor, the wilfully idle and the involuntarily unemployed, those who can do some kind of work and those who cannot). An analysis of idleness—and its conditions and effects—tends to replace the somewhat global charitable sacralisation of 'the poor'. This analysis has as its practical objective at best to make poverty useful by fixing it to the apparatus of production, at worst to lighten as much as possible the burden it imposes on the rest of society. The problem is to set the 'able-bodied' poor to work and transform them into a useful labour force, but it is also to assure the self-financing by the poor themselves of the cost of their sickness and temporary or permanent incapacitation, and further to render profitable in the short or long term the educating of orphans and foundlings. Thus, a complete utilitarian decomposition of poverty is marked out and the specific problem of the sickness of the poor begins to figure in the relationship of the imperatives of labour to the needs of production.

But one must also note another process which is more general than the first, and more than its simple elaboration. This is the emergence of the health and physical well-being of the population in general as one of the essential objectives of political power. Here it is not a matter of offering support to a particularly fragile, troubled and troublesome margin of the population, but of how to raise the level of health of the social body as a whole. Different power apparatuses are called upon to take charge of 'bodies', not simply so as to exact blood service from them or levy dues, but to help and if necessary constrain them to ensure their own good health. The imperative of health: at once the duty of each and the objective of all.

Taking a longer perspective, one could say that from the heart of the Middle Ages power traditionally exercised two great functions: that of war and peace, which it exercised through the hard-won monopoly of arms, and that of the arbitration of lawsuits and punishments of crimes, which it ensured through its control of judicial functions. *Pax et justitia*. To these functions were added—from the end of the Middle Ages—those of the maintenance of order and the organisation of enrichment. Now in the eighteenth century we find a further function emerging, that of the disposition of society as a milieu of physical well-being, health and optimum longevity. The exercise of these three latter functions—order, enrichment and health—is assured less through a single apparatus than by an ensemble of multiple regulations and institutions which in the eighteenth century take the generic name of 'police'. Down to the end of the *ancien régime*, the term 'police' does not signify, at least not exclusively, the institution of police in the modern sense; 'police' is the ensemble of mechanisms serving to ensure order, the properly channelled growth of wealth and the conditions of preservation of health 'in general'. Delamare's *Treatise* on police, the great charter of police functions in the Classical period, is significant in this respect. The eleven headings under which it classifies police activities can readily be distinguished in terms of three main sets of aims: economic regulation (the circulation of commodities, manufacturing processes, the obligations of tradespeople both to one another and to their clientele), measures of public order (surveillance of dangerous individuals, expulsion of vagabonds and, if necessary, beggars and the pursuit of criminals) and general rules of hygiene (checks on the quality of foodstuffs sold, the water supply and the cleanliness of streets).

At the point when the mixed procedures of police are being broken down into these elements and the problem of sickness among the poor is identified in its economic specificity, the health and physical well-being of populations comes to figure as a political objective which the 'police' of the social body must ensure along with those of economic regulation and the needs of order. The sudden importance assumed by medicine in the eighteenth century originates at the point of intersection of a new, 'analytical' economy of assistance with the emergence of a general 'police' of health. The new noso-politics inscribes the specific question of the sickness of the poor within the general problem of the health of populations, and makes the shift from the narrow context of charitable aid to the more general form of a 'medical police', imposing its constraints and dispensing its services. The texts of Th. Rau (the *Medizinische Polizei ordnung* of 1764), and above all the great work of J. P. Frank, *System einer medizinische Polizei*, give this transformation its most coherent expression.

What is the basis for this transformation? Broadly one can say that it has to do with the preservation, upkeep and conservation of the 'labour force'. But no doubt the problem is a wider one. It arguably concerns the economico-political effects of the accumulation of men. The great eighteenth-century demographic upswing in Western Europe, the necessity for co-ordinating and integrating it into the apparatus of production and the urgency of controlling it with finer and more adequate power mechanisms cause 'population', with its numerical variables of space and chronology, longevity and health, to emerge not only as a problem but as an object of surveillance, analysis, intervention, modification etc. The project of a technology of population begins to be sketched: demographic estimates, the calculation of the pyramid of ages, different life expectations and levels of mortality, studies of the reciprocal relations of growth of wealth and growth of population, various measures of incitement to marriage and procreation, the development of forms of education and professional training. Within this set of problems, the 'body'—the body of individuals and the body of populations—appears as the bearer of new variables, not merely as between the scarce and the numerous, the submissive and the restive, rich and poor, healthy and sick, strong and weak, but also as between the more or less utilisable, more or less amenable to profitable investment, those with greater or lesser prospects of survival, death and illness, and with more or less capacity for being usefully trained. The biological traits of a population become relevant factors for economic management, and it becomes necessary to organise around them an apparatus which will ensure not only their subjection but the constant increase of their utility.

This enables us to understand the main characteristics of eighteenth-century noso-politics as follows:

(1) *The privilege of the child and the medicalisation of the family.* The problem of 'children' (that is, of their number at birth and the relation of births to mortalities) is now joined by the problem of 'childhood' (that is, of survival to adulthood, the physical and economic conditions for this survival, the necessary and sufficient amount of investment for the period of child development to become useful, in brief the organisation of this 'phase' perceived as being both specific and finalised). It is no longer just a matter of producing an optimum number of children, but one of the correct management of this age of life.

New and highly detailed rules serve to codify relations between adults and children. The relations of filial submission and the system of signs that these entail certainly persist, with few changes. But they are to be henceforth invested by a whole series of obligations imposed on parents and children alike: obligations of a physical kind (care, contact, hygiene, cleanliness, attentive proximity), suckling of children by their mothers, clean clothing, physical exercise to ensure the proper development of the organism: the permanent and exacting corporal relation between adults and their children. The family is no longer to be just a system of relations inscribed in a social status, a kinship system, a mechanism for the transmission of property. It is to become a dense, saturated, permanent, continuous physical environment which envelops, maintains and develops the child's body. Hence it assumes a material figure defined within a narrower compass; it organises itself as the child's immediate environment, tending increasingly to become its basic framework for survival and growth. This leads to an effect of tightening, or at least intensification, of the elements and relations constituting the restricted family (the group of parents and children). It also leads to a certain inversion of axes: the conjugal bond no longer serves only, nor even perhaps primarily, to establish the junction of two lines of descent, but to organise the matrix of the new adult individual. No doubt it still serves to give rise to two lineages and hence produce a descent, but it serves also to produce—under the best possible conditions—a human being who will live to the state of adulthood. The new 'conjugality' lies rather in the link between parents and children. The family, seen as a narrow, localised pedagogical apparatus, consolidates itself within the interior of the great traditional family-as-alliance. And at the same time health, and principally the health of children, becomes one of the family's most demanding objectives. The rectangle of parents and children must become a sort of homeostasis of health. At all events, from the eighteenth century onwards the healthy, clean, fit body, a purified, cleansed aerated domestic space, the medically optimal siting of individuals, places, beds and utensils, and the interplay of the 'caring' and the 'cared for' figure among the family's essential laws. And from this period the family becomes the most constant agent of medicalisation. From the second half of the eighteenth century, the family is the target for a great enterprise of medical acculturation. The first wave of this offensive bears on care of children, especially babies. Among the principal texts are Audrey's *L'orthopédie* (1749), Vandermonde's *Essai sur la manière de perfectionner l'espèce humaine* (1756), Cadogan's *An essay upon nursing, and the management of children, from their birth to three years of age* (1748; French translation, 1752), des Essartz's *Traité de l'éducation corporelle en bas age* (1760), Ballex-sert's *Dissertation sur l'Éducation physique des enfants* (1762), Raulin's *De la conservation des enfants* (1768), Nicolas' *Le cri de la nature en faveur des enfants nouveaux-nés* (1775), Daignan's *Tableau des sociétés de la vie humaine*

(1786), Saucerotte's *De la conservation des enfants* (year
IV), W. Buchan's *Advice to mothers on the subject of their
own health; and on the means of promoting the health,
strength and beauty of their offspring* (1803; French translation, 1804), J. A. Millot's *Le Nestor francais* (1807), Laplace
Chanvre's *Dissertation sur quelques points de l'éducation
physique et morale des enfants* (1813), Leretz's *Hygiène des
enfants* (1814) and Prévost Leygonie's *Essai sur l'éducation
physique des enfants* (1813). This literature gains even
further in extension in the nineteenth century with the
appearance of a whole series of journals which address
themselves directly to the lower classes.

The long campaign of inoculation and vaccination has its
place in this movement to organise around the child a
system of medical care for which the family is to bear the
moral responsibility and at least part of the economic cost.
Via different routes, the policy for orphans follows an
analogous strategy. Special institutions are opened: the
Foundling Hospital, the Enfants Trouvés in Paris; but there
is also a system organised for placing children with nurses or
in families where they can make themselves useful by taking
at least a minimal part in domestic life, and where, moreover, they will find a more favourable milieu of development at less cost than in a hospital where they would be
barracked until adolescence.

The medical politics outlined in the eighteenth century in
all European countries has as its first effect the organisation
of the family, or rather the family–children complex, as the
first and most important instance for the medicalisation of
individuals.The family is assigned a linking role between
general objectives regarding the good health of the social
body and individuals' desire or need for care. This enables a
'private' ethic of good health as the reciprocal duty of
parents and children to be articulated on to a collective
system of hygiene and scientific technique of cure made
available to individual and family demand by a professional
corps of doctors qualified and, as it were, recommended by
the State. The rights and duties of individuals respecting
their health and that of others, the market where supply and
demand for medical care meet, authoritarian interventions
of power in the order of hygiene and illness accompanied at

the same time by the institutionalising and protection of the private doctor–patient relation, all these features in their multiplicity and coherence characterise the global function-ing of the politics of health in the nineteenth century, yet they cannot be properly understood if one abstracts them from this central element formed in the eighteenth century, the medicalised and medicalising family.

(2) *The privilege of hygiene and the function of medicine as an instance of social control.* The old notion of the régime, understood at once as a rule of life and a form of preventive medicine, tends to become enlarged into that of the collec-tive 'régime' of a population in general, with the disap-pearance of the great epidemic tempests, the reduction of the death-rate and the extension of the average life-span and life-expectation for every age group as its triple objective. This programme of hygiene as a régime of health for populations entails a certain number of authoritarian medical interventions and controls.

First of all, control of the urban space in general: it is this space which constitutes perhaps the most dangerous en-vironment for the population. The disposition of various quarters, their humidity and exposure, the ventilation of the city as a whole, its sewage and drainage systems, the siting of abattoirs and cemeteries, the density of population, all these are decisive factors for the mortality and morbidity of the inhabitants. The city with its principal spatial variables appears as a medicalisable object. Whereas the medical topographies of regions analyse climatic and geological conditions which are outside human control, and can only recommend measures of correction and compensation, the urban topographies outline, in negative at least, the general principles of a concerted urban policy. During the eighteenth century the idea of the pathogenic city inspires a whole mythology and very real states of popular panic (the Charnel House of the Innocents in Paris was one of these high places of fear); it also gave rise to a medical discourse on urban morbidity and the placing under surveillance of a whole range of urban developments, constructions and institutions.[2]

In a more precise and localised fashion, the needs of hygiene demand an authoritarian medical intervention in what are regarded as the privileged breeding-grounds of disease: prisons, ships, harbour installations, the *hôpitaux généraux* where vagabonds, beggars and invalids mingle together, the hospitals themselves, whose medical staffing is usually inadequate, and which aggravate or complicate the diseases of their patients, to say nothing of their diffusing of pathological germs into the outside world. Thus priority areas of medicalisation in the urban environment are isolated and are destined to constitute so many points for the exercise and application of an intensified medical power. Doctors will, moreover, have the task of teaching individuals the basic rules of hygiene which they must respect for the sake of their own health and that of others: hygiene of food and habitat, exhortations to seek treatment in case of illness.

Medicine, as a general technique of health even more than as a service to the sick or an art of cures, assumes an increasingly important place in the administrative system and the machinery of power, a role which is constantly widened and strengthened throughout the eighteenth century. The doctor wins a footing within the different instances of social power. The administration acts as a point of support and sometimes a point of departure for the great medical enquiries into the health of populations, and conversely doctors devote an increasing amount of their activity to tasks, both general and administrative, assigned to them by power. A 'medico-administrative' knowledge begins to develop concerning society, its health and sickness, its conditions of life, housing and habits, which serves as the basic core for the 'social economy' and sociology of the nineteenth century. And there is likewise constituted a politico-medical hold on a population hedged in by a whole series of prescriptions relating not only to disease but to general forms of existence and behaviour (food and drink, sexuality and fecundity, clothing and the layout of living space).

A number of phenomena dating from the eighteenth century testify to this hygienist interpretation of political and medical questions and the 'surplus of power' which it bestows on the doctor: the increasing presence of doctors in the Academies and learned societies, the very substantial medical participation in the production of the Encyclopedias, their presence as counsellors to representatives of power, the organisation of medical societies officially charged with a certain number of administrative responsibilities and qualified to adopt or recommend authoritarian measures, the frequent role of doctors as programmers of a well-ordered society (the doctor as social or political reformer is a frequent figure in the second half of the eighteenth century), and the super-abundance of doctors in the Revolutionary Assemblies. The doctor becomes the great advisor and expert, if not in the art of governing, at least in that of observing, correcting and improving the social 'body' and maintaining it in a permanent state of health. And it is the doctor's function as hygienist rather than his prestige as a therapist that assures him this politically privileged position in the eighteenth century, prior to his accumulation of economic and social privileges in the nineteenth century.

The challenge to the hospital institution in the eighteenth century can be understood on the basis of these three major phenomena: the emergence of 'population' with its bio-medical variables of longevity and health, the organisation of the narrowly parental family as a relay in a process of medicalisation for which it acts both as the permanent source and the ultimate instrument, and the interlacing of medical and administrative instances in organising the control of collective hygiene.

The point is that in relation to these new problems the hospital appears in many respects as an obsolete structure. A fragment of space closed in on itself, a place of internment of men and diseases, its ceremonious but inept architecture multiplying the ills in its interior without preventing their outward diffusion, the hospital is more the seat of death for the cities where it is sited than a therapeutic agent for the population as a whole. Not only the difficulty of admission and the stringent conditions imposed on those seeking to enter, but also the incessant disorder of comings and goings, inefficient medical surveillance and the difficulty of effective treatment cause the hospital to be regarded, from the moment the population in general is specified as the object of medicalisation and the overall improvement in its level of health as the objective, as an inadequate instrument. The hospital is perceived as an area of darkness within the urban space that medicine is called upon to purify. And it acts as a deadweight on the economy since it provides a mode of assistance that can never make possible the diminution of poverty, but at best the survival of certain paupers—and hence their increase in number, the prolongation of their sicknesses, the consolidation of their ill-health with all the consequent effects of contagion.

Hence there is the idea, which spreads during the eighteenth century, of a replacement of the hospital by three principal mechanisms. The first of these is the organisation of a domestic form of 'hospitalisation'. No doubt this has its risks where epidemics are concerned, but it has economic advantages in that the cost to society of the patient's upkeep is far less as he is fed and cared for at home in the normal manner. The cost to the social body is hardly more than the loss represented by his forced idleness, and then only where he had actually been working. The method also offers medical advantages, in that the family—given a little advice—can attend to the patient's needs in a constant and adjustable manner that would be impossible under hospital administration: each family will be enabled to function as a small, temporary, individual and inexpensive hospital. But such a procedure requires the replacement of the hospital to be backed by a medical corps dispersed throughout the social body and able to offer treatment either free or as cheaply as possible. A medical staffing of the population, provided it is permanent, flexible and easy to make use of, should render unnecessary a good many of the traditional hospitals. Lastly, it is possible to envisage the care, consultation, and distribution of medicaments already offered by certain hospitals to out-patients being extended to a general basis, without the need to hold or intern the patients: this is the method of the dispensaries which aim to retain the technical advantages of hospitalisation without its medical and economic drawbacks.

These three methods gave rise, especially in the latter half of the eighteenth century, to a whole series of projects and programmes. They inspired a number of experiments. In 1769 the Red Lion Square dispensary for poor children was opened in London. Thirty years later almost every district of the city had its dispensary and the annual number of those receiving free treatment there was estimated at nearly 50,000. In France it seems that the main effort was towards the improvement, extension and more-or-less homogeneous distribution of medical personnel in town and country. The reform of medical and surgical studies (in 1772 and 1784), the requirement of doctors to practice in boroughs and small towns before being admitted to certain of the large cities, the work of investigation and coordination performed by the Royal Society of Medicine, the increasing part occupied by control of health and hygiene in the responsibilities of the Intendants, the development of free distribution of medicaments under the authority of doctors designated by the administration, all these measures are related to a health policy resting on the extensive presence of medical personnel in the social body. At the extreme point of these criticisms of the hospital and this project for its replacement, one finds under the Revolution a marked tendency towards 'dehospitalisation'; this tendency is already perceptible in the reports of the *Comité de mendicité*, with the project to establish a doctor or surgeon in each rural district to care for the indigent, supervise children under assistance and practice inoculation. It becomes more clearly formulated under the Convention, with the proposal for three doctors in each district to provide the main health care for the whole population. However, the disappearance of the hospital was never more than the vanishing point of a utopian perspective. The real work lay in the effort to elaborate a complex system of functions in which the hospital comes to have a specialised role relative to the family (now considered as the primary instance of health), to the extensive and continuous network of medical personnel, and to the administrative control of the population. It is within this complex framework of policies that the reform of the hospitals is attempted.

The first problem concerns the spatial adaptation of the hospital, and in particular its adaptation to the urban space in which it is located. A series of discussions and conflicts arise between different schemes of implantation, respectively advocating massive hospitals capable of accommodating a sizeable population, uniting and thus rendering more coherent the various forms of treatment, or alternatively smaller hospitals where patients will receive better attention and the risks of contagion will be less grave. There was another, connected problem: should hospitals be sited outside the cities where ventilation is better and there is no risk of hospital miasmas being diffused among the population— a solution which in general is linked to the planning of large architectural installations; or should a multiplicity of small hospitals be built at scattered points where they can most easily be reached by the population which is to use them, a solution which often involves the coupling of hospital and dispensary? In either case, the hospital is intended to become a functional element in an urban space where its effects must be subject to measurement and control.

It is also necessary to organise the internal space of the hospital so as to make it medically efficacious, a place no longer of assistance but of therapeutic action. The hospital must function as a 'curing machine'. First, in a negative manner, all the factors which make the hospital dangerous for its occupants must be suppressed, solving the problem of the circulation of air which must be constantly renewed without its miasmas or mephitic qualities being carried from one patient to another, solving as well the problem of the changing, transport and laundering of bed-linen. Secondly, in a positive manner, the space of the hospital must be organised according to a concerted therapeutic strategy, through the uninterrupted presence and hierarchical prerogatives of doctors, through systems of observation, notation and record-taking which make it possible to fix the knowledge of different cases, to follow their particular evolution, and also to globalise the data which bear on the long-term life of a whole population, and finally through substituting better-adapted medical and pharmaceutical cures for the somewhat indiscriminate curative régimes which formed the essential part of traditional nursing. The hospital tends towards becoming an essential element in medical technology, not simply as a place for curing, but as an instrument which, for a certain number of serious cases, makes curing possible.

Consequently it becomes necessary in the hospital to

articulate medical knowledge with therapeutic efficiency. In the eighteenth century there emerge specialised hospitals. If there existed certain establishments previously reserved for madmen or venereal patients, this was less for the sake of any specialised treatment than as a measure of exclusion or out of fear. The new 'unifunctional' hospital on the other hand comes to be organised only from the moment when hospitalisation becomes the basis, and sometimes the condition, for a more-or-less complex therapeutic approach. The Middlesex Hospital, intended for the treatment of smallpox and the practice of vaccination, was opened in London in 1745, The London Fever Hospital dates from 1802, and the Royal Ophthalmic Hospital from 1804. The first Maternity Hospital was opened in London in 1749. In Paris, the Enfants Malades was founded in 1802. One sees the gradual constitution of a hospital system whose therapeutic function is strongly emphasised, designed on the one hand to cover with sufficient continuity the urban or rural space whose population it has charge of, and on the other to articulate itself with medical knowledge and its classifications and techniques.

Lastly, the hospital must serve as the supporting structure for the permanent staffing of the population by medical personnel. Both for economic and medical reasons, it must be possible to make the passage from treatment at home to a hospital régime. By their visiting rounds, country and city doctors must lighten the burden of the hospitals and prevent their overcrowding, and in return the hospital must be accessible to patients on the advice and at the request of their doctors. Moreover, the hospital as a place of accumulation and development of knowledge must provide for the training of doctors for private practice. Clinical teaching in the hospital, the first rudiments of which appear in Holland with Sylvius and then Boerhaave, at Vienna with Van Swieten, and at Edinburgh through the linking of the School of Medicine with the Edinburgh Infirmary, becomes at the end of the eighteenth century the general principle around which the reorganisation of medical studies is undertaken. The hospital, a therapeutic instrument for the patients who occupy it, contributes at the same time, through its clinical teaching and the quality of the medical knowledge acquired there, to the improvement of the population's health as a whole.

The return of the hospitals, and more particularly the projects for their architectural, institutional and technical reorganisation, owed its importance in the eighteenth century to this set of problems relating to the urban space, the mass of the population with its biological characteristics, the close-knit family cell and the bodies of individuals. It is in the history of these materialities, which are at once political and economic, that the 'physical' process of transformation of the hospitals is inscribed.

Notes

1 Cf. G. Rosen, *A History of Public Health*, New York 1958.
2 Cf. for example, J. P. L. Morel, *Dissertation sur les causes qui contribuent le plus à rendre cachectique et rachitique la constitution d'un grand nombre d'enfants de la ville de Lille* (A dissertation on the causes which most contribute to rendering the constitution of a great number of children in the city of Lille cachectic and rachitic), 1812.

10 THE HISTORY OF SEXUALITY

Interviewer: Lucette Finas

Michel Foucault, *The Will to Know*, the first volume of your 'History of Sexuality', strikes me as being from every point of view a work revolutionary in its impact. The position you maintain, which is unexpected and at first glance simple, is progressively revealed to be very complex. One way of summarising it might be to say that the relation between power and sex is not one of repression, far from it. But before we go any further, could we talk about *The Order of Discourse*, your inaugural lecture given at the Collège de France in December 1970. There, you analyse the factors which control the production of discourse, among which are interdiction, the old dichotomy between reason and madness, and the will to truth. Could you clarify for us the connections between *The Will to Know* and *The Order of Discourse* and tell us whether or not during the course of your argument the will to know and the will to truth will be re-united?

I think that in *The Order of Discourse* I conflated two concepts, or rather that for what I take to be a legitimate problem (that of articulating the data of discourse with the mechanisms of power) I provided an inadequate solution. It was a piece I wrote at a moment of transition. Till then, it seems to me, I accepted the traditional conception of power as an essentially judicial mechanism, as that which lays down the law, which prohibits, which refuses, and which has a whole range of negative effects: exclusion, rejection, denial, obstruction, occultation, etc. Now I believe that conception to be inadequate. It had, however, been adequate to my purpose in *Madness and Civilisation* (not that that book is in itself either satisfactory or sufficient) since madness is a special case—during the Classical age power over madness was, in its most important manifestation at least, exercised in the form of exclusion; thus one sees madness caught up in a great movement of rejection. So in my analysis of this fact I was able, without too many problems, to use a purely negative conception of power. There came a time when this struck me as inadequate. It was during the course of a concrete experience that I had with prisons, starting in 1971–2. The case of the penal system convinced me that the question of power needed to be formulated not so much in terms of justice as in those of technology, of tactics and strategy, and it was this substitution for a judicial and negative grid of a technical and strategic one that I tried to effect in *Discipline and Punish* and then to exploit in 'The History of Sexuality'. So I should be only too glad to discard everything in *The Order of Discourse* which might seem to identify the relations of power to discourse with negative mechanisms of selection.

> The reader of your *Madness and Civilisation* is left with the picture of a great Baroque madness locked away and reduced to silence. In the middle of the seventeenth century asylums were hurriedly constructed all over Europe. Should that lead us to say that, whereas silence was imposed on madness by modern history, sex was rendered articulate? To put it another way, did anxiety about madness and anxiety about sex lead to results, at the level of discourse as at that of events, that were the direct opposite for the one and for the other? If so, why?

In fact I believe there are a series of historical relations between madness and sexuality which are important and of which I was certainly unaware when I wrote *Madness and Civilisation*. At that time I had it in mind to write two parallel histories: on the one hand the history of the exclusion of madness and the oppositions which came into play following on from it; on the other, a history of how various forms of circumscription were brought into effect within the field of sexuality (forms of sexuality that are permitted or forbidden, normal or abnormal, male or female, adult or child); I was thinking of a whole series of binary oppositions which had each in its own way fed on the great opposition between reason and unreason that I had tried to re-constitute *à propos* of madness. But I don't think that will do: whereas madness was, for at least a century, essentially an object of negative operations, sexuality became during that same period the domain of quite precise and positive investments. However, in the nineteenth century, an absolutely fundamental phenomenon made its appearance: the inter-weaving, the intrication of two great technologies of power: one which fabricated sexuality and the other which segregated madness. The technology of madness changed from negative to positive, from being binary to being complex and multiform. There came into being a vast technology of the psyche, which became a characteristic feature of the nineteenth and twentieth centuries; it at once turned sex into the reality hidden behind rational consciousness and the sense to be decoded from madness, their common content, and hence that which made it possible to adopt the same modalities for dealing with both.

> One ought perhaps to eliminate three possible mis-understandings. Would it be true to say that your rejection of the hypothesis of repression consists neither in a simple shift of emphasis nor in imputing to power an attitude of denial or ignorance with respect to sex? One might, instead of stressing the repression to which heretics were subject, choose to emphasise the 'will to know' which presided over their torture! This is not, is it, a line that you would take? Now would you say, would you, either that power conceals from itself its own interest in sex, or that sex speaks unbeknown to a power which it surreptitiously outflanks?

I don't in fact think that any of these aims or preoccupations, which you call misunderstandings, are to be found in my book. To call them misunderstandings is a little too severe on these interpretations, or rather on these attempts at circumscribing my book. Take the first one; I did indeed want to change the emphasis and make positive mechanisms appear where one would normally stress the negative ones.

Thus in discussions of the penitential it is always emphasised that Christianity imposes sanctions on sexuality, that it authorises certain forms of it and punishes the rest. But one ought, I think, also to point out that at the heart of Christian penitence there is the confessional, and so the admission of guilt, the examination of conscience, and arising from that the production of a whole body of knowledge and a discourse on sex which engendered a range of effects on both theory (for example the vast analysis of concupiscence in the seventeenth century) and practice (a pedagogy of sexuality, subsequently laicised and medicalised). In the same way I have described the way in which different instances and stages in the transmission of power were caught up in the very pleasure of their exercise. There is something in surveillance, or more accurately in the gaze of those involved in the act of surveillance, which is no stranger to the pleasure of surveillance, the pleasure of the surveillance of pleasure, and so on. I wanted to make that point, but that was not all I wanted to indicate. There is no doubt, for example, that the outbreaks of hysteria in psychiatric hospitals during the second half of the nineteenth century were really a mechanism in reverse, a counter-blow against the very exercise of psychiatry: psychiatrists were brought face to face with the hysterical body of their patients (I mean given total acquaintance with it whilst still in total ignorance), without their having either sought this or even known how it came about. These too are elements in my book but they are not what is essential to it. It seems to me that they cannot be understood except in relation to the establishing of a power exercised on the body itself. What I want to show is how power relations can materially penetrate the body in depth, without depending even on the mediation of the subject's own representations. If power takes hold on the body, this isn't through its having first to be interiorised in people's consciousnesses. There is a network or circuit of bio-power, or somato-power, which acts as the formative matrix of sexuality itself as the historical and cultural phenomenon within which we seem at once to recognise and lose ourselves.

On page 121 of *La Volonté de savoir*, in what seems to be a response to the reader's expectation, you distinguish between 'Power' as a set of institutions and apparatuses, and power as a multiplicity of relations of force immanent in the domain in which they are inscribed. You present this play of power as generating itself at each moment, at each point, and in every relation between one point and another. Is it power in this sense, if I have understood you correctly, that is not external to sex but in fact quite the reverse?

For me, the whole point of the project lies in a re-elaboration of the theory of power. I'm not sure that the mere pleasure of writing about sexuality would have provided me with sufficient motivation to start this sequence of at least six volumes, if I had not felt impelled by the necessity of re-working this problem of power a little. It seems to me that the problem is too often reduced—following the model imposed by the juridico-philosophical thinking of the sixteenth and seventeenth centuries—to the problem of sovereignty (what is the sovereign? how is he constituted as sovereign? what bond of obedience ties individuals to the sovereign?). This is the problem posed by monarchist and anti-monarchist jurists alike from the thirteenth to the nineteenth centuries, the problem which continues to haunt us, and which seems to me to preclude the analysis of a whole range of areas; I realise that these can seem over-empirical and secondary, but after all, they concern our bodies, our lives, our day-to-day existences. As against this privileging of sovereign power, I wanted to show the value of an analysis which followed a different course. Between every point of a social body, between a man and a woman, between the members of a family, between a master and his pupil, between every one who knows and every one who does not, there exist relations of power which are not purely and simply a projection of the sovereign's great power over the individual; they are rather the concrete, changing soil in which the sovereign's power is grounded, the conditions which make it possible for it to function. The family, even now, is not a simple reflection or extension of the power of the State; it does not act as the representative of the State in relation to children, just as the male does not act as its representative with respect to the female. For the State to function in the way that it does, there must be, between male and female or adult and child, quite specific relations of domination which have their own configuration and relative autonomy.

I think one must be wary of the whole thematic of representation which encumbers analyses of power. For a long time, the great problem was how it was possible for the will of individuals to be represented in or by the general will. Nowadays the same thematic is evoked in the oft-repeated statement that fathers, husbands, employers, teachers all represent a state power which itself 'represents' the interests of a class. This takes no account of the complexity of the mechanisms at work, their specificity, nor the effects of inter-dependence, complementarity, and sometimes of blockage, which this very diversity produces.

In general terms, I believe that power is not built up out of 'wills' (individual or collective), nor is it derivable from interests. Power is constructed and functions on the basis of particular powers, myriad issues, myriad effects of power. It is this complex domain that must be studied. That is not to say that it is independent or could be made sense of outside of economic processes and the relations of production.

> In reading what might be considered to be an attempt, in your book, to elaborate a new conception of power, one is split between the image of the computer and that of the individual, isolated, or supposedly so, but also having a specific power at his disposal.

The idea that the State must, as the source or point of confluence of power, be invoked to account for all the apparatuses in which power is organised, does not seem to me very fruitful for history, or one might rather say that its fruitfulness has been exhausted. The opposite approach seems at present more promising: I have in mind studies like that of Jacques Donzelot on the family (he shows how the absolutely specific forms of power exerted within the family have, as a result of the development and expansion of the school system, been penetrated by more general mechanisms of State power, but also how State and familial forms of power have each retained their specificity and have only been able to interlock so long as the specific ways in which they each operate have been respected). Similarly, Francois Ewald has written a study of the mines, showing the role played by the owners' systems of control and the way those systems have survived the absorption of the mines by the State without losing their effectiveness.

> Once the question of what we call 'power' is re-opened in this way, can one adopt a political standpoint regarding power? You speak of sexuality as a political apparatus. Could you define the sense you give to the word 'political'?

If it is true that the set of relations of force in a given society constitutes the domain of the political, and that a politics is a more-or-less global strategy for co-ordinating and directing those relations, then I believe one can answer your questions in the following way: the political is not something which determines in the last analysis (or over-determines) relations that are elementary and by nature 'neutral'. Every relation of force implies at each moment a relation of power (which is in a sense its momentary expression) and every power relation makes a reference, as its effect but also as its condition of possibility, to a political field of which it forms a part. To say that 'everything is political', is to affirm this ubiquity of relations of force and their immanence in a political field; but this is to give onself the task, which as yet has scarcely even been out-lined, of disentangling this indefinite knot. Such an analysis must not be telescoped by laying everything at the door of individual responsibility, as was done above all a decade or two ago by the existentialism of self-flagellation—you know, how everyone is responsible for everything, there is not an injustice in the world to which we are not accomplices—it must not be evaded by those displacements that are glibly practiced today: everything derives from the market economy, or from capitalist exploitation, or simply from the rottenness of our society (so that sexual problems, or problems of delinquency or insanity are put off until there is a 'different' society).

Political analysis and criticism have in a large measure still to be invented—so too have the strategies which will make it possible to modify the relations of force, to co-ordinate them in such a way that such a modification is possible and can be inscribed in reality. That is to say, the problem is not so much that of defining a political 'position' (which is to choose from a pre-existing set of possibilities) but to imagine and to bring into being new schemas of politicisation. If 'politicisation' means falling back on ready-made choices and institutions, then the effort of analysis involved in uncovering the relations of force and mechanisms of power is not worthwhile. To the vast new techniques of power correlated with multinational economies and bureaucratic States, one must oppose a politicisation which will take new forms.

> One of the aspects and results of your research is the elaboration of a very subtle and complex distinction between sex and sexuality. Could you clarify that distinction and tell us accordingly how to read the title of your 'History of Sexuality'?

This question was the central difficulty with my book. I had begun to write it as a history of the way in which sex was obscured and travestied by this strange life-form, this strange growth which was to become sexuality. Now, I believe, setting up this opposition between sex and sexuality leads back to the positing of power as law and prohibition, the idea that power created sexuality as a device to say no to sex. My analysis was still held captive by the juridical conception of power. I had to make a complete reversal of direction. I postulated the idea of sex as internal to the apparatus of sexuality, and the consequent idea that what must be found at the root of that apparatus is not the rejection of sex, but a positive economy of the body and of pleasure.

Now there is a trait which is fundamental to the economy of pleasures as it functions in the West, namely that sex acts as a principle of measure and intelligibility. For millennia the tendency has been to give us to believe that in sex, secretly at least there was to be found the law of all pleasure, and that this is what justifies the need to regulate sex and makes its control possible. These two notions, that sex is at the heart of all pleasure and that its nature requires that it should be restricted and devoted to procreation, are not of Christian but of Stoic origin; and Christianity was obliged to incorporate them when it sought to integrate itself in the State structure of the Roman Empire in which Stoicism was virtually the universal philosophy. Sex then became the 'code' of pleasure. Whereas in societies with a heritage of erotic art the intensification of pleasure tends to desexualise the body, in the West this systematisation of pleasure according to the 'laws' of sex gave rise to the whole apparatus of sexuality. And it is this that makes us believe that we are 'liberating' ourselves when we 'decode' all pleasure in terms of a sex shorn at last of disguise, whereas one should aim instead at a desexualisation, at a general economy of pleasure not based on sexual norms.

> Your analysis makes the genealogy of psychoanalysis seem rather suspicious and shameful. Psychoanalysis is revealed as springing, primordially at least, from confession in the age of the Inquisition on the one hand, and from the medicalisation of psychiatry on the other. Does that really represent your view of the matter?

One can say certainly that psychoanalysis grew out of that formidable development and institutionalisation of confessional procedures which has been so characteristic of our civilisation. Viewed over a shorter span of time, it forms part of that medicalisation of sexuality which is another strange phenomenon of the West: whereas in erotic art what is medicalised is rather the means (pharmaceutical or somatic) which serve to intensify pleasure, one finds in the West a medicalisation of sexuality itself, as though it were an area of particular pathological fragility in human existence. All sexuality runs the risk at one and the same time of being in itself an illness and of inducing illnesses without number. It cannot be denied that psychoanalysis is situated at the point where these two processes intersect. How it was possible for psychoanalysis to take the form it did, at the time it did, is something I will try and establish in the later volumes. I am afraid that the same situation will arise with psychoanalysis as arose with psychiatry after I had written *Madness and Civilisation*; I had attempted to narrate there what took place up to the beginning of the nineteenth century, but psychiatrists took my analysis to be an attack on present-day psychiatry. I don't know what will happen with the psychoanalysts but I very much fear that they will take for an 'anti-psychoanalysis' what will merely be a genealogy.

Why should an archaeology of psychiatry function as an 'anti-psychiatry', when an archaeology of biology does not function as an anti-biology? Is it because of the partial nature of the analysis? Or is it not rather that psychiatry is not on good terms with its own history, the result of a certain inability on the part of psychiatry, given what it is, to accept its own history? We shall see how psychoanalysis responds when faced with the question of its own history.

> Do you feel that your 'History of Sexuality' will advance the women's question? I have in mind what you say about the hysterisation and psychiatrisation of the female body.

There are few ideas there, but only hesitant ones, not yet fully crystallised. It will be the discussion and criticism after each volume that will perhaps allow them to become clarified. But it is not up to me to lay down how the book should be used.

> *The Will to Know* deals with modes of discourse and questions of fact which are themselves caught up in your own discourse, in this order of your discourse which seems rather to be an anti-order. You flit from one point of your argument to another, you engender within your own text discourses that contradict your own, as though the space occupied by your analysis were there in advance and constrained you. Your writing, moreover, strives to depict, before the very eyes of the reader, relations that are abstract and remote. Would you accept this view of the dramatic organisation your analysis and its fictive nature?

This book does not have the function of a proof. It exists as a sort of prelude, to explore the keyboard, sketch out the themes and see how people react, what will be criticised, what will be misunderstood, and what will cause resentment — it was in some sense to give the other volumes access to these reactions that I wrote this one first. As to the problem of fiction, it seems to me to be a very important one; I am well aware that I have never written anything but fictions. I do not mean to say, however, that truth is therefore absent. It seems to me that the possibility exists for fiction to function in truth, for a fictional discourse to induce effects of truth, and for bringing it about that a true discourse engenders or 'manufactures' something that does not as yet exist, that is, 'fictions' it. One 'fictions' history on the basis of a political reality that makes it true, one 'fictions' a politics not yet in existence on the basis of a historical truth.

11 THE CONFESSION OF THE FLESH

A conversation with Alain Grosrichard, Gerard Wajeman, Jaques-Alain Miller, Guy Le Gaufey, Dominique Celas, Gerard Miller, Catherine Millot, Jocelyne Livi and Judith Miller.

GROSRICHARD: Let's begin with the general title of this new project of yours: the 'History of Sexuality'. What is the nature of this new historical object which you term 'sexuality'? Evidently it isn't sexuality in the sense that botanists or biologists speak or have spoken of it, something which is more a matter for historians of science. Nor is it a question of sexuality in the sense that traditional histories of ideas or customs might have understood the term, the point of view which you are now contesting with your doubts about the 'repressive hypothesis'. Nor even, finally, do you seem to be talking about sexual practices such as historians study today using new methods and techniques of analysis. You talk about an 'apparatus of sexuality'. What is the meaning or the methodological function for you of this term, *apparatus (dispositif)*?

FOUCAULT: What I'm trying to pick out with this term is, firstly, a thoroughly heterogeneous ensemble consisting of discourses, institutions, architectural forms, regulatory decisions, laws, administrative measures, scientific statements, philosophical, moral and philanthropic propositions — in short, the said as much as the unsaid. Such are the elements of the apparatus. The apparatus itself is the system of relations that can be established between these elements. Secondly, what I am trying to identify in this apparatus is precisely the nature of the connection that can exist between these heterogeneous elements. Thus, a particular discourse can figure at one time as the programme of an institution, and at another it can function as a means of justifying or masking a practice which itself remains silent, or as a secondary re-interpretation of this practice, opening out for it a new field of rationality. In short, between these elements, whether discursive or non-discursive, there is a sort of interplay of shifts of position and modifications of function which can also vary very widely. Thirdly, I understand by the term 'apparatus' a sort of—shall we say—formation which has as its major function at a given historical moment that of responding to an *urgent need*. The apparatus thus has a dominant strategic function. This may have been, for example, the assimilation of a floating population found to be burdensome for an essentially mercantilist economy: there was a strategic imperative acting here as the matrix for an apparatus which gradually undertook the control or subjection of madness, mental illness and neurosis.

WAJEMAN: So an apparatus is defined by a structure of heterogeneous elements, but also by a certain kind of genesis?

FOUCAULT: Yes. And I would consider that there are two important moments in this genesis. There is a first moment which is the prevalent influence of a strategic objective. Next, the apparatus as such is constituted and enabled to continue in existence insofar as it is the site of a double process. On the one hand, there is a process of *functional overdetermination*, because each effect—positive or negative, intentional or unintentional—enters into resonance or contradiction with the others and thereby calls for a re-adjustment or a re-working of the heterogeneous elements that surface at various points. On the other hand, there is a perpetual process of *strategic elaboration*. Take the example of imprisonment, that apparatus which had the effect of making measures of detention appear to be the most efficient and rational method that could be applied to the phenomenon of criminality. What did this apparatus produce? An entirely unforeseen effect which had nothing to do with any kind of strategic ruse on the part of some meta- or trans-historic subject conceiving and willing it. This effect was the constitution of a delinquent milieu very different from the kind of seedbed of illegalist practices and individuals found in eighteenth-century society. What happened? The prison operated as a process of filtering, concentrating, professionalising and circumscribing a criminal milieu. From about the 1830s onwards, one finds an immediate re-utilisation of this unintended, negative effect within a new strategy which came in some sense to occupy this empty space, or transform the negative into a positive. The delinquent milieu came to be re-utilised for diverse political and economic ends, such as the extraction of profit from pleasure through the organisation of prostitution. This is what I call the strategic completion (*remplissement*) of the apparatus.

GROSRICHARD: In *The Order of Things* and *The Archaeology of Knowledge*, you talked about the *episteme*, knowledge and discursive formations. Now you are more inclined to talk about 'apparatuses' and 'disciplines'. Are these new concepts intended to replace the previous ones, which you would now want to abandon? Or do they rather reproduce them in a different register? Does this amount to a change in the way you would like your books to be used? Are you now selecting your objects of study, your way of approach and your conceptual instruments in terms of new objectives, namely the contemporary struggles that have to be fought, the world which has to be changed rather than interpreted? I am asking this now so that the questions we put to you afterwards won't be at cross purposes with what you are trying to do.

FOUCAULT: But bear in mind that it may be just as well if they're at cross purposes: that would show that my own undertaking is at cross purposes. But you are right to ask the question. With the notion of the apparatus, I find myself in a difficulty which I haven't yet been properly able to get out of. I said that the apparatus is essentially of a *strategic* nature, which means assuming that it is a matter of a certain manipulation of relations of forces, either developing them in a particular direction, blocking them, stabilising them, utilising them, etc. The apparatus is thus always inscribed in a play of power, but it is also always linked to certain coordinates of knowledge which issue from it but, to an equal degree, condition it. This is what the apparatus consists in: strategies of relations of forces supporting, and supported by, types of knowledge. In seeking in *The Order of Things* to write a history of the *episteme*, I was still caught in an impasse. What I should like to do now is to try and show that what I call an apparatus is a much more general case of the *episteme*; or rather, that the *episteme* is a specifically *discursive* apparatus, whereas the apparatus in its general form is both discursive and non-discursive, its elements being much more heterogeneous.

J.-A. MILLER: The complex which you are introducing under the term of apparatus is certainly conceived in a much more heterogeneous form than what you termed the *episteme*. You mingled together or distributed within your epistemes statements of very diverse kinds, those of philosophers, savants, obscure authors, practitioners theorising their practice: hence the effect of surprise your work produced, but it was still finally concerned with discursive utterances.

FOUCAULT: Certainly.

J.-A. MILLER: With the introduction of 'apparatuses', you want to get beyond discourse. But these new ensembles, which articulate together so many different elements, remain nonetheless *signifying* ensembles. I can't quite see how you could be getting at a 'non-discursive' domain.

FOUCAULT: In trying to identify an apparatus, I look for the elements which participate in a rationality, a given form of co-ordination, except that . . . .

J.-A. MILLER: One shouldn't say rationality, or we would be back with the *episteme* again.

FOUCAULT: If you like, I would define the *episteme* retrospectively as the strategic apparatus which permits of separating out from among all the statements which are possible those that will be acceptable within, I won't say a scientific theory, but a field of scientificity, and which it is possible to say are true or false. The *episteme* is the 'apparatus' which makes possible the separation, not of the true from the false, but of what may from what may not be characterised as scientific.

LE GAUFEY: But going back to this question of the 'non-discursive', what is there in an apparatus, over and above the discursive utterances, except the 'institutions'?

FOUCAULT: The term 'institution' is generally applied to every kind of more-or-less constrained, learned behaviour. Everything which functions in a society as a system of constraint and which isn't an utterance, in short, all the field of the non-discursive social, is an institution.

J.-A. MILLER: But clearly the institution is itself discursive.

FOUCAULT: Yes, if you like, but it doesn't much matter for my notion of the apparatus to be able to say that this is discursive and that isn't. If you take Gabriel's architectural plan for the Military School together with the actual construction of the School, how is one to say what is discursive and what institutional? That would only interest me if the building didn't conform with the plan. But I don't think it's very important to be able to make that distinction, given that my problem isn't a linguistic one.

The Analytic of Power

GROSRICHARD: In *The Will to Know*, you study the constitution and the history of an apparatus: the apparatus of sexuality. Very schematically, one can say that this apparatus is articulated, on the one hand, on to what you call power (*le pouvoir*), for which it serves as a means and expression, and that on the other hand it produces, as one might put it, an imaginary, historically datable object, namely sex. There follow from this two major series of questions about power, about sex, and about their relation to the apparatus of sexuality. Concerning power, you voice doubts about the conception of it that has been traditionally held. And what you are proposing is not so much a new theory of power as an '*analytic of power*'. How does this term, 'analytic' help you to throw light on what you refer to here as 'power' and its connection with the apparatus of sexuality?

FOUCAULT: Power in the substantive sense, '*le*' *pouvoir*, doesn't exist. What I mean is this. The idea that there is either located at — or emanating from — a given point something which is a 'power' seems to me to be based on a misguided analysis, one which at all events fails to account for a considerable number of phenomena. In reality power means relations, a more-or-less organised, hierarchical, co-ordinated cluster of relations. So the problem is not that of constituting a theory of power which would be a remake of Boulainvilliers on the one hand and Rousseau on the other. Both these authors start off from an original state in which all men are equal, and then, what happens? With one of them, a historical invasion, with the other a mythico-juridical event, but either way it turns out that from a given moment people no longer have rights, and power is constituted. If one tries to erect a theory of power one will always be obliged to view it as emerging at a given place and time and hence to deduce it, to reconstruct its genesis. But if power is in reality an open, more-or-less coordinated (in the event, no doubt, ill-coordinated) cluster of relations, then the only problem is to provide oneself with a grid of analysis which makes possible an analytic of relations of power.

GROSRICHARD: And yet in your book, speaking of the repercussions of the Council of Trent, you propose to study 'via what channels and through what discourses power is able to gain access to the slightest, most individual forms of behaviour, by what routes it is enabled to reach into the most insubstantial, imperceptible forms of desire' . . . . Here the language you use still suggests a power beginning from a single centre which, little by little, through a process of diffusion, contagion or carcinosis, brings within its compass the minutest, most peripheral details. Now it seems to me that elsewhere, when you talk about the multiplication of 'disciplines', you show power as having its beginnings in the 'little places', organising itself in terms of the 'little things', before it gets to the stage of concentrated organisation. How can one reconcile these two representations of power, the one describing it as exercised from the top downwards, from the centre to the perimeter, by the important over the trivial, and the other, which seems to be the exact opposite?

FOUCAULT: I inwardly blushed while listening to you reading, thinking to myself, it's true, I did use that metaphor of the point which progressively irradiates its surroundings. But that was in a very particular case, that of the Church after the Council of Trent. Generally speaking I think one needs to look rather at how the great strategies of power encrust themselves and depend for their conditions of exercise on the level of the micro-relations of power. But there are always also movements in the opposite direction,

whereby strategies which co-ordinate relations of power
produce new effects and advance into hitherto unaffected
domains. Thus up to the middle of the sixteenth century the
Church only supervised sexuality in a fairly distant manner.
The requirement of annual confession, with its avowal of the
different kinds of sins committed, ensured that in fact one
wouldn't have to relate very many sexual adventures to
one's curé. With the Council of Trent, around the middle of
the sixteenth century, there emerge, alongside the ancient
techniques of the confessional, a new series of procedures
developed within the ecclesiastical institution for the
purpose of training and purifying ecclesiastical personnel.
Detailed techniques were elaborated for use in seminaries
and monasteries, techniques of discursive rendition of daily
life, of self-examination, confession, direction of conscience
and regulation of the relationship between director and
directed. It was this technology which it was sought to inject
into society as a whole, and it is true that the move was
directed from the top downwards.

J.-A. MILLER: This is the phenomenon which Pierre
Legendre has studied.

FOUCAULT: I haven't been able to read his most recent
book yet, but what he did in *L'Amour du Censeur* seems to
me to be an absolutely necessary undertaking. What he
describes there is a process that really existed. But I don't
believe that relations of power are *only* engendered like
that, from the top downwards.

GROSRICHARD: Then you think this representation of
power as exercised from above, and in a negative or
repressive way, is an illusion? Isn't it a necessary illusion,
one engendered by power itself? At all events, the illusion is
a very persistent one, and after all it's against just this kind
of power that people have struggled in the hope of being
able to change things.

G. MILLER: I would add this: even if one accepts that
power, on the scale of a whole society, doesn't proceed
downwards from the top but can be analysed rather as a
cluster of relations, don't the 'micro-powers' on which these
relations are founded themselves still operate from above?

FOUCAULT: Yes, if you like. In so far as power relations
are an unequal and relatively stable relation of forces, it's

clear that this implies an above and a below, a difference of potentials.

GROSRICHARD: One always needs to have someone smaller than oneself.

FOUCAULT: Agreed, but what I meant was that in order for there to be a movement from above to below there has to be a capillarity from below to above at the same time. Take a simple example, the feudal form of power relation. Between the serfs tied to the land and the lord who levies rent from them, there exists a local, relatively autonomous relation, almost a *tête-à-tête*. For this relation to hold, it must indeed have the backing of a certain pyramidal ordering of the feudal system. But it's certain that the power of the French kings and the apparatuses of State which they gradually established from the eleventh century onward had as their condition of possibility a rooting in forms of behaviour, bodies and local relations of power which should not at all be seen as a simple projection of the central power.

J.-A. MILLER: What is it, then, this 'power relation'? It isn't just the relation of obligation . . . .

FOUCAULT: Ah no! I was just trying to answer the question that was asked a moment ago, about this power from above, which is supposed to be 'negative'. All power, whether it be from above or from below, whatever level one examines it on, is actually represented in a more-or-less uniform fashion throughout Western societies under a negative, that is to say a *juridical* form. It's the characteristic of our Western societies that the language of power is law, not magic, religion, or anything else.

GROSRICHARD: But the language of love, for example, as it's formulated in courtly literature and in the whole history of love in the West, isn't a juridical language; yet it does nothing but talk of power, never ceases establishing relations of domination and servitude. Take the term 'mistress', for instance.

FOUCAULT: Yes indeed. But Duby has an interesting explanation there. He connects the emergence of courtly literature with the existence in medieval society of the '*juvenes*': the *juvenes* were the young people, the descendants who had no rights of inheritance and had to live on the margins of the linear genealogical successions which characterised the feudal system. They waited for deaths among the male legitimate heirs, or for an heiress obliged to procure a husband capable of taking charge of the inheritance and the functions of head of a family. The *juvenes* thus constituted the turbulent surplus necessarily engendered by the mode of transmission of power and property. And Duby sees this as the origin of courtly literature: courtly literature was a sort of fictive joust between the *juvenes* and the head of a family, the lord, the King even, for the stake of the already appropriated wife. In the intervals between wars and the leisure of the long winter evenings there was woven around the wives the web of these courtly relations which at bottom were the very inverse of relations of power since it was still only an affair of a landless knight turning up at a chateau to seduce the lord of the manor's wife. So what one had here, engendered by the institutions themselves, was a sort of loosening of constraints, an acceptable unbridling, which yielded this real–fictive joust one finds in the themes of courtly love. It's a comedy around power relations which functions in the interstices of power but isn't itself a real power relation.

GROSRICHARD: Perhaps, but even so courtly literature derives, via the troubadours, from Arabic and Moslem civilisation. Does Duby's analysis work there as well? But let's return to the question of power and its relation to the notion of the apparatus.

MILLOT: Discussing what you call 'general apparatuses' (*'dispositifs d'ensemble'*) you write in *The Will to Know* that 'here the logic is perfectly clear, the aims decipherable, yet it turns out that no one can have conceived and very few formulated them: such is the implicit character of the great, anonymous, almost mute strategies which coordinate the voluble tactics whose "inventors" or directors are often devoid of all hypocrisy . . . .' You define here something like a strategy without a subject. How is this conceivable?

FOUCAULT: Let's take an example. From around 1825 to 1830 one finds the local and perfectly explicit appearance of definite strategies for fixing the workers in the first heavy industries at their work-places. At Mulhouse and in northern France various tactics are elaborated: pressuring people to marry, providing housing, building *cités ouvrières*, practising that sly system of credit-slavery that Marx talks about, consisting in enforcing advance payment of rents while wages are paid only at the end of the month. Then there are the savings-bank systems, the truck-system with grocers and wine-merchants who act for the bosses, and so on. Around all this there is formed little by little a discourse, the discourse of philanthropy and the moralisation of the working class. Then the experiments become generalised by way of the institutions and societies consciously advocating programmes for the moralisation of the working class. Then on top of that there is superimposed the problem of women's work, the schooling of children and the relations between the two issues. Between the schooling of children, which is a centralised, Parliamentary measure, and this or that purely local initiative dealing with workers' housing, for example, one finds all sorts of support mechanisms (unions of employers, chambers of commerce, etc.) which invent, modify and re-adjust, according to the circumstances of the moment and the place—so that you get a coherent, rational strategy, but one for which it is no longer possible to identify a person who conceived it.

MILLOT: But then what role does the social class play?

FOUCAULT: Ah, here we are at the centre of the problem, and no doubt also of the obscurities of my own discourse. A dominant class isn't a mere abstraction, but neither is it a pre-given entity. For a class to become a dominant class, for it to ensure its domination and for that domination to reproduce itself is certainly the effect of a number of actual pre-meditated tactics operating within the grand strategies that ensure this domination. But between the strategy which fixes, reproduces, multiplies and accentuates existing relations of forces, and the class which thereby finds itself in a ruling position, there is a reciprocal relation of pro-duction. Thus one can say that the strategy of moralising the working class is that of the bourgeoisie. One can even say that it's the strategy which allows the bourgeois class to be the bourgeois class and to exercise its domination. But what I don't think one can say is that it's the bourgeois class on the level of its ideology or its economic project which, as a sort of at once real and fictive subject, invented and forcibly imposed this strategy on the working class.

J.-A. MILLER: So there is no subject, but there is an effect of finalisation.

FOUCAULT: An effect of finalisation relative to an objective—.

J.-A. MILLER: —An objective which is imposed, then.

FOUCAULT: Which turns out to be imposed. To reiterate: the moralisation of the working class wasn't imposed by Guizot, through his schools legislation, nor by Dupin through his books. It wasn't imposed by the employers' unions either. And yet it was accomplished, because it met the urgent need to master a vagabond, floating labour force. So the objective existed and the strategy was developed, with ever-growing coherence, but without it being necessary to attribute to it a subject which makes the law, pronouncing it in the form of 'Thou shalt' and 'Thou shalt not'.

G. MILLER: But how is one to distinguish between the different subjects involved in this strategy? Mustn't one be able to distinguish, for instance, between those who produce it and those who only undergo it? Even if their respective initiatives often end by converging, are they all merged into one or do they singularise themselves? And if so, in what terms?

GROSRICHARD: Or to put it another way, is your model Mandeville's *Fable of the Bees*?

FOUCAULT: I wouldn't exactly say that, but I'll take another example: that of the constitution of a medico-legal apparatus, through which on the one hand psychiatry is utilised in the penal system while, conversely, penal types of controls and interventions are developed and multiplied to deal with the actions or behaviour of abnormal subjects. This led to that vast theoretical and legislative edifice constructed around the question of degeneracy and degenerates. What took place here? All sorts of subjects intervened, administrative personnel for example, for reasons of public order, but above all it was the doctors and magistrates. Can one talk of interests here? In the case of the doctors, why should they have wanted to intervene so directly in the penal domain, just when they had barely, and then only with difficulty, succeeded in detaching psychiatry from the sort of magma constituted by the practices of internment which occupied precisely the heart of the 'medico-legal' domain except for the fact that they were neither medical nor legal. Just when the alienists have barely isolated and marked out the theory and practice of mental alienation, here they are saying, 'There are crimes which are our business, these people belong to us!' Where is their interest as doctors in this? To say that there was a sort of imperialist dynamic of psychiatry aiming to annex crime and submit it to its rationality doesn't get us anywhere. I would be tempted to say that there was, in fact, a necessity here (which one doesn't have to call an interest) linked to the very existence of a psychiatry which had made itself autonomous but needed thereafter to secure a basis for its intervention by gaining recognition as a component of public hygiene. And it could establish this basis only through the fact that there was a disease (mental alienation) for it to mop up. There had also to be a danger for it to combat, comparable with that of an epidemic, a lack of hygiene, or suchlike. Now, how can it be proved that madness constitutes a danger except by showing that there exist extreme cases where madness, even though not apparent to the public gaze, without manifesting itself beforehand through any symptom except a few minute fissures, minuscule murmurings perceptible only to the highly trained observer, can suddenly explode into a monstrous crime. This was how the diagnosis of homicidal mania was constructed. Madness is a redoubtable danger precisely in that it is not foreseeable by any of those persons of good sense who claim to be able to recognise it. Only a doctor can spot it, and thus madness becomes exclusively an object for the doctor, whose right of intervention is grounded by the same token. In the case of the magistrates, one can say that it is a different necessity which leads them, despite their reluctance, to accept the intervention of the doctors. Along with the edifice of the Penal Code, the punitive machine of the prison which had been placed in their hands could function effectively only if it operated at the level of the individuality of the individual, the criminal and not the crime, so as to transform and reform him. But, once given that there were crimes whose reasons and motives could not be established, punishment became impossible. To punish a person whom one doesn't fully know is impossible for a penal system which no longer works through the *supplice* but through internment. (This is so much the case that the other day someone, an admirable person moreover, uttered this astounding sentence which ought to have left us all gaping: 'You cannot execute Patrick Henry, you don't understand him'. What does that mean? If they had understood him, would it have been all right to kill him?) The magistrates, therefore, so as to combine a penal code which was still based on punishment and expiation with a punitive practice which had become one of reform and imprisonment, were forced to make room for the psychiatrists. So here you have strategic necessities which are not exactly interests . . . .

G. MILLER: You substitute for the notion of 'interest' those of 'problem' (for the doctors) and 'necessity' (for the magistrates). The gain appears very slight, and things remain still very imprecise.

LE GAUFEY: It seems to me that the metaphorical system governing your analysis is that of the organism, which makes possible the elimination of reference to a thinking, willing subject. A living organism tends always to persist in its being, and all means for its attaining that objective are good ones.

FOUCAULT: No, I don't agree with that at all. Firstly, I have never used the metaphor of the organism. Secondly, the problem isn't one of self-preservation. When I speak of strategy, I am taking the term seriously: in order for a certain relation of forces not only to maintain itself, but to accentuate, stabilise and broaden itself, a certain kind of manoeuvre is necessary. The psychiatrist had to manouvre in order to make himself recognised as part of the public hygiene system. This isn't an organism, any more than in the case of the magistrature, and I can't see how what I'm saying can imply that these are organisms.

GROSRICHARD: What is striking, however, is that it was during the nineteenth century that a theory of society conceived on the model of the organism was constituted— that of Auguste Comte for instance. But let's leave that. All the examples you have given us to show how you conceive this 'strategy without a subject' are drawn from the nine-teenth century, a period where society and the State already possess a very centralised, technicised form. Are things equally clear for earlier periods?

J.-A. MILLER: In short, it's just at the moment when the strategy appears to have a subject that Foucault shows that it hasn't . . . .

FOUCAULT: In a sense, I would agree. I heard someone talking about power the other day—it's in fashion. He observed that the famous 'absolute' monarchy in reality had nothing absolute about it. In fact it consisted of a number of islands of dispersed power, some of them functioning as geographical spaces, others as pyramids, others as bodies, or through the influence of familial systems, kinship networks and so forth. One can see perfectly well why grand strategies couldn't emerge in such a system. The French monarchy was equipped with a very strong, but very rigid, administrative apparatus: one which let a tremendous amount slip through its grip. Certainly there was a King, the manifest representative of power, but in reality power wasn't centralised and didn't express itself through grand strategies, at once fine, supple and coherent. On the other hand, in the nineteenth century one finds all kinds of mechanisms and institutions—the parliamentary system, diffusion of information, publishing, the great exhibitions, the university, and so on: 'bourgeois power' was then able to elaborate its grand strategies, without one needing for all that to impute a subject to them.

J.-A. MILLER: As far as the space of 'theory' was concerned, after all, the old 'transcendental space without a subject' never really worried many people, whatever the reproaches that were made against you from the direction of *Les Temps Modernes* when you published *The Order of Things* complaints about the absence of any kind of causality from your shifts from one *episteme* to the next. But perhaps there is a problem when one is dealing not with the 'theoretical' but the 'practical' field. Given that there are relations of forces, and struggles, the question inevitably arises of who is doing the struggling and against whom? Here you can't escape the question of the subject, or rather the *subjects*.

FOUCAULT: Certainly, and this is what is preoccupying me. I'm not too sure what the answer is. But after all, if one considers that power has to be analysed in terms of relations of power, then it seems to me that one has a much better chance than in other theoretical procedures of grasping the relation that exists between power and struggles, and especially the class struggle. What I find striking in the majority—if not of Marx's texts then those of the Marxists (except perhaps Trostsky)—is the way they pass over in silence what is understood by *struggle* when one talks of class struggle. What does struggle mean here? Is it a dialectical confrontation? An economic battle? A war? Is civil society riven by class struggle to be seen as a war continued by other means?

CELAS: Perhaps one should take account here of the party, that other institution, which can't be assimilated to those others which don't have 'taking power' as their goal . . . .

GROSRICHARD: And then again, the Marxists do all the same ask the question, 'Who are our friends, who are our enemies?', the question which serves to determine the real lines of confrontation within this field of struggles . . . .

J.-A. MILLER: So who ultimately, in your view, are the subjects who oppose each other?

FOUCAULT: This is just a hypothesis, but I would say it's all against all. There aren't immediately given subjects of the struggle, one the proletariat, the other the bourgeoisie. Who fights against whom? We all fight each other. And there is always within each of us something that fights something else.

J.-A. MILLER: Which would mean that there are only ever transitory coalitions, some of which immediately break up, but others of which persist, but that strictly speaking individuals would be the first and last components?

FOUCAULT: Yes, individuals, or even sub-individuals.

J.-A. MILLER: Sub-individuals?

FOUCAULT: Why not?

G. MILLER: Regarding this question of power, if I could give my impression as a reader of your book, there are places where I would say it's too neat . . . .

FOUCAULT: That's what '*La Nouvelle Critique*' said about my previous book: it's too neat not to be harbouring lies . . . .

G. MILLER: What I mean is that this business of strategies

is all too neat. I don't think it's harbouring lies, but, after seeing everything so tidily arranged and organised on the local, the regional and the national level, and over periods of centuries, I wonder if one doesn't still have to leave room for the shambles?

FOUCAULT: Oh, I quite agree. Judiciary and psychiatry join hands, but only after such a mess, such a shambles! Only my position is as if I were dealing with a battle: if one isn't content with descriptions, if one wants to try and explain a victory or a defeat, then one does have to pose the problems in terms of strategies, and ask, 'Why did that work? How did that hold up?' That's why I look at things from this angle, which may end up giving the impression the story is too pretty to be true.

Sex from Tertullian to Freud

GROSRICHARD: Now let's talk about sex. You treat it as a historical object, engendered in some sense by the apparatus of sexuality.

J.-A. MILLER: Your previous book dealt with criminality. Sexuality, apparently, is a different kind of object. Unless it were more interesting to show that it's the same? Which would you prefer?

FOUCAULT: I would say, let's try and see if it isn't the same. That's the stake in the game, and if I'm thinking of writing six volumes, it's precisely because it's a game! This book is the only one I've written without knowing beforehand what I would call it, and right up to the last moment I couldn't think of a title. I use 'History of Sexuality' for want of anything better. The first projected title, which I subsequently dropped, was 'Sex and Truth'. All the same, that was my problem: what had to happen in the history of the West for the question of truth to be posed in regard to sexual pleasure? And this has been a problem that has exercised me ever since I wrote *Madness and Civilisation*. About that book historians say 'Yes, that's fine, but why didn't you look at the different mental illnesses that are found in the seventeenth and eighteenth centuries? Why didn't you do the history of the epidemics of mental illnesses during that period?' I can't seem to be able to explain to them that indeed that is all extremely interesting, but that wasn't my problem. Regarding madness, my problem was to find out how the question of madness could have been made to operate in terms of discourses of truth, that is to say, discourses having the status and function of *true* discourses. In the West that means scientific discourse. That was also the angle from which I wanted to approach the question of sexuality.

GROSRICHARD: How would you define what you call 'sex' in relation to this apparatus of sexuality? Is it an imaginary object, a phenomenon, an illusion?

FOUCAULT: Well, I'll tell you what happened when I was writing the book. There were several successive drafts. To start with, sex was taken as a pre-given datum, and sexuality figured as a sort of simultaneously discursive and institutional formation which came to graft itself on to sex, to overlay it and perhaps finally to obscure it. That was the first line of approach. Then I showed some people the manuscript and came to realise that it wasn't very satisfactory. Then I turned the whole thing upside down. That was only a game, because I wasn't sure . . . . But I said to myself, basically, couldn't it be that sex—which seems to be an instance having its own laws and constraints, on the basis of which the masculine and feminine sexes are defined—be something which on the contrary is *produced* by the apparatus of sexuality? What the discourse of sexuality was initially applied to wasn't sex but the body, the sexual organs, pleasures, kinship relations, interpersonal relations, and so forth.

J.-A. MILLER: A heterogeneous ensemble.

FOUCAULT: Yes, a heterogeneous ensemble, one which was finally completely overlaid by the apparatus of sexuality, which in turn at a certain moment produced, as the keystone of its discourse and perhaps of its very functioning, the idea of sex.

G. MILLER: But isn't this idea of sex contemporaneous with the establishment of the apparatus of sexuality?

FOUCAULT: No, no! It seems to me that one sees sex emerging during the course of the nineteenth century.

G. MILLER: We have only had sex since the nineteenth century?

FOUCAULT: We have had sexuality since the eighteenth century, and sex since the nineteenth. What we had before that was no doubt the flesh. The basic originator of it all was Tertullian.

J.-A. MILLER: You'll have to explain that for us.

FOUCAULT: Well, Tertullian combined within a coherent theoretical discourse two fundamental elements: the essentials of the imperatives of Christianity—the '*didaske*'—and the principles by way of which it was possible to escape from the dualism of the Gnostics.

J.-A. MILLER: I can see you are looking for the devices that will enable you to erase the break that is located with Freud. You recall how at the time when Althusser was proclaiming the Marxian break, you were already there with your eraser. And now Freud is going to go the same way, at any rate I think that's your objective, no doubt within a complex strategy, as you would say. Do you really think you can erase the break between Tertullian and Freud?

FOUCAULT: I'll say this, that for me the whole business of breaks and non-breaks is always at once a point of departure and a very relative thing. In *The Order of Things*, I took as my starting-point some very manifest differences, the transformations of the empirical sciences around the end of the eighteenth century. It calls for a degree of ignorance (which I know isn't yours) to fail to see that a treatise of medicine written in 1780 and a treatise of pathological anatomy written in 1820 belong to two different worlds. My problem was to ascertain the sets of transformations in the régime of discourses necessary and sufficient for people to use these words rather than those, a particular type of discourse rather than some other type, for people to be able to look at things from such and such an angle and not some other one. In the present case, for reasons which are conjunctural, since everyone is putting the stress on breaks, I'm saying, let's try to shift the scenery and take as our starting point something else which is just as manifest as the 'break', provided one changes the reference points. One then finds this formidable mechanism emerging—the machinery of the confession, within which in fact psychoanalysis and Freud figure as episodes.

J.-A. MILLER: You're constructing a machine which swallows an enormous amount at a time . . . .

FOUCAULT: An enormous amount at a time, and then I'll try and establish what the transformations are . . . .

J.-A. MILLER: Making sure, of course, that the principal transformation doesn't come with Freud. You'll show, for example, that the focussing of sexuality on the family began prior to Freud, or that—.

FOUCAULT: —It seems to me that the mere fact that I've adopted this course undoubtedly excludes for me the possibility of Freud figuring as the radical break, on the basis of which everything else has to be re-thought. I may well attempt to show how around the eighteenth century there is installed, for economic reasons, historical reasons, and so forth, a general apparatus in which Freud will come to have his place. And no doubt I'll show how Freud turned the theory of degeneracy inside out, like a glove—which isn't the usual way of situating the Freudian break as an event in terms of scientificity.

J.-A. MILLER: Yes, you like to accentuate the artificial character of your procedure. Your results depend on the choice of reference points, and the choice of reference points depends on the conjuncture. It's all a matter of appearances, is that what you're telling us?

FOUCAULT: Not a delusive appearance, but a fabrication.

J.-A. MILLER: Right, and so it's motivated by what you want, your hopes, your . . . .

FOUCAULT: Correct, and that's where the polemical or political objective comes in. But as you know, I never go in for polemics, and I'm a good distance away from politics.

J.-A. MILLER: And what effects do you hope to produce regarding psychoanalysis?

FOUCAULT: Well, I would say that in the usual histories one reads that sexuality was ignored by medicine, and above all by psychiatry, and that at last Freud discovered the sexual aetiology of neuroses. Now everyone knows that that isn't true, that the problem of sexuality was massively and manifestly inscribed in the medicine and psychiatry of the nineteenth century, and that basically Freud was only taking literally what he heard Charcot say one evening: it is indeed all a question of sexuality. The strength of psychoanalysis consists in its having opened out on to something quite different, namely the logic of the unconscious. And there sexuality is no longer what it was at the outset.

J.-A. MILLER: Certainly. When you say psychoanalysis there, one could say Lacan, couldn't one?

FOUCAULT: I would say Freud and Lacan. In other words, the important part is not the *Three Essays on the Theory of Sexuality* but *The Interpretation of Dreams*.

J.-A. MILLER: Not the theory of development, but the logic of the signifier.

FOUCAULT: Not the theory of development, nor the sexual secret behind the neuroses or psychoses, but a logic of the unconscious . . . .

J.-A. MILLER: That's very Lacanian, opposing sexuality and the unconscious. And moreover it's one of the axioms of that logic that there is no sexual relation.

FOUCAULT: I didn't know there was this axiom.

J.-A. MILLER: It implies that sexuality isn't historical in the sense that everything else is, through and through from the start. There isn't a history of sexuality in the way that there is a history of bread.

FOUCAULT: No, but there is one in the sense that there is a history of madness, I mean of madness as a question, posed in terms of truth, within a discourse in which human madness is held to signify something about the truth of what man, the subject, or reason is. From the day when madness ceased to appear as the mask of reason but was inscribed as a prodigious Other which is nevertheless present in every reasonable man, sole possessor of a part, if not of the essence of the secrets of reason: from that moment, something like a history of madness begins, or at least a new episode in the history of madness. And we have still not emerged from this episode. I would say in the same way that from the day when it was said to man, 'You shall not merely make yourself pleasure with your sex, you will make yourself truth, and that truth will be your truth', from the day Tertullian began saying to the Christians, 'Where your chastity is concerned . . .'

J.-A. MILLER: Here you are looking for an origin again, and now it's all Tertullian's fault . . . .

FOUCAULT: I was only joking there.

J.-A. MILLER: Obviously, you're going to say things are much more complicated, there are heterogeneous levels, movements from above to below and below to above . . . ! But seriously, this search for the point where it all may have begun, all this malady of speech, do you . . . ?

FOUCAULT: I say that in a fictive manner, as a joke, to make a fable.

J.-A. MILLER: But if one wasn't joking, what would one say?

FOUCAULT: What would one say? One would arguably find in Euripides, and linking this with certain elements of Jewish mysticism, and others from Alexandrian philosophy, and the notion of sexuality among the Stoics, and including also the notion of *enkrateia*, that assumption of a quality not to be found in the Stoics, chastity . . . . But what I'm concerned with, what I'm talking about, is how it comes about that people are told that the secret of their truth lies in the region of their sex.

GROSRICHARD: You talk about techniques of confession. There are also, it seems to me, techniques of listening. One finds, for example, in most of the manuals for confessors or dictionaries of cases of conscience, an article on 'morose delectation' which treats of the nature and gravity of the sin that consists in taking a lingering pleasure (that's the *morositas*) in the *representation*, through thought or speech, of a past sexual pleasure. And here is what is directly of concern for the confessor: how is one to lend one's ear to the recital of abominable scenes without sinning oneself, that is, taking pleasure oneself? There is a whole technique and casuistry of listening here, which evidently depends on the one hand on the relation of the thing itself to the thought of the thing, and on the other hand on the relation of the thought of the thing to the words which say it. Now, this double relationship has varied through time, as you clearly showed in *The Order of Things* where you delimited the initial and terminal bounds of the '*episteme* of representation'. This long history of the confessional, this will to hear the other speak the truth of his sex, which today still hasn't ceased to exercise itself, is thus accompanied by a history of techniques of listening which have passed through profound changes. Is the line you trace from the

Middle Ages down to Freud a continuous one? When Freud—or any psychoanalyst—listens, is the way he listens, what he listens to, or the place occupied in this by the signifier still comparable with how things were for the confessors?

FOUCAULT: This first volume of my book is concerned with getting an overview on something whose permanent existence in the West is difficult to deny: regulated procedures for the confession of sex, sexuality and sexual pleasures. But it's true that these procedures were often profoundly altered at certain moments, under conditions which are often difficult to explain. In the eighteenth century one finds a very sharp falling away, not in pressure and injunctions to confess, but in the refinement of techniques of confession. During this period, where the direction of conscience and the confessional have lost the essential force of their role, one finds brutal medical techniques emerging, which consist in simply demanding that the subject tell his or her story, or narrate it in writing . . . .

J.-A. MILLER: But do you believe that throughout this long period there perdures one and the same concept, not of sex, but of truth? Is truth localised and collected in the same way? Is it attributed causal powers?

FOUCAULT: What was constantly assumed and accepted, subject no doubt to all sorts of possible variations, was the notion that the production of truth is charged with effects on the subject . . . .

J.-A. MILLER: Don't you ever have the feeling that you're putting together an argument, which—amusing as it is—is destined to let slip the essentials? That your net is so coarse-meshed that it will let all the fish through? Why, instead of using your microscope, are you now taking a telescope, and looking through the wrong end at that? The only way we will be able to understand why you're doing it is if you'll tell us what you hope to gain by it.

FOUCAULT: Is it permissible to talk of hope here? The term of confession (*aveu*) that I'm using is perhaps a little too broad. But I think I gave it a fairly precise meaning in my book. What I mean by 'confession', even though I can well see that the term may be a little annoying, is all those procedures by which the subject is incited to produce a discourse of truth about his sexuality which is capable of having effects on the subject himself.

J.-A. MILLER: I'm not very happy with the huge concepts you're employing here. They seem to me to dissolve as soon as one looks at things more closely.

FOUCAULT: But they're meant to be dissolved, these are only very general definitions . . . .

J.-A. MILLER: In confessional procedures it is assumed that the subject *knows* the truth. Isn't there a radical change at the point where it's assumed that the subject *doesn't* know this truth?

FOUCAULT: I see what you're getting at, but one of the fundamental points of the Christian method of direction of conscience is precisely that the subject doesn't know the truth.

J.-A. MILLER: And you want to show that his non-knowledge has the status of an unconscious? But re-inscribing the subject's discourse within a grid of reading, re-coding it in accordance with a questionnaire to establish whether such and such an act is a sin or not, this has nothing to do with imputing a knowledge to the subject whose truth he does not himself know.

FOUCAULT: In the direction of conscience, what the subject doesn't know is something quite different from whether an act is or isn't a sin, or whether it's a mortal or a venial sin. He doesn't know what takes place within him. And when the Christian comes in search of his director, and says to him, 'Listen . . .' .

J.-A. MILLER: So the relation of director and directed is exactly the analytical situation?

FOUCAULT: Listen, I want to finish. The Christian says, 'Listen, the trouble is that I can't pray at present, I have a feeling of spiritual dryness which has made me lose touch with God.' And the director says to him, 'Well, there is something happening in you which you don't know about. We will work together to find it out.'

J.-A. MILLER: I'm sorry, but I don't find the comparison quite convincing.

FOUCAULT: I fully realise we are touching here on what is, for you, for me, for all of us, the fundamental question. I'm not seeking to construct this notion of confession into a framework enabling me to reduce everything to the same thing, from the confessors to Freud. On the contrary, as in *The Order of Things*, it's a matter of making the differences stand out more clearly. My field of objects here is the procedures for the extortion of truth: in the next volume, which will be concerned with the Christian notion of the flesh, I shall try to study the characteristics of these discursive procedures, from the tenth to the eighteenth century. And that will bring me to this transformation, one which seems to me enigmatic in a much profounder sense than that of psychoanalysis, since the question it poses was what led me to transform what was only meant to be a little book into this current rather mad project of mine: within the space of twenty years, throughout Europe, doctors and educators came to be exclusively obsessed with that incredible epidemic threatening the whole human race: child masturbation. Something that no one was supposed to have previously practiced!

LIVI: Concerning child masturbation, do you think you are giving sufficient importance to the difference between the sexes? Or do you think pedagogical institutions functioned in the same way for girls as for boys?

FOUCAULT: At first sight, the differences prior to the nineteenth century seemed slight to me.

LIVI: I think it all seems to happen much more discreetly with girls. It's less talked about, whereas with boys there are very detailed descriptions.

FOUCAULT: Yes . . . . The problem of sex in the eighteenth century was the problem of the male sex, and the discipline of sex was put into effect in boys' colleges, military schools, etc. Then, from the moment the woman begins to take on importance in medico-social terms, with the connected problems of child-bearing, breast-feeding, etc., at that point female masturbation comes to be on the order of the day. In the nineteenth century this seems to become the dominant problem. At the end of the nineteenth century, at any rate, great surgical operations are performed on girls, veritable tortures: cauterisation of the clitoris with red-hot irons was, if not habitual, at least fairly frequent at that time. In terms of the masturbation problem, this was a dramatic development.

WAJEMAN: Could you clarify what you were saying about Freud and Charcot?

FOUCAULT: Freud comes to Charcot's clinic. He sees interns giving women inhalations of amyl nitrate, and they then bring them, intoxicated, for Charcot to see. The women adopt certain postures, say things. They are listened to and watched, and then at a certain moment Charcot declares that this is getting ugly. What we have here, then, is a superb gadget by means of which sexuality is actually extracted, induced, incited and titillated in all manner of ways, and then suddenly Charcot says that that's enough of that. As for Freud, he will ask why that is enough. Freud doesn't need to go hunting for anything other than what he had seen *chez* Charcot. Sexuality was there before his eyes in manifest form, orchestrated by Charcot and his worthy aides . . . .

WAJEMAN: That isn't quite what you say in your book. All the same there did take place what you call the intervention of 'the most famous of Ears'. No doubt sexuality did pass from a mouth to an ear, Charcot's mouth to Freud's ear, and it's true that Freud saw the manifestation at La Salpétrière of something of the order of sexuality. But did Charcot recognise the sexuality? Charcot had hysterical fits induced, like the circular-arc posture. Freud recognised in that something akin to coitus. But can one say that Charcot saw what Freud was to see?

FOUCAULT: No, but I was speaking as an apologist for Freud. I meant that Freud's great originality wasn't discovering the sexuality hidden beneath neurosis. The sexuality was already there, Charcot was already talking about it. Freud's originality was taking all that literally, and then erecting on its basis the *Interpretation of Dreams*, which is something other than a sexual aetiology of neuroses. If I were to be very pretentious, I would say that I'm doing something a bit similar to that. I'm starting off from an apparatus of sexuality, a fundamental historical given which must be an indispensable point of departure for us. I'm taking it literally, at face value: I'm not placing myself outside it, because that isn't possible, but this allows me to get at something else.

J.-A. MILLER: And in the *Science of Dreams* aren't you

aware of seeing a truly unprecedented form of relation between sex and discourse being instituted?

FOUCAULT: Possibly. I don't exclude that at all. But the relation instituted with the direction of consciences after the Council of Trent is also unprecedented. It was a gigantic cultural phenomenon: this is undeniable.

J.-A. MILLER: And psychoanalysis isn't?

FOUCAULT: Yes, of course, I'm not saying that psychoanalysis is already there with the directors of conscience. That would be an absurdity.

J.-A. MILLER: Yes, yes, you aren't saying that, but all the same, you are! Would you say in the last analysis that the history of sexuality, in the sense of your understanding of that term, culminates in psychoanalysis?

FOUCAULT: Certainly! A culminating point is arrived at here in the history of procedures that set sex and truth in relation. In our time there isn't a single one of the discourses on sexuality which isn't, in one way or another, oriented in relation to that of psychoanalysis.

J.-A. MILLER: Well, what I find amusing is that a declaration like that is only conceivable in the French context and the conjuncture of today. Don't you agree?

FOUCAULT: It's true that there are countries where, owing to the way the cultural domain is institutionalised and functions, discourses on sex don't perhaps have that position of subordination, derivation and fascination *vis-à-vis* psychoanalysis which they have here in France, where the intelligentsia, because of its place in the pyramidal hierarchy of recognised values, accords psychoanalysis a privileged value that no one can escape, not even Ménie Grégoire.[1]

J.-A. MILLER: Perhaps you could say a little about the women's and the homosexuals' liberation movements?

FOUCAULT: Well, regarding everything that is currently being said about the liberation of sexuality, what I want to make apparent is precisely that the object 'sexuality' is in reality an instrument formed a long while ago, and one which has constituted a centuries-long apparatus of subjection. The real strength of the women's liberation movements is not that of having laid claim to the specificity of their sexuality and the rights pertaining to it, but that they have actually departed from the discourse conducted within the apparatuses of sexuality. These movements do indeed emerge in the nineteenth century as demands for sexual specificity. What has their outcome been? Ultimately, a veritable movement of de-sexualisation, a displacement effected in relation to the sexual centering of the problem, formulating the demand for forms of culture, discourse, language, and so on, which are no longer part of that rigid assignation and pinning-down to their sex which they had initially in some sense been politically obliged to accept in order to make themselves heard. The creative and interesting element in the women's movements is precisely that.

J.-A. MILLER: The inventive element?

FOUCAULT: Yes, the inventive element . . . . The American homosexual movements make that challenge their starting-point. Like women, they begin to look for new forms of community, co-existence, pleasure. But, in contrast with the position of women, the fixing of homosexuals to their sexual specificity is much stronger, they reduce everything to the order of sex. The women don't.

LE GAUFEY: All the same it was these movements that succeeded in removing homosexuality from the nomenclature of mental illnesses. There is still a fantastic difference in the fact of saying, 'You want us to be homosexuals, well, we are'.

FOUCAULT: Yes, but the homosexual liberation movements remain very much caught at the level of demands for the right to their sexuality, the dimension of the sexological. Anyway that's quite normal since homosexuality is a sexual practice which is attacked, barred and disqualified as such. Women on the other hand are able to have much wider economic, political and other kinds of objectives than homosexuals.

LE GAUFEY: Women's sexuality doesn't lead them to depart from the recognised kinship systems, while that of homosexuals places them immediately outside them. Homosexuals are in a different position *vis-à-vis* the social body.

FOUCAULT: Yes, yes.

LE GAUFEY: Look at the women's homosexual movements: they fall into the same traps as the male homosexuals. There is no basic difference between them, precisely because they both refuse the kinship systems.

GROSRICHARD: Does what you say in your book about perversions apply equally to sado-masochism? People who have themselves whipped for sexual pleasure have been talked about for a very long time . . . .

FOUCAULT: Listen, that's something that's hard to demonstrate. Do you have any documentation?

GROSRICHARD: Yes, there exists a treatise *On the Use of the Whip in the Affairs of Venus*, written by a doctor and dating, I think, from 1665, which gives a very complete catalogue of cases. It's cited precisely at the time of the convulsions at St Médard, in order to show that the alleged miracle actually concealed a sexual story.

FOUCAULT: Yes, but this pleasure in having oneself whipped isn't catalogued as a disease of the sexual instinct. That comes much later. I think, although I'm not certain, that the first edition of Krafft-Ebing only contains the one case of Sacher-Masoch. The emergence of perversion as a medical object is linked with that of instinct, which, as I've said, dates from the 1840s.

WAJEMAN: And yet when one reads a text by Plato or Hippocrates, one finds the uterus described as an animal which wanders about in the woman's insides, at the behest, precisely, of her instinct. But this instinct . . .

FOUCAULT: Yes, you no doubt understand very well that there is a difference between saying that the uterus is an animal which moves about, and saying that there exist organic and functional diseases, and that among the functional diseases there are some which affect the organs and others which affect the instincts, and that among the instincts, the sexual instinct can be affected in various classifiable ways. This difference corresponds to a wholly unprecedented type of medicalisation of sexuality. Compared with the idea of an organ that wanders about like a fox in its earth, one has a discourse which is, after all, of a different epistemological texture!

J.-A. MILLER: Ah yes, and what does the 'epistemological texture' of Freud's theory suggest to you, precisely on the matter of instinct? Do you think, as indeed people thought before Lacan, that Freud's instinct has the same 'texture' as your instinct introduced in 1840? What are you going to make of that?

FOUCAULT: At present I've no idea!

J.-A. MILLER: Do you think the death-instinct stands in the direct line of this theory of the instinct which you show to appear in 1844?

FOUCAULT: I'd have to re-read the whole of Freud before I could answer that!

J.-A. MILLER: But you have read *The Interpretation of Dreams*?

FOUCAULT: Yes, but not the whole of Freud.

Racism

GROSRICHARD: To come now to the last part of your book . . . .

FOUCAULT: Yes, no one wants to talk about that last part. Even though the book is a short one, but I suspect people never got as far as this last chapter. All the same, it's the fundamental part of the book.

GROSRICHARD: You articulate the theme of racism there on to both the apparatus of sexuality and the question of degeneracy. But the theme seems to have been articulated much earlier than that in the West, in particular by the old French nobility hostile to Louis XIV's absolutism which favoured the commonalty. In Boulainvilliers, who represents this nobility, one finds already a whole history of the superiority of Germanic blood, from which the nobility was descended, over Gaulish blood.

FOUCAULT: This idea that the nobility came from Germany in fact goes back to the Renaissance, and it was a theme utilised first of all by the French Protestants, who said that France was formerly a Germanic state, and in German law there were limits to the power of the sovereign. It was this idea which was subsequently taken over by a fraction of the French nobility.

GROSRICHARD: Regarding the nobility, you talk in your book of a myth of blood, blood as a mythical object. But what strikes me as remarkable, apart from its symbolic function, is that blood was also regarded by this nobility as a biological object. Its racism wasn't founded on a mythical tradition, but on a veritable theory of heredity by blood. It's already a biological racism.

FOUCAULT: But I say that in my book.

GROSRICHARD: I had the impression that you were talking of blood mainly as a symbolic object.

FOUCAULT: Yes, it's true that at the moment when historians of the nobility like Boulainvilliers were singing the praises of noble blood, saying that it was the bearer of physical qualities, courage, *vertu*, energy, there was a correlating of the themes of generation and of nobility. But what is new in the nineteenth century is the appearance of a racist biology, entirely centred around the concept of degeneracy. Racism wasn't initially a political ideology. It was a scientific ideology which manifested itself everywhere, in Morel and the others. And the political utilisation of this ideology was made first of all by the socialists, those of the Left, before those of the Right.

LE GAUFEY: This was when the Left was nationalist?

FOUCAULT: Yes, but above all with the idea that the rotten, decadent class was that of the people at the top, and that a socialist society would have to be clean and healthy. Lombroso was a man of the Left. He wasn't a socialist in the strict sense, but he had a lot of contacts with the socialists, and they took up his ideas. The breach only took place at the end of the nineteenth century.

LE GAUFEY: Couldn't one see a confirmation of what you are saying in the nineteenth century vogue for vampire novels, in which the aristocracy is always presented as the beast to be destroyed? The vampire is always an aristocrat, and the saviour a bourgeois . . . .

FOUCAULT: In the eighteenth century, rumours were already circulating that debauched aristocrats abducted little children to slaughter them and regenerate themselves by bathing in their blood. The rumours even led to riots . . . .

LE GAUFEY: Yes, but that's only the beginning. The way the idea becomes extended is strictly bourgeois, with that whole literature of vampires whose themes recur in films today: it's always the bourgeois, without the resources of the police or the curé, who gets rid of the vampire.

FOUCAULT: Modern antisemitism began in that form. The new forces of antisemitism developed, in socialist milieus, out of the theory of degeneracy. It was said that the Jews are necessarily degenerates, firstly because they are rich, secondly because they intermarry. They have totally aberrant sexual and religious practices, so it is they who are the carriers of degeneracy in our societies. One encounters this in socialist literature down to the Dreyfus affair. Pre-Hitlerism, the nationalist antisemitism of the Right, adopted exactly the same themes in 1910.

GROSRICHARD: The Right will say that it's in the homeland of socialism that one encounters the same theme today . . . .

J.-A. MILLER: Did you know that a first congress on psychoanalysis is going to be held in the USSR?

FOUCAULT: So I've been told. Will there be Soviet psycho-analysts there?

J.-A. MILLER: No, they're trying to get psychoanalysts from elsewhere to come . . . .

FOUCAULT: So it will be a psychoanalysis congress in the Soviet Union where the speakers will be foreigners! Incredible! Although there was a Congress of Penal Sciences at St Petersburg in 1894, where a French criminologist, someone whose name is too little known—he was called Monsieur Larrivée—said to the Russians: everyone is now in agreement that criminals are impossible people, born criminals. What is to be done with them? In our countries, which are too small, we don't know how to dispose of them. But you Russians have Siberia: couldn't you put them there in sorts of great labour camps, and thus at the same time exploit that extraordinarily rich territory?

GROSRICHARD: Weren't there any labour camps then in Siberia?

FOUCAULT: No! I was very surprised about that.

CELAS: Sibera was just a zone of exile. Lenin went there in 1898, got married, went hunting, had a maid, etc. There were also some penal colonies. Chekhov visited one on the Sakhalin Islands. The massive concentration camps where people were set to work were a socialist invention! They arose notably from initiatives like those of Trotsky, who organised the wreckage of the Red Army into a sort of labour army, which then constituted disciplinary camps which rapidly became places of internment. It came about through a combination of deliberate planning, pursuit of efficiency through militarisation, re-education, coercion . . . .

FOUCAULT: In fact that idea came from the French relegation laws. The idea of utilising prisoners during the period of their sentences as labour or for some useful purpose is as old as the prisons. But the idea that there is a basic group of criminals who are absolutely irredeemable and must somehow or other be eliminated from society, yet at the same time put to some use, that was the idea of relegation. In France, after a certain number of repeated convictions, the fellow was deported to Guyana or New Caledonia, and then became a settler there. This was what Monsieur Larrivée suggested to the Russians, so as to develop Siberia. It's incredible all the same that the Russians hadn't thought of that before. But if they had, there would have been a Russian there at the Congress to say, 'But Monsieur Larrivée, we have already thought of this wonderful idea!' And there wasn't. In France we don't have a Gulag, but we have ideas . . . .

GROSRICHARD: Maupertuis — yet another Frenchman, but one who was the Secretary of the Royal Academy in Berlin — suggested to sovereigns, in a *Letter on the Progress of the Sciences*, the utilisation of prisoners for carrying out useful experiments. That was in 1752.

J. MILLER. And apparently La Condamine, using an ear-trumpet because he had gone deaf after his expedition to Peru, went to listen to the words of those sentenced to the *supplice*, right to the moment of their death.

GROSRICHARD: In this idea of making the *supplice* serve a useful purpose, utilising this absolute power of execution for the profit of a better knowledge of life by in a sense forcing the condemned to confess a truth concerning life, there is a link with what you were saying about the confession, and the phenomena you analyse in the final section of your book. You write that there is a shift at a certain moment from a power exercised in the form of a right to put to death, to a 'power over life'. One might ask you this: is this power over life, this concern to master its excesses or defects, specific to modern Western societies? Take an example: Book XXIII of Montesquieu's *Esprit des Lois* is entitled, 'Of laws in their relation to the number of inhabitants'. He discusses as a grave problem the depopulation of Europe, and contrasts Louis XIV's edict of 1666 in favour of marriages with the different and much more effective measures practiced by the Romans. As though, under the Roman Empire, the question of a power over life—a discipline of sexuality from the standpoint of reproduction —had been posed and then forgotten, re-emerging finally in the middle of the eighteenth century. So is this shift from a power of death to a power over life really something un-precedented, or is it not rather periodic, linked for instance to ages and civilisations where urbanisation and the concen-tration of population, or conversely the depopulation caused by wars and epidemics seem to imperil the nation?

FOUCAULT: Certainly the problem of population in the form: 'Aren't we getting too numerous?' or 'Aren't we getting too few?' has long been posed, and there have long been different legislative solutions for it: taxes on bachelors, grants for numerous families, etc. But what is interesting in the eighteenth century is, firstly, the generalisation of these problems: account begins to be taken of all aspects of the phenomena of population (epidemics, conditions of habi-tats, hygiene . . .), and these aspects begin to be integrated into a central problem. Secondly, one finds all sorts of new types of knowledge being applied: the emergence of demography, observations regarding the spread of epi-demics, enquiries into nurses and conditions of breast-feeding. Thirdly, the establishment of apparatuses of power making possible not only observation but also direct inter-vention and manipulation in all these areas. I would say that at that moment, where hitherto there had only been vague improvisatory measures of promotion designed to alter a situation which was scarcely known, something begins to develop which can be called a power over life. In the eighteenth century, for instance, despite significant efforts made in statistics, people were convinced that the popu-lation was falling, whereas historians now know that on the contrary there was a massive growth in population.

GROSRICHARD: Is there any light you can throw, in con-nection with the work of historians like Flandrin, on the development of contraceptive practices in the eighteenth century?

FOUCAULT: There I have to rely on these historians. They

have very sophisticated techniques for interpreting the notaries' registers, baptismal registers, etc. Flandrin brings out a point which seems very interesting to me, relating to the interplay between breast-feeding and contraception, which is that the real issue was the survival of children, not their creation. In other words, contraception was practiced, not so much so in order that children should not be born as that those that were born should survive. Contraception encouraged by a natalist policy: it's pretty amazing!

GROSRICHARD: But that's something that the doctors and demographers of the period declare openly.

FOUCAULT: Yes, but there was a sort of countervailing effect which meant that children were nevertheless born at close intervals. Medical and popular traditions demanded that a woman who was still suckling her child was not permitted to have sexual intercourse, since otherwise her milk would spoil. So women, especially among the rich, sent their children to a wet-nurse, in order to be able to resume having sexual intercourse, and hence keep their husbands. There was a veritable nursing industry. Poor women did it so as to earn some money. But there was no way of checking how the nurse brought up the child, or even whether it was dead or alive, so that the nurses, and in particular the go-betweens with the parents, continued getting paid for a child which was already dead. Some nurses were scoring nineteen dead infants out of twenty entrusted to them. It was appalling! It was to prevent this mess, to re-establish a little order, that mothers were encouraged to feed their own children. The rule of incompatibility between sexual intercourse and suckling was broken at a stroke, but only on condition that women didn't immediately get pregnant again. Hence the need for contraception. And the whole business ultimately turns on this idea that once you have made a child, you keep it.

GROSRICHARD: The astonishing thing is that a new argument appears among those used to get mothers to breast-feed. Suckling indeed enables the mother and child to keep in good health, but also what pleasure it gives! So the problem of weaning is posed in terms which are now psychological as well as physiological. How is the child to be separated from its mother? A well known doctor invented a sort of spiked disc which the mother or nurse was to put on her teat. The child when it sucks experiences a pleasure mixed with pain, and if one increases the calibre of the spikes it has enough and detaches itself from the breast.

FOUCAULT: Is that a fact?

LIVI: Madame Roland recounts that when she was a little girl her nurse put mustard on her breast to wean her. She made fun of the child when the mustard got up her nose!

GROSRICHARD: This was also the time when the modern feeding-bottle was introduced.

FOUCAULT: I don't know the date of that!

GROSRICHARD: 1786, with the French translation of *The Way of Hand-feeding Children in the Absence of Nurses*, by an Italian, Baldini. It had a great success.

FOUCAULT: I renounce all my public and private functions! Shame overwhelms me! I cover myself with ashes! I didn't know the date the feeding-bottle was introduced!

Transcript edited by Alain Grosrichard.

Note

1 Celebrated family agony-columnist on French radio.

AFTERWORD

The history of the sciences brings in play a theme which introduced itself into philosophy almost surreptitiously at the end of the eighteenth century; at that time, the question was first addressed to rational thought not only as to its nature, its ground, its powers and rights, but as to its history and geography, its immediate past and present actuality, its moment and place. This is the question which Mendelssohn, followed by Kant, sought to answer in the *Berlinische Monatschrift* in 1784: *Was ist Aufklärung?* [What is Enlightenment?] . . . Such an undertaking always comprises two objectives which are, in fact, indissociable and inter-dependent: on the one hand, the search to identify in its chronology, constituent elements and historical conditions the moment when the West first affirmed the autonomy and sovereignty of its own mode of rationality —Lutheran Reform, 'Copernican revolution', Cartesian philosophy, Galilean mathematisation of nature, Newtonian physics? And, on the other hand, an analysis of the 'present' moment which seeks to define, in terms both of the history of this Reason and of its current balance-sheet, its relation to that founding act: a relation of rediscovery, renewal of a forgotten meaning, completion and fulfilment, or alternatively one of rupture, return to a prior epoch, and so forth.

Michel Foucault, Preface to Georges Canguilhem,
The normal and the pathological.[1]

The way the question of power and knowledge has recently been posed in France by Foucault and others clearly has to do with the impact of the events of May 1968, and not least the fact that the academic world happened to act as one of the principal focusses of a spectacular series of political and social upheavals. The effect of this circumstance was to cast a fresh light on questions concerning the relation of knowledge and politics in general; it also gave renewed currency and pertinence to some issues that Foucault's previous work had been an attempt to formulate. And through this retro-active effect it became possible to read these books in a different way. 'When I think back now, I ask myself what else it was that I was talking about, in *Madness and Civilisation* or *The Birth of the Clinic*, if not power? Yet I'm perfectly aware that I scarcely ever used the word and never had such a field of analyses at my disposal then.' (above p. 115).

In order to analyse this phenomenon of recurrence properly, its origins would have to be traced back to a whole number of post-war currents in French thought, notably those of the penetration of Marxism into the universities, the renaissance in Hegel studies associated with the names of Hyppolite and Kojève, and the importation (in fact dating back to the early 1930s) by Sartre, Merleau-Ponty and others of Husserlian phenomenology. But perhaps both the backcloth and the centre of preoccupation for Foucault's early work is above all that of the spectacular modern growth and ascent in influence and prestige of the series of disciplines collectively known as the social or human sciences. Two particular aspects of this development in post-war France are worth briefly noting here. The first, the school of historians associated with the journal *Annales* and led successively by Lucien Febvre and Fernand Braudel, promoted a synthesising research programme involving the collaboration of specialists in geography, economics, demography, sociology, ethnology and psychology. The Braudelian conception of 'general history' which crowned this interdisciplinary edifice was moreover intensely humanist; 'general history' was explicitly conceived as the history of Man. The breadth of influence of the *Annales* project is reflected in the efforts of Marxist philosophers as different as Sartre and Althusser to reach a certain accommodation between their respective positions and this 'new kind of history'. With regard to the second current which approached the centre of the stage during the 1960s, designated under the somewhat dubious rubric of 'structuralism' and embracing an even more heterogeneous cluster of disciplines, it is worth here simply noting the fact that, for all the aggressively 'anti-humanist' ideology of some of its manifestations, its overall effect was emphatically one of reinforcing the implicit claims of the human sciences to constitute something like the self-evident rationality of the age.

Now the impossibility, or at least the extreme difficulty and inaccessibility of Foucault's venture during this period lay in the fact that, in contrast with those of Sartre or Althusser, it sought to problematise this universal credo by asking the question: how are the human sciences historically possible, and what are the historical consequences of their existence? The point of Foucault's efforts in *Madness and Civilisation, The Birth of the Clinic* and *The Order of Things* to reconstruct and to de-mythologise the origins of modern knowledges of Man was condemned to remain obscure so long as the sense of this underlying interrogation of a whole contemporary order of rationality remained ungrasped or ungraspable. Discussion of these books tended instead to centre on their supposed affiliation with one or other of the main currents *within* the human sciences, the first being read as a 'history of mentalities' *à la* Lucien Febvre, the last as a structuralist extravaganza forming a companion piece to those of Lévi-Strauss, Lacan and Althusser, and the second as something of an uneasy synthesis of both. The discussion which the books were actually attempting to open remained blocked by a number of obstacles. The Left remained indifferent to their historical material, which it regarded as unimportant or marginal (p. 109f); the books themselves were complex and elusive in their philosophical armature, lacked any overt declarations of ideological allegiance, and maintained an increasingly formidable effort of historical synthesis and abstraction. With hindsight one can also suspect that some of the external obstacles to their reception are internalised at those points where these texts anticipate in prophetically Nietzschean tones the impending dissolution of the figure of 'Man'.

Now while the effect of '68 in the universities had less the character of a fundamental interrogation of the human sciences than that of a fresh impetus for their renovation, developments elsewhere gave a topical point to questions previously posed by Foucault and others on the institutional matrices of the human sciences (the psychiatric asylum, the clinical hospital). The waves of new forms of working-class revolt (factory occupations, sequestrations of bosses, 'popular justice') and the dispersed struggles in a whole range of social institutions (housing, schools, prisons, asylums, hospitals, the army, social workers, magistrates and lawyers . . .) made the existing social forms of the exercise of power, and the particular roles of certain forms of specialised knowledge in the functioning of these apparatuses, increasingly visible. Yet another series of effects of

'68 are also pertinent, at a more subterranean level, to the trend of Foucault's work. One might say that the trouble with Foucault's work was that its originality was in inverse proportion to its utility for Marxism. Now factors such as the rather obvious discrepancy between the events of 1968 and after, and the revolutionary time-table of the Communist Party, both made it increasingly difficult for the organised Left to impose on its loyal intellectuals the strict conditions of service customary in the era of Zhdanov, and opened up the possibility on the Left for a reconsideration of some of the problematic features of Marxism. Among these features it is relevant here to mention two paradoxes about Marxism's relation to history.

It can be argued that Marxism's intellectual victory over other nineteenth-century forms of socialism had less to do with either the wonders of the dialectic of nature or the theorems on the rate of profit than with its comprehensive absorption of the theoretical advances of British, German and French historians over the preceding century. Yet it is also clear that communism as a political institution has exercised the most rigorous and exclusive control over the political utilisation of historical knowledge, an ideological policing codified in the axioms of 'determination in the last instance' and the Leninist/Stalinist strategic lore of the 'objective conditions' of the 'current conjuncture'. Secondly, whereas historical materialism has seemed in principle pre-eminently destined to construct a history of Western forms of rationality and scientificity superior to idealist narratives in terms of progress, spirit, 'influence' or the sublime accidents of genius, its actual achievement in this domain has remained depressingly meagre and problematic, paralysed all too often by the universal explanatory nostrums of class consciousness, class ideology and class interest. One must recognise, all the same, that the problems here do not arise only for Marxists. If, no doubt in direct or indirect response to the challenge of Marxism, a certain broad consensus endorses the project of some kind of materialistic history of 'ideas', what is less often remarked on is the extreme sparseness of the fragments of such a project which have been convincingly realised, to say nothing of the very uncertainty regarding what is to count as success on this terrain, what kind of intelligibility is to be aimed for, what kinds of 'material' conditions are to be accepted as explanatory and what contemporary significance, if any, might attach to the results of such investigations.

It is against these problems that the value of Foucault's work needs to be measured. What one in fact finds in the researches he has pursued since 1968–9, often in parallel with a direct personal participation in a number of the struggles evoked above, is a progressive re-working and re-formulation of these paradoxes and difficulties in terms of a characteristic set of basic questions: (1) A 'genealogical' question: what kind of political relevance can enquiries into our past have in making intelligible the 'objective conditions' of our social present, not only its visible crises and fissures but also the solidity of its unquestioned rationales? (2) An 'archaeological' question: how can the production in our societies of sanctioned forms of rational discourse be analysed according to their material, historical conditions of possibility and their governing systems of order, appropriation and exclusion? (3) An 'ethical' question: what kind of relations can the role and activity of the intellectual establish between theoretical research, specialised knowledge and political struggles? (4) Lastly, a further question fundamental to the possibility of analysing the preceding ones, the question of the proper use to be made of the concept of power, and of the mutual enwrapping, interaction and interdependence of power and knowledge.

This last question, which Foucault designates as that of *pouvoir-savoir*, 'power/knowledge', constitutes the strategic fulcrum of his recent work. Yet the very generality of these two terms 'power' and 'knowledge' is liable to obscure the particularity and originality of the manner in which Foucault conceives their interaction. We can begin here by pointing out a few differences between this approach and the earlier, and in some respects analogous, contribution made by the Critical Theory of the Frankfurt School with its analysis of the dialectics of *Vernunft* and *Herrschaft*, reason and domination. (It is of interest that the one prior study of the general practice of punishment discussed by Foucault in

Discipline and Punish, Kirschheimer and Rusche's *Punishment and Social Structure*, was published in America in 1939 under the auspices of the exiled Frankfurt Institute for Social Research.) Adorno and Horkheimer's *Dialectic of Enlightenment*, probably the Institute's central historical text, takes as its point of departure the seventeenth-century thought of Bacon and Descartes, the revolutions in the mathematical and physical sciences, and the technological project of the mastery of nature (Bacon's 'Knowledge is power'), the objectification of the world articulated in the philosophical divorce between the subject and the object of knowledge. Foucault's studies, on the other hand, repeatedly centre around the latter part of the eighteenth century and the decades around 1800 as the period of the initial constitution of the human sciences in their modern forms and of the elaboration of certain new 'technologies' for the governance of people, both developments being linked to a new philosophical conception of 'Man' as a simultaneous subject and object of knowledge.

The purpose of this comparison is not to set up a controversy about the exact nature and chronology of 'the' scientific revolution, but to illustrate through the differences we have noted here the methodological shifts encapsulated in Foucault's view of power and 'power/knowledge'. Within the horizon of contemporary political theory it is difficult indeed to entertain the possibility of any basic change in our conceptualisation of power. Outstanding issues in this area are treated as matters of nuance, of the synthesis and harmonisation of alternative approaches, the equitable administration of complementary insights. If nevertheless it is to be argued that Foucault's work marks a new departure here, one must begin by noting the novelty of a reflection on power in terms beyond good and evil, located, that is to say, outside the fields of force of two antithetical conceptions of power whose conjunction and disjunction determine the ground rules of most modern political thought: on the one hand, the benign sociological model of power as the agency of social cohesion and normality, serving to assure the conditions of existence and survival of the community, and on the other the more polemical representation of power as an instance of repression, violence and coercion, eminently represented in the State with its 'bodies of armed men'. Each of these conceptions of power carries with it a framework of moral and political objectives: either the optimal instrumentalisation and distribution of power, or its overthrow, dismantling and 'withering away'. The appeal of the Leninist conception of revolutionary politics is perhaps that of the fusion of these dual projects within a single scenario. In any case, the very possibility of such a synthesis derives from the common presuppositions of these opposed politico-philosophical theorems. Foucault's initiative marks a break with this shared premise that power, whether localised or invested in a monarch, a community of citizens or a class dictatorship, consists in some substantive instance or agency of *sovereignty*. He introduces the double methodological principle of neutrality or scepticism of an analysis of power — or rather, an analysis *in terms of* power, which bases itself neither on a moral philosophy nor on a social ontology. It is through this dual precaution of method that the positive sense of Foucault's notion of power/knowledge becomes apparent. One can say that in these two respects his thought is at once intensely Nietzschean and profoundly Kantian, inspired both by the *Critique of Pure Reason* and the *Genealogy of Morals*.

It may appear an implausible move within the problematic of materialist history to invoke the precedent of Kant's transcendental idealism. Yet it is in fact at this point that Foucault's work, from *Madness and Civilisation* to *The Will to Know*, manifests a certain characteristic philosophical and historical irony. The 'Histoire de la Folie' and the projected 'History of Sexuality' are in fact not histories of madness or sexuality at all. Nor is the former text even a history of attitudes to, or modes of treatment of, madness. Its working hypothesis could be taken on the contrary to be that 'madness' does not signify a real historical-anthropological entity at all but is rather the name for a fiction or a historical construct: the problem which it addresses is hence that of the series of conceptual and practical operations through which madness, as mental illness, has been constituted in our societies as an object of certain forms of knowledge and a target of certain institutional practices. Foucault's general attitude to 'power' is somewhat analogous. 'Power in the

substantive sense, '*le pouvoir*, doesn't exist.' (p. 198)
'Clearly it is necessary to be a nominalist: power is not an
institution, a structure, or a certain force with which certain
people are endowed; it is the name given to a complex
strategic relation in a given society.'[2] So, as with Kant, the
task is not that of fixing an ontologically primitive, definitively 'real' stratum of historical reality, but in tracing the
mobile systems of relationships and syntheses which provide
the conditions of possibility for the formation of certain
orders and levels of objects and of forms of knowledge of
such objects: the uncovering of what Foucault terms a
'historical *a priori*'. This methodology does not mean an
indefinite phenomenological 'bracketing' of the history of
material life, although it does imply certain reservations
about the historical materialism which posits the real in the
fore of a total process, a general, continuous and unitary
human substance. On the contrary, Foucault would no
doubt say that 'sexuality', for example, is all the more a
historical object because it is a fictive or constituted entity,
and that working hypotheses of this form serve not to
supplant or invalidate such parallel investigations as those of
historical sociology and ethnology but to make available to
historical analysis a whole additional range of objects and
relations.

The other aspect of Foucault's methodological scepticism
emerges if it is recalled that the historicisation of the
Kantian problem is a pre-eminently Nietzschean theme.
The function of the notion of 'power/knowledge' belongs
within a version of the Nietzschean project of genealogy,
dependent on the principle of ethical as well as ontological
scepticism. At first sight, Foucault's concern with the intrinsic links between knowledge and power might be taken
for a variant of certain radical currents in sociology and
'critique of ideology' influenced by the Frankfurt School and
The German Ideology: that point of view which (to carica-
ture it a little) condemns all dominant and socially ratified
forms of knowledge as masks and instruments of oppression.
But the purpose of the concept of power/knowledge is not
thus to cut through the Gordian knots of epistemology and
history, nor to act as an offensive weapon of ideological
struggle by confronting various 'bourgeois' academic disci-

plines with the complicities inscribed in their origin. It is not a scalpel serving to extract from the body of good, true science those ideologies which act as comprador allies of repressive power. What is at issue is indeed a certain series of historical connections which become visible and intelligible in terms of power, but these relations are not for Foucault the symptom of a violent transgression of the bounds of legitimate knowledge. On the contrary, if certain knowledges of 'Man' are able to serve a technological function in the domination of people, this is not so much thanks to their capacity to establish a reign of ideological mystification as to their ability to define a certain field of empirical truth. And the history of their utilisation in this field is perfectly compatible with their authentic espousal of the humanist values of self-emancipation, self-improvement and self-realisation. Nor are such values automatically taken as being 'objectively' a ruse or a fraud: Foucault is perhaps less of an anti-humanist than Nietzsche on this point.

It is these features of Foucault's genealogy which make it into the opposite of a critique of ideology that give point to his insistence on the *positive*, *productive* characteristics of modern apparatuses of power and his contention that their effectivity rests on the installation of what he calls a politics or a regime of truth – as opposed to a reign of falsity (p. 131ff). His object is not to arrive at *a priori* moral or intellectual judgments on the features of our society produced by such forms of power, but to render possible an analysis of the process of production itself. It turns out in fact that this scrutiny of power in terms of knowledge and of knowledge in terms of power becomes all the more radical — and this is indeed the condition of its possibility— through its rigorous insistence on this particular kind of neutrality. In fact, if one takes the contrasts drawn above between Foucault and the Frankfurt School, it becomes possible now to see how this seemingly innocuous methodology depends on the confrontation of a series of blockages and obstacles which span the fields of the history of science and political theory; one can decipher a logic whereby Foucault's initial and seemingly unspectacular explorations and subject-matter lead to a series of unexpected consequences concerning the question of power.

One notion of Foucault's which has a particular tendency to jar on the sensibilities is that of 'technologies' of power, a term which has the sound of a strange and tendentious metaphor when applied to the mastery of people rather than that of nature. It is worth asking why this is the case. First there is the fact that, as Foucault remarks (p. 110), philosopher-historians of science have concentrated largely on the great transformations of the physical and mathematical, rather than the social and biological sciences. Perhaps as a consequence of this, there is a tendency to consider the social and political effects of scientific technology as historically derivative from the growth of these same sciences. Power as exercised over people has, in its modern forms, largely been interpreted as a particular form or effect of the mastery of nature and of the resources of violence or coercion assured by that mastery. What corresponds here, and particularly in the thought of the Frankfurt School, to a technology of power is the oppressive process of the objectification of human beings, which falsifies their real essence as it does that of the natural world as well. Moreover, where technology as such is a theme of nineteenth- and twentieth-century philosophy, notably within the hermeneutical tradition of Dilthey and Heidegger, it is used as a criterion for distinguishing the activity of the physical sciences from that of the human sciences or *Geisteswissenschaften*. Again, in *The Crisis of the European Sciences* Husserl attributes the disasters of twentieth-century history to the 'mathematisation of the world' inaugurated by Galileo. The extent to which the very idea of 'technologies of power' has a lurid and disagreeable ring in some ears is a testimony to the enduring strength of the humanist conviction that technology is intrinsically alien to the human sphere. The employment of this notion depends on the violation of a multiple system of taboos. It is first of all not the empirical contestation of certain quasi-orthodoxies regarding natural science, human science and technology which is crucial but the conceptual displacements necessary in order for the issue to be posed at all. Foucault's position involves neither the dismissal of the vexed question of the epistemological differences between natural and human science,[3] nor does it assert the radical autonomy of 'human'

from 'physical' technologies.[4] Its minimum thesis is that the
historical matrix of conditions of possibility for the modern
human sciences must be understood in relation to the
elaboration of a whole range of techniques and practices for
the discipline, surveillance, administration and formation of
populations of human individuals. These forms of knowledge and these apparatuses of power are linked in a
constitutive interdependence.[5] In order for a genealogy of
this relationship to be possible, two complementary shifts of
philosophical perspective are necessary: firstly, the discard-
ing of that ethical polarisation of the subject–object relationship which privileges subjectivity as the form of moral
autonomy, in favour of a conception of domination as able
to take the form of a subjectification as well as of an
objectification; and secondly, the rejection of the assumption
that domination falsifies the essence of human subjectivity,
and the assertion that power regularly promotes and utilises
a 'true' knowledge of subjects and indeed in a certain
manner constitutes the very field of that truth. The whole of
Foucault's work from *Madness and Civilisation* to *The Will
to Know* can be read as an exposition of these two theses; it
is possible to think that their significance may be com-
mensurate with the influences and assumptions which have
hitherto rendered them inadmissible. It must be pointed out
that the 'subject' here is thought of by Foucault as a fictive
or constructed entity (as are certain objects) though this
does not mean that it is *false* or *imaginary*. Power does not
itself give birth to actual people, but neither does it dream
subjects into existence. The key here to Foucault's position
is his methodological scepticism about both the ontological
claims and the ethical values which humanist systems of
thought invest in the notion of subjectivity. To repeat: the
point is not to judge or to subvert these values, only
to investigate how they become possible and not to
content oneself with ascribing them to the teleology of
progress.

The question of progress in fact marks the point where the
rather shallow antithesis between neutrality and critique
implied in the preceding remarks can be transcended. The
various precautions of method and displacements of perspective that have been described are indeed preliminaries

to the deployment of a certain form of critique, one whose terms and objects must now be stated. At the same time we may be able to see how a number of very wide-ranging theses are developed in Foucault's work from a starting-point in a fairly restricted sector of the history of the sciences. The uncertainty of the interface within historiography between general history and the history of the sciences itself comprises or symptomatises one of the major obstacles to the quest for a materialist history of forms of rationality. It is this complex set of relationships between the notions of historicity and rationality that form the framework of Foucault's critical thought.

Foucault has acknowledged that one of the initial reasons for his opting to work in the history of sciences which were not the philosophically 'noble' disciplines of physics and mathematics was the example of Georges Canguilhem who, since the 1940s, has produced a remarkable body of studies devoted entirely to the history of the biological sciences.[6] What this work has shown is that the philosophically recalcitrant aspects of the development of these sciences imposes on the historian certain methodological reflections which yield a series of novel philosophical insights. Precisely because the biological sciences do not emerge out of discoveries validated through the adequacy and rigour of their mathematical formalisation, it becomes unsatisfactory and inadequate for their historian to assume the present standpoint of a more-or-less definitive scientific truth and to reconstruct their development as the immanent logic of a series of ordered transformations through which that truth is attained or revealed. The history of biology does not thus transparently unfold itself before the gaze of present truth. But neither can it be made intelligible through a simple descriptive sociology of the beliefs and practices of successive generations of savants. Nor does the solution lie in an amalgamation of these two approaches. Rather, the standard of truth/falsity is a necessary internal component of a history of science, but this history must be given the form, not of a history of the truth itself, but of a history of what Canguilhem (following Bachelard) terms *veridical* discourses, practices governed by the norm of a specified project for the formulation of true propositions. Such discourses are scientific not directly through the actual truth-content of their propositions but through the veridical normativity of their organisation as a practice: not their truth but their relation towards a truth. Canguilhem also shows how the manner in which this norm is defined in the biological and biologistic sciences has a further important property which we will return to below, namely that this norm is internally related both to conceptions of the intrinsic normativity of its natural objects, the phenomena of life, and also to various other normative forms of social practice. But a further thesis of Canguilhem's that interests us here is that the relation between truth and historicity is an intrinsic element in the rationality of these sciences; the advance of biological knowledge involves a particular kind of continual re-evaluation, a retrospective transformation and re-utilisation of different preceding stages of that knowledge. Biology thus progresses through a constantly open-ended and provisional critique of its own progress.

Foucault's thought performs a further elaboration and extension of these considerations. The scientific model of progressivity, at least in its formal attributes as a sequence of cumulative and non-reversible transformations, corresponds to a more global and general accumulative process characteristic of our societies, a process whose reality, however enigmatic, is obvious and indisputable. The uncertain and yet suggestive status of the history of the sciences consists in the fact that it exhibits a kind of rationality which may be taken either as a formal model, an exemplar, a component or an explanation of this ensemble of social-historical processes. Now there is an important and essential corollary to the manner in which the phenomenon of historical progressivity in general is experienced: this experience always engenders and is incorporated in a certain conception of *the present*. And here Foucault's method of genealogy utilises Canguilhem's analysis and critique of this conception of the present as a standpoint of scientific thought and a standpoint of the history of that thought. We can say that the object of Foucault's critique is the status of the present. It is in this sense that Foucault characterises his enterprise as the 'history of the present'. Not a history for which the present means the real terminal point of explanatory narratives, nor a history for which the present functions as the given existential site determining the questions that the historian addresses to a past, but a history of the present as 'modernity': the present as the form of a particular kind of domain of rationality, constituted by its place on a diachronic gradient; a 'régime of truth' composed of a field of problems, questions and responses determined by the continuity or discontinuity, clarity or obscurity of the administered ensemble of relations which constitute the partition between present and past, 'new' and 'old'. (It is here that the wider critical import of Foucault's concern with establishing that the failure of the prisons is an older problem, and 'sexuality' a newer problem than is officially maintained, becomes fully apparent.) The present is a fundamental figure of power/knowledge, the correlate of a form of social practice within which historiography is only one aspect or component. Here again one has a certain kind of nominalism. If Foucault poses a philosophical challenge to history, it is not to question the reality of 'the past' but to interrogate the rationality of the 'present'.

As an account of Foucault's views this probably strays into the margins of exegetical fiction. It must be said in any case that Foucault's genealogy is certainly not a master-schema purporting to govern all possible forms of historical explanation (though it may offer them a supplementary dimension of reflection). What it may possibly provide is a principle of intelligibility for some, at least, of the historical relations covered by the category of power/knowledge, insofar as these are constituents of an effect of progressivity/ modernity. More precisely, it suggests a mode of examination of the general signification of the history of particular forms of rationality and scientificity. This would consist in the exact opposite of the rationalist historicism where the truth of history is interpreted as the effect of a meta-historical process of rationalisation; it would mean a study of the specific effects of practices whose rationale is the installation of a regime of truth. Alternatively, one might say: the study of rational practices whose effects are intelligible in that they 'secrete' a certain kind of historicity.

In the remainder of this background sketch we will attempt to look more closely at some of the details of Foucault's method, beginning with two of Foucault's earlier texts and turning our attention from the 'genealogical' question to the 'archaeological' question. *The Birth of the Clinic* (1963) contains one of the most remarkable studies to date relating the transformation of a field of knowledge during a specific period to its context in the field of extra-theoretical material circumstances and events. It demonstrates how the conceptual and epistemological mutations effected in medical knowledge during the first decades of the nineteenth century were bound up with the re-definition of the social and medical function of the hospital, the incidence of revolution and war on the organisation of, and relations between medical teaching, research and practice, the ethical, epistemological and political transformation of the relation between medicine and its patients and of the professional status of medical personnel, and the complementary projects of a science of the individual case and a hygienic policing of an entire population (see chapter 9). What is interesting about Foucault's method here is that it does not conduct an ontological search for the determinant-in-the-last-instance, nor attempt to deduce these diverse orders of events from causal principles of sufficient reason such as an economic mode of production or the intentions and interests of a class. Instead it analyses a multiplicity of political, social, institutional, technical and theoretical *conditions of possibility*, re-constructing a heterogeneous system of relations and effects whose contingent interlocking makes up what Foucault calls the historical *a priori* of the 'clinical gaze'. What it thus achieves is a form of historical intelligibility whose concreteness and materiality resides in the very irreducibility of the distinct orders of events whose relations it plots.

The Archaeology of Knowledge develops this approach further by proposing a theoretical re-working of certain problems traditionally assigned under the histories of science, ideas and ideologies. This project of an 'archaeology' is conceived as the study of forms of knowledge and rationality at the level of their material manifestation as bodies of discourse composed of finite sets of effective oral or written utterances. The aim is to render these discourses accessible to description and analysis as constituting a specific order of historical reality whose organisation is irreducible to either the history of the careers, thought and intentions of individual agents (the authors of utterances) or to a supra-individual teleology of discovery and intellectual evolution (the truth of utterances). His conception of an order of discourse presents Foucault with a specific area in which to examine one aspect of the general problem of the intelligibility of the historically contingent. His procedure is that of the re-construction of 'rules of formation' for particular discourses such that not only is the formulation of certain individual utterances *possible* in these discourses (in the sense of conforming to a model of acceptability comparable to that of a grammar) but it is these utterances (and not others) that are effectively *produced*. The material for this double descriptive/analytical investigation is thus a set of phenomena or object-events whose conditions of possibility are at the same time their conditions of existence. At the same time, the particular rules of formation of discourses specify these intrinsic forms of regularity in terms of relations with other orders of historical phenomena: the roles and qualifications for the utterers of specific discourses, the mode of specification of their objects of knowledge, the conceptual frameworks for the derivation, formalisation and systematisation of utterances, and the strategic relations of conditioning and effect operating between discourses and other forms of social practice. While at first sight reductionist in its focusing on one narrowly defined 'level' of historical objects, this approach in fact yields through the very delicacy and rigour of its discriminations an enriched conception of the historical interaction of logical, epistemological and social relations.

It is sometimes supposed that Foucault's subsequent thematisation of power tacitly jettisons as obsolete the ambitious methodological edifice of the *Archaeology*. In fact the features of the latter which we have just evoked form the essential ground for the further concepts Foucault was to introduce. The extension and enrichment of these earlier analyses was undertaken through two successive and complementary moves. First, in his 1970 lecture *The Order of*

Discourse, Foucault shows how the rules of formation of discourses are linked to the operation of a particular kind of social power. Discourses not only exhibit immanent principles of regularity, they are also bound by regulations enforced through social practices of appropriation, control and 'policing'. Discourse is a political commodity. It is true that here Foucault adopts a somewhat negative view of the articulation of discourse and power as a phenomenon of exclusion, limitation and prohibition (somewhat as in *Madness and Civilisation*, see p. 183 above). But his more recent books bring to attention a different and converse form of articulation whose effects are much more positive and productive in character. This phenomenon consists in the singular emergence in Western thought during the past four centuries of discourses which construct programmes for the formation of a social reality. The existence of these discourses, whose object-domains are defined simultaneously as a target area for intervention and a functioning totality to be brought into existence, has a significance for historical analysis which prior to Foucault seems never to have been fully exploited. Our world does not follow a programme, but we live in a world of programmes, that is to say in a world traversed by the effects of discourses whose object (in both senses of the word) is the rendering rationalisable, transparent and programmable of the real.

Before proceeding further we need to recall Foucault's insistence on the use of the concept of power in a relational rather than a substantialising mode. Power for Foucault is not an omnipotent *causal* principle or shaping spirit but a perspective concept. Thus it is not a question here of simply re-interpreting the kinds of relations of conditions and effects studied in *The Birth of the Clinic* as relations programmed by a power. On the other hand this *is* a conception of the exercise of power as a practice which *establishes* certain relationships between heterogeneous elements. If we say that all human practices are possible only within relations and subject to conditions which are only finitely modifiable at a given point and time, then the exercise of power can be conceived as the general aspect of practice within which these relations and conditions function as a material and a terrain of operation. Power is exercised not only subject to, but through and by means of conditions of possibility. Hence for Foucault power is omnipresent in the social body because it is coterminous with the conditions of social relations in general.

Foucault employs three concepts of general forms of rationality pertinent to the study of power/knowledge: the concepts of *strategies*, *technologies* and *programmes* of power. The two latter terms have already been introduced here. All three concepts serve as means of conceiving relations of power in terms of the differential and differentiated interaction between distinct orders of historical events. In order to understand these concepts, it is necessary to keep in mind a basic distinction between three such general orders of events: that of certain forms of explicit, rational, reflected *discourse*; that of certain non-discursive social and institutional *practices*; and that of certain *effects* produced within the social field. These three orders do not of course represent watertight ontological compartments; the same events can be considered in turn under each of them. The point is to clarify certain of the ways in which they intersect and interact. Readers of Foucault sometimes emerge with the dismaying impression of a paranoid hyper-rationalist system in which the strategies-technologies-programmes of power merge into a monolithic regime of social subjection. The misunderstanding here consists in a conflation of historical levels which reads into the text two massive illusions or paralogisms: an illusion of 'realisation' whereby it is supposed that programmes elaborated in certain discourses are integrally transposed to the domain of actual practices and techniques, and an illusion of 'effectivity' whereby certain technical methods of social domination are taken as being actually implemented and enforced upon the social body as a whole. (These misunderstandings are perhaps both metaphysically rooted in a neo-Hegelian tendency to identify realisation with effectivity, both notions being copresent in the Hegelian concept of *Wirklichkeit*. For Foucault's thought it is essential that they remain distinguished from one another.) One needs to beware the pitfalls inherent in the word 'power' itself. Foucault's thesis of the *omnipresence* of relations of power or power/knowledge is all too easily run together with the idea that all power, in so far as it is held, is a kind of sovereignty amounting to untrammelled mastery, absolute rule or command. Hence Foucault is taken to attribute an absolute *omnipotence* to 'apparatuses' of power. It hardly needs to be pointed out that, if this were the case, history would assume the form of a homogeneous narrative of perpetual despotism, and the subtleties of genealogical analysis would be entirely superfluous. In fact the concepts of strategies, programmes and technologies of power serve to analyse not the perfect correspondence between the orders of discourse, practice and effects, but the manner in which they fail to correspond and the positive significance that can attach to such discrepancies.

This kind of non-correspondence is not a new discovery, of course. But the ways in which it is most commonly treated, in terms for example of the gulf between the intentions of human agents and the results of their actions, leaves a number of options unexplored. This point is admirably stated by Albert O. Hirschman in a recent essay which connects at a number of points with the current researches of Foucault and others.[7] In *The Passions and the Interests: Political Arguments for Capitalism before its Triumph* (Princeton, 1977), Hirschman compares his own discussion of the intellectual antecedents of capitalism with that of Max Weber's *The Protestant Ethic and the Spirit of Capitalism*. As Hirschman remarks, Weber's thesis of the paradoxical effects on economic behaviour of Calvinist theology and morality 'spelled out one of those remarkable unintended effects of human actions (or in this case, thoughts) whose discovery has become the peculiar province and highest ambition of the social scientists since Vico, Mandeville and Adam Smith' (p. 130). He goes on to suggest that:

> discoveries of the symmetrically opposite kind are both possible and valuable. On the one hand, there is no doubt that human actions and social decisions tend to have consequences that were entirely unintended at the outset. But, on the other hand, these actions and decisions are often taken because they are earnestly and fully expected to have certain effects that then wholly fail to materialise.

The latter phenomenon, while being the structural obverse of the former, is also likely to be one of its causes; the illusory expectations that are associated with certain social decisions at the time of adoption may keep their *real* future effects from view. Moreover, once these desired effects fail to happen and refuse to come into the world, the fact that they were originally counted on is likely to be not only forgotten but actively repressed. (p. 131)

Thus the empirical non-correspondence between the level of discourses and the level of historical effects can be analysed in other terms than the sociological inference of a hidden hand which orchestrates the unexpected, without lapsing into the interpretation of history as the realisation of some (articulate or inarticulate) project. And just because non-realised programmes tend to be dropped from the official record, it becomes all the more important and fascinating to investigate what may have been their mode of their real but unprogrammed effects.

Foucault's work suggests a further means of exploring the positive significance of the phenomena Hirschman describes. If the effects of a programme transcend the criterion of whether its intentions are fulfilled, this is largely because a programme is always something more than a formulation of wishes or intentions. Every programme also either articulates or presupposes a *knowledge* of the field of reality upon which it is to intervene and/or which it is calculated to bring into being. The common axiom of programmes is that an effective power is and must be a power which *knows* the objects upon which it is exercised. Further, the condition that programmatic knowledge must satisfy is that it renders reality in the form of an object which is *programmable*. This operation is reminiscent of the function Kant attributes in the *Critique of Pure Reason* to the concept of the schema which, as Deleuze puts it, 'does not answer the question, how are phenomena made subject to the understanding, but the question, how does the understanding apply itself to the phenomena which are subject to it?'[8]

A characteristic solution to this problem is the positing of a reality which is programmable by virtue of an intrinsic mechanism of self-regulation, an inherent *economy*. Hirschman brings out certain properties of such systems in his remarks on Steuart's *Inquiry into the Principles of Political Oeconomy* (1767):

> The basic consistency of Steuart's thinking is best under-
> stood through his metaphor of the watch to which he
> likens the 'modern oeconomy'. He uses it on two different
> occasions to illustrate in turn . . . two aspects of state
> intervention . . . . On the one hand, the watch is so
> delicate that it 'is immediately destroyed if . . . touched
> with any but the gentlest hand'; this means that the
> penalty for old-fashioned arbitrary *coups d'autorité* is so
> stiff that they will simply have to cease. On the other
> hand, these same watches are continually going wrong;
> sometimes the spring is found too weak, at other times
> too strong for the machine . . . and the workman's hand
> becomes necessary to set it right'; hence well-intentioned,
> delicate interventions are frequently required. (pp. 86–7)

Here the genius of the programme consists in positing a real mechanism which itself 'programmes' the appropriate form of intervention upon it. Even more sophisticated schemas can be constructed, of course. Those which Foucault has discussed most extensively are the programmes which invent forms of automatism for the correction of the automatism of the economy and in particular the rectification of the human elements of its materials. Such a model is that of Bentham's *Panopticon* (cf. Chapter 7). Bentham completes the economy of exchange with an economy of power. In such models, where one begins to approach the thematic field of the human sciences, the notion of a mechanism is sup-plemented with a perhaps even more powerful conception, that of the *norm* of behaviour and functioning of human individuals and collectivities.

Here one encounters a complex and intimate series of relations between programmes of power and technologies of power. One property of human norms is that deviation is no longer, as with the watch, an adventitious consequence of the imperfection of its construction. Abnormalities come to be understood as effects of a human and social pathogeny which is as natural as the norm itself, and hence the object of a complementary form of knowledge. Further, the concept of a norm is inseparable, as Canguilhem has shown,[9] from concepts of normativity and normalisation; the specification of a norm is inseparable from the specification of natural and technical operations which effect or correct this normativity. Indeed without the availability of means of normalisation a norm is hardly knowable. In turn, techniques of normalisation themselves suffer from defects which necessitate correction and adjustment.

Thus a programmatic schema fulfils its vocation only in so far as it is complemented by the elaboration of a technology. This internal relation between the programmatic and the technological, the normal and the normative, is in turn the outcome of the conceptualisation within the discursive form of the programme itself of an ineluctable discrepancy between discourse and actuality. Now this programmatic point of view on phenomena of 'non-correspondence' is not the last word on this matter for the genealogist of programmes. But it does already allow one to indicate one basic mode of the historical effects of 'unsuccessful' programmes, namely the manner in which every programme caters in advance for the eventuality of its own failure. What Foucault illustrates here is a curious anti-functionality of the norm: the failure of prisons to fulfil their planned function as reformatories, far from precipitating their breakdown acts instead as the impulse for a perpetual effort to reform the prison which continually reinvokes the model of its original, aborted programme. The prison is one of many such epics of failure in the annals of social policy. Failure here is the norm.[10] Yet a further factor, the complement of this one, is the possibility that the untoward effects of a technique which mark a failure within one programme can still be recouped as 'successes' within the coordinates of another one. This is exactly what happens with the prisons (cf. Chapter 2).

But *Discipline and Punish* does not, finally, take this absurd historical logic as defining the ineluctable, immovable truth of 'the social'. The effects described above belong within what Foucault terms the domain of *strategies* of power. In contrast with the normative logic of the programme, the characteristic of strategy is its artificial, improvisational, factitious nature. Whereas programmes/ technologies of power have essentially to do with the *formation* of the social real, strategic activity consists in the *instrumentalisation* of the real. In effect Foucault's notion of strategy defines that minimum form of rationality of the exercise of power in general which consists in the mobile sets of operations whereby a multiplicity of heterogeneous elements (forces, resources, the features of a terrain, the disposition and relation of objects in space-time) are invested with a particular functionality relative to a dynamic and variable set of objectives. Strategy is the exploitation of possibilities which it itself discerns and creates. What is important is to avoid merging the concept of strategy into that of the programme by way of the image of the grand strategist and his plan. (It is necessary here to distinguish clearly between Foucault and his authors. Bentham's *Panopticon* may well be described as a design for an automatic strategy of social power. But Foucault for his part is not under the illusion that such an integrated strategy has ever been translated into reality. Nor is his position the futile hypothesis that everything happens 'as though' such a plan had been implemented.) The basic difference is that strategy, unlike the programme, is an essentially non-discursive rationality. Discourse is not a medium for strategy but a resource. And the point where the perspective of strategy becomes indispensable for genealogy is where the non-correspondence of discourse, practices and effects creates possibilities for operations whose sense is, in various ways, either unstated or unstateable within any one discourse. Strategy is the arena of the cynical, the promiscuous, the tacit, in virtue of its general logical capacity for the synthesis of the heterogeneous. This is what Foucault calls the 'anonymity' of certain effects within the field of power-relations: it is not that these effects lack an agent but that they lack a programmer.

What is at first less clear is why Foucault asserts that these effects manifest, at certain points and in certain circumstances, a recognisable overall coherence in terms of strategy. A field of strategy is one which is traversed by a multiplicity of more-or-less coordinated or uncoordinated, intelligent or stupid agencies. (And it must be remembered that the human 'elements' of the field are themselves not an inert and passive material.) Thus the logic of strategy cannot in itself entail any necessary coherence whatever. In other words, a history cannot be *based* on the concept of strategy. The concept only becomes pertinent as an instrument for historical decipherment at the point where the instrumentalisation of the social terrain interacts with its formation by programmes and technologies of power. The latter (conceptual and practical) operations, by establishing certain new forms of objects and relations, engender strategic possibilities and, in particular, provide a matrix of crystallisation for organised effects of strategy. What is meant by a strategy of power is the interplay between one or more programmes/technologies and an operational evaluation in terms of strategy: a logically hybrid (and sometimes elusive) function which integrates the production of effects with the utilisation of those effects.

In what follows we will briefly sketch some of the general forms of this interplay. But it must be stressed that these concepts do not compose any self-sufficient 'theory' of history: their concrete utility can only be seen and tested at the level of their empirical, narrative deployment in studies such as *Discipline and Punish*.

(1) Clearly the effectivity of the discursive form of the programme does not reduce itself to some magical efficacy attributed to the thought of the programmer as mastermind. Rather it possesses an inherent strategic utility as a public space for the articulation of problems and the contention, negotiation and collaboration of different forces and interests. The paradigm of strategy as a zero-sum war game is inappropriate here. Where the terrain of strategy is the social, there is always a likelihood that the outcome of two competing or conflicting strategy-programmes will be the composition of a third one. The built-in logical coherence of the programme serves here as a vehicle for the improvisational flexibility of strategy.

(2) Over and above the internal relation that links the elaboration of human technologies of power to the rationality of the programme, technology possesses an intrinsic rationality of its own, independent of the phenomena

whereby particular techniques either fail to produce the results prescribed by a programme or produce other, unforeseen results. In fact this is true of any technology: the concept of technology signifies precisely the specific level of intelligence, progressivity and rationality characteristic of the technical. The history of this rationality cannot be reduced to that of its individual or institutional users, to the times and places, or to the ulterior purpose of its applications. Foucault's account in *Discipline and Punish* of the development of technologies of discipline and surveillance comprises, in terms of all these extra-technological dimensions, a random collage of scattered and heterogeneous elements. But this does not vitiate the analysis: the coherence of the phenomena described is to be found in the order of the technological itself, rather than in some other order. (It should be added that conscious forms of technological experimentation regularly occur in the forms of institutional 'models': the model eighteenth-century prisons in the USA, for example.) This 'relative autonomy' of the technical permits it to act as an independent principle for the multiplication, adaptation and reorganisation of effects. Whatever its *logical* interdependence with the framework of the programme in general, a technology of normalisation always admits of a certain free play with respect to any specific programmatic norm. This opens up a whole range of strategic possibilities. The autonomous diffusion and adaptation of techniques makes it possible for programmes based on quite different normative analyses (political economy, social, economy, eugenicist psychology, psychoanalysis . . .) to enter into a complex play of permutation, exchange or complementarity of technical roles. It is also possible for a technological apparatus like the prison to continue operating while adapting itself to a strategic role diametrically opposite to that of its initial programme: not the elimination of criminality, but its exploitation.

(3) To grasp the full range of these possibilities we must consider more closely the notion of the norm. The term has been partly used here as a shorthand notation for a whole cluster of what Kant might have termed 'regulative ideas', ideas conceptually affiliated with the entire gamut of forms of knowledge of Man: system, structure, rule, order, and

exchange, for example.[11] But beneath this multiplicity of alternative and complementary concepts it is possible to identify a basic structural bipolarity which characterises modern projects of human governance. This characteristic is clearly formulated above by Fontana and Pasquino (p. 123f). If the general object-material for the relations and networks of power studied by Foucault is that of the concrete forms of conduct and behaviour of human beings, then one can say that operations designed to form or re-form this material articulate themselves according to two broad modalities, 'microscopic' and 'macroscopic': techniques which effect an orthopaedic training of the body and soul of an individual, and techniques which secure and enhance the forms of life and well-being of a population or 'social body'. Now it is possible to effect a partial classification of programmes, strategies and technologies according to how their field of operation focusses within one or other of these modalities, and how a double epistemological-practical activity of shaping their material into a normal-normative-normalisable form is weighted towards the focus of the individual or that of the population. But at the same time every such practice is conceived as having necessarily to be evaluated simultaneously on both levels. Modern forms of governance are thus conceptualised in terms of a double surface of effects, or by means of a double-entry system of calculation. And the *ratio* of this bipolarity is the basic premise of modern forms of governmental practices which requires that a good and legitimate government or governance of men must be one which is *omnium et singulorm*, of all and of each. What underpins the evergreen moral and ontological arguments in social and political theory about 'the individual and society', including their current forms as theories of 'the subject' and of 'socialisation' is the strategic rule by which organised relations of power are called upon to integrate these dual imperatives of good government.

Two supplementary clarifications must be added here. Firstly, the 'macroscopic' focus of the population is not to be equated with Foucault's conception of the field of strategic effects in the real. The logic of the processes he describes is not that of an inexorable globalisation of effects of power towards the ideal horizon of a perfectly subjected totality. Thus Foucault distinguishes his characterisation of our societies as *disciplinary* from the fantasy of a *disciplined* society populated by docile, obedient, normalised subjects. Secondly, although Foucault locates the basis of power in minute, capillary relations of domination, relations which act as the lasting substratum for the transitory politico-historical edifices of State and Revolution, this is not to assert that the governance of collectivities is simply a resultant or a projection of a discipline of individuals pioneered in closed institutions such as the prison. The different forms of exercise of power focussed around the regulative ideas of individual and society are genealogically interdependent and coeval. A social government is as much constituted out of minute capillary relations as is individual pedagogics. The 'capillary' is not equivalent to the in-dividual: it may be sub-individual or trans-individual. And the State is neither the definitive form assumed by govern-ment nor its subject, but rather one of its effects or instruments.[12]

Foucault's thought on strategy has certain political and ethical applications and corollaries. Perhaps it is now clear that if Foucault's reflection on power is rather more extended than those which historians usually permit them-selves, it is not the kind of obsessive serenade which sublimates the desire to personally lay hands on the levers of control. It does not produce a mock-up of a political control room. Nor do its illustrations of the multiplicity, fecundity and productivity of power-relations imply their collective imperviousness to resistance. The study of the history of forms of rationality imposes a certain bias which neces-sitates greater attention being paid to forms of domination than to forms of insubordination. But the facts of resistance are nevertheless assigned an irreducible role within the analysis. The field of strategies is a field of conflicts: the human material operated on by programmes and tech-nologies is inherently a *resistant* material. If this were not the case, history itself would become unthinkable.

The strategically coordinated apparatuses of power which

Foucault identifies do not have the status of a trans-
historical law. Those which he describes, organised during
the nineteenth century around the 'objects' of criminality and
sexuality, are implicitly situated as local episodes within a
more general history of the political. They constitute an
inherently fragile structure and their instruments and techniques are always liable to forms of re-appropriation,
reversibility and re-utilisation not only in tactical re-
alignments from 'above' but in counter-offensives from
'below'. This is why no one good or bad ideology of
oppression or subversion is possible: thematic implements
of power—individual conscience, norms of sexuality, the
security of a population—have been and are constantly
being 'turned round', in both directions.

Even so, it may be objected that Foucault never locates
his theoretical enterprise 'on the side of' resistance by
undertaking to formulate a strategy of resistance, and hence
inferred that the cunning of strategy is taken as being the
exclusive property of forms of domination. Foucault does
indeed refuse the kind of articulation with the political
whereby theory undertakes to provide proof that its
ideological identity papers are in proper order. He also
consistently refuses to assume the standpoint of one speaking for and in the name of the oppressed.[13] These refusals
correspond to a certain caution about the project of
formulating, at last and once again, the lines of a 'correct'
political strategy. In conclusion we will attempt to formulate
some of these reservations as they arise from Foucault's
discussions of power, strategy and resistance.

The identification of resistances. Every programme of
revolution or subversion which espouses the dictum that 'It
is right to revolt' is obliged to limit its generosity by
distinguishing those acts which it authenticates as right and
as revolts from those other occurrences and agents which it
disqualifies as adventurisms, provocations, left-wing in-
fantilisms, criminality, hooliganism or whatever. What
needs to be problematised here is the subordination of the
category of resistance to the normative criteria of a political
programme. A corollary of Foucault's desubstantialisation
of power is a certain desacralisation of canonical forms of
resistance identified by a politico-ideological affiliation.

Without rushing to the opposite extreme of a romanticism of noble savagery, it can be argued that within a general reflection in terms of power, the category of resistance cannot be made to exclude its (supposedly) 'primitive' or 'lumpen' forms of manifestation. There is another problem about the political definition of resistance. If one turns, not to the fictitious schema of the disciplined subject but to the question of what is it for real people to reject or refuse, or on the other hand in some manner to consent to, acquiesce in, or accept the subjection of themselves or of others, it becomes apparent that the binary division between resistance and non-resistance is an unreal one. The existence of those who seem not to rebel is a warren of minute, individual, autonomous tactics and strategies which counter and inflect the visible facts of overall domination, and whose purposes and calculations, desires and choices resist any simple division into the political and the apolitical. The schema of a strategy of resistance as a vanguard of politicisation needs to be subjected to re-examination, and account must be taken of resistances whose strategy is one of evasion or defence – the Schweijks as well as the Solzhenitsyns. There are no good subjects of resistance.

The focussing of resistances. Certain contemporary apparatuses of power are evocative of a different kind of mechanism from that envisaged by a Steuart or a Bentham. Foucault has likened France's legal system to the constructions of Tinguely: 'one of those immense pieces of machinery, full of impossible cog-wheels, belts which turn nothing and wry gear-systems: all these things which 'don't work' and ultimately serve to make the thing 'work''.[14] Even the stupidities, the failures, the absurdities, the 'weak links' (p. 143f) of the existing order of things are capable of a positive utility within the strategic field. For this and other reasons a certain prudence is advisable regarding revolutionary strategies which utilise these phenomena as levers for the realisation of a programme which is more rational, more intelligent, and hence more acceptable and better than that of the prevailing regime. There is a different kind of challenge which might be considered here: what if instead of stigmatising the unacceptable in order to supplant it by the acceptable, one were to call in question the very rationality which grounds the establishment of a regime of acceptability and the programmatic logic whereby the 'unacceptable' is regularly restored to the 'acceptability' of a norm? It is at the points where the role of a whole species of rationality and the status of a whole regime of truth can be made to open itself to interrogation that the possibility of a profounder logic of revolt may begin to emerge. Here, as Foucault says in Chapter 5, the object is neither a denunciation of the effects of knowledge in general, nor the fabrication of a knowledge for the instruction, correction and guidance of every possible resistance. At this point the contribution of the intellectual as historical analyst ends and gives way to the reflection and decisions, not of the managers and theoreticians of resistance but of those who themselves choose to resist. For the recent eruptions of 'popular knowledge' and 'insurrections of subjugated knowledges' which he celebrates (p. 81f), what Foucault may have to offer is a set of possible tools, tools for the identification of the conditions of possibility which operate through the obviousnesses and enigmas of our present, tools perhaps also for the eventual modification of those conditions.

COLIN GORDON

Notes

1 Forthcoming: see Bibliography.
2 *La Volonté de savoir* p. 123, trans. C. Gordon.
3 This issue is discussed in Chapter 4.
4 See the discussion of the 'man–machine' motif in *Discipline and Punish*. Part III Chapter 1. On machinofacture and the body, see Didier Deleule and Francois Guéry, *Le corps productif* (Paris, 1972).
5 It is worth re-reading the final two chapters of *The Order of Things*, dealing with 'Man' and the human sciences, in parallel with the morphology of discipline set out in Part III of *Discipline and Punish*.
6 Especially valuable on this question are Canguilhem's 'Introduction' to his *Idéologie et rationalité dans l'histoire des sciences de la vie* (1977), and Foucault's Preface to a forthcoming English translation of Canguilhem's *Le Normal et le pathologique* (1966).
7 In his 1978 and 1979 lectures at the Collège de France, Foucault has been concerning himself with the characteristics of liberalism and neo-liberalism as rationalities of governmental practices. For analyses in a similar perspective, see the articles by Pasquale Pasquino, Giovanna

Procacci and Jacques Donzelot in *Ideology and Consciousness* 4 (Autumn 1978) and 5 (Spring 1979); one of Foucault's 1978 lectures is translated as 'Governmentality' in No. 6 of the same journal (Autumn 1979). See also Robert Castel, *L'Ordre psychiatrique* (1976) and Jacques Donzelot, *La police des familles* (1977).

8 *La philosophie critique de Kant* (1963).
9 See *Le Normal et le pathologique*.
10 J. Donzelot's *La police des familles* analyses the 'failure' of the modern family to accomplish its imputed functions, and the processes of the functionalisation of that failure.
11 See *The Order of Things*, p. 355ff.
12 See note 7. Since *Discipline and Punish* Foucault's work has been increasingly—though not exclusively—concerned with the governmental focus of relations of power. This does not signal any theoretical 'break'; the theme is already broached in *Discipline and Punish*. In *The Will to Know* Foucault identifies the strategic importance of sexuality as a point of interchange between the 'microscopic' and the 'macroscopic' dimensions. See Chapters 10 and 11 above.
13 See Foucault's discussion with Gilles Deleuze on 'Intellectuals and Power' (1973).
14 *Le Monde*, 21 October 1978.

BIBLIOGRAPHY: Writings of Michel Foucault

Note: This Bibliography lists as nearly as possible all writings and translations by Michel Foucault published in French or English under his own name, alone or in collaboration, up to June 1979, together with some forthcoming items and some pieces originally published in Italian.

Entries are arranged in each section according to the date of their first published version, accompanied by details of their English translations(s) (if any). Entries which include details of an English-language text, either original or in translation, are marked with an asterisk.

Information on any errors or omissions will be gratefully received.

The following previous bibliographies have been consulted:

(1) F. Lapointe, 'Michel Foucault. A Bibliographic Essay', *Journal of the British Society for Phenomenology* Vol. 4 No. 2 (May 1973).

(2) W. Seitter, 'Bibliographie des Scriften Michel Foucaults' in W. Seitter ed., *Michel Foucault, Von der Subversion des Wissens* (Munich, 1974).

(3) C. Jambet, 'Bibliographie', *Magazine litteraire* No. 101 (1975).

(4) M. Morris and P. Patton, 'Bibliography' in M. Morris and P. Patton eds., *Michel Foucault: Power, Truth, Strategy* (Sydney, 1979).

(1), (3) and (4) also cover writings on Foucault. (4) gives a helpful selection of (mainly recent) writings in French and English. There is a full secondary bibliography by F. Lapointe and W. Seitter in *Philosophischen Jahrbuch*, Jg. 81 (1974), 1 Hb.

All French-language texts listed are published in Paris unless otherwise indicated.

1 Books

* *Maladie mentale et personnalité* (1954). Editions since 1955 retitled: *Maladie mentale et psychologie*. Revised edition (1966). *Mental illness and psychology* trans. A. Sheridan (New York, 1976).

* *Folie et déraison. Histoire de la folie à l'âge classique* (1961). Pocket edition abridged by the author (1964). Second edition: *Histoire de la folie à l'âge classique* (1972) with new Preface and two Appendices: 'La folie, l'absence d'oeuvre' and 'Mon corps, ce papier, ce feu'.

Madness and Civilisation. A History of Insanity in the Age of Reason trans. R. Howard, based on the pocket edition (New York, 1965).

* *Naissance de la clinique. Une archéologie du regard médical* (1963). Revised edition (1972). *The Birth of the Clinic. An Archaeology of Medical Perception* trans. A. M. Sheridan (London, 1973).

Raymond Roussel (1963).

* *Les Mots et les Choses. Une archéologie des sciences humaines* (1966). *The Order of Things, An Archaeology of the Human Sciences* with a 'Foreword to the English edition' (London, 1970).

* *L'archéologie du savoir* (1969). *The Archaeology of Knowledge* trans. A. M. Sheridan Smith (London, 1972).

* *L'ordre du discours. Leçon inaugurale au Collège de France prononcée le 2 décembre 1970* (1971). 'Orders of discourse' trans. R. Swyer in *Social Science Information* Vol. 10. No. 2 (April, 1971) republished as 'The Discourse on Language' in Michel Foucault, *The Archaeology of Knowledge* (New York, 1972).

Ceci n'est pas une pipe (Montpellier, 1973). Augmented text of an article (same title, 1968) with two letters and four drawings by R. Magritte.

* *Surveiller et punir. Naissance de la prison* (1975). *Discipline and Punish. Birth of the Prison* trans. A. Sheridan (London, 1977).

* *Histoire de la sexualité 1: La volonté de savoir* (1976). *The History of Sexuality. Volume I: An Introduction* trans. R. Hurley (New York, 1978).

In collaboration

* *Moi, Pierre Rivière, ayant égorgé ma mère, ma soeur et mon frère . . . Un cas de parricide au XIXe siècle* (1973). See below, under Articles. *I, Pierre Rivière, having slaughtered my mother, my sister and my brother . . . A Case of Parricide in the 19th Century* trans. F. Jellinek (New York, 1975).

Les machines à guérir (1976). (Dossiers et documents d'architecture, Institut de l'environnement). See below, under Articles.

Collected translations

* *Language, Counter-Memory, Practice: Selected Essays and Interviews* edited and translated with an Introduction by D. F. Bouchard (New York, 1977). (Cited below as *LCMP*).

2 Translations, editions, prefaces

L. Binswanger, *Le rêve et l'existence* trans. from the German with an Introduction by M.F. (1954).

V. von Weizsäcker, *Le cycle du structure* trans. from the German by M.F. and D. Rocher (1958).

J.-J. Rousseau, *Rousseau juge de Jean-Jacques*. Introduction by M.F. (1962).

L. Spitzer, *Études de style* trans. from the German by E. Kaufholz, A. Couchon and M.F. (1962).

I. Kant, *Anthropologies du point de vue pragmatique* trans. from the German with Introduction and Notes by M.F. (1964).

F. Nietzsche, *Oeuvres philosophiques complètes: Le gai savoir. Les fragments posthumes (1881–1882)*. Foreword by M.F. and G. Deleuze (1967).

Arnauld and Lancelot, *Grammaire générale et raisonnée*. Introduction by M.F. (1969).

G. Bataille, *Oeuvres complètes*. Vol. 1. Introduction by M.F. (1970).

J.-P. Brisset, *La grammaire logique. La science de Dieu*. Preface by M.F. '7 propos sur le 7e ange' (1970).

G. Flaubert, *La tentation de Saint Antoine*. Preface by M.F. (1971).

S. Livrozet, *De la prison à la révolte*. Preface by M.F. (1973).

B. Jackson, *Leurs prisons*. Preface by M.F. (1974).

Le désir est partout, Fromanger. Exhibition catalogue, Galérie Jeanne Bucher. Preface by M.F. (1975).

B. Cuau, *L'affaire Mirval ou Comment le récit abolit le crime*. Prefaces by M.F. 'Une mort inacceptable', and P. Vidal-Naquet (1976).

WIAZ En attendant le grand soir (Drawings). Preface by M.F. (1976).

My secret life (Abridged French translation). Preface by M.F. (1977).

M. Debard and J.-L. Hennig, *Les juges kaki*. Preface by M.F. (1977). Preface reprinted in *Le Monde* 1–2 December 1977.

J. M. Aillaume *et al.*, *Politiques de l'habitat 1800–1850*. Under the auspices of Comité de recherche et du développement en architecture (CORDA), directed by M.F. (1977).

G. Deleuze and F. Guattari, *Anti-Oedipus*. Preface by M.F. to English translation (New York, 1977).

Herculine Barbin dite Alexina B. Compiled and presented by M.F. (1978).

P. Brückner, *Ennemi de l'État*. Preface by M.F. (1979).

* G. Canguilhem, *The Normal and the Pathological*. Preface by M.F. to forthcoming English translation.

3 Articles, reviews and lectures

'La recherche du psychologue' in *Des chercheurs Français s'interrogent* (1957).

* 'Le "non" du père', review of J. Laplanche: *Hölderlin et la question du père, Critique* 178 (1962). 'The Father's "No" ' trans. D. F. Bouchard, in *LCMP*.

'Un si cruel savoir', on Cl. Crébillon and J. A. Reveroni de Saint-Cyr, *Critique* 182 (1962).

* 'Préface à la transgression', on G. Bataille, *Critique* 195–6 (1963). 'A Preface to Transgression' trans. D. F. Bouchard, in *LCMP*.

'Distance, aspect, origine', on the *Tel Quel* novelists, *Critique* 198 (1963). Reprinted in *Tel Quel, Théorie d'ensemble* (1968).

* 'Le langage à l'infini', *Tel Quel* 15 (1963). 'Language to Infinity' trans. D. F. Bouchard, in *LCMP*.

'La métamorphose et le labyrinthe', on R. Roussel, *Nouvelle Revue Française* 124 (1963).

'Guetter le jour qui vient', on R. Laporte, *Nouvelle Revue Française* 130 (1963).

'Le langage de l'espace', on Laporte, Le Clezio, Ollier, Butor, *Critique* 203 (1964).

'La prose d'Actéon', on P. Klossowski, *Nouvelle Revue Française* 135 (1964).

'L'obligation d'écrire', *Arts* 11 (1964).

'Le Mallarmé de R.-P. Richard', *Annales* 5 (1964).

'La folie, l'absence d'oeuvre', *La table ronde* (May 1964). Reprinted in M.F., *Histoire de la folie à l'âge classique,* 2nd edn. (1972).

'La prose du monde', *Diogène* 53 (1966).

'L'arrière-fable', on Jules Verne, *L'Arc* 29 (Aix-en-Provence, 1966).

'Une histoire restée muette', on E. Cassirer: *The Philosophy of the Enlightenment, La Quinzaine littéraire* 8 (1966).

'La pensée du dehors', on M. Blanchot, *Critique* 229 (1966).

* 'Un "fantastique de bibliothèque" ', on G. Flaubert: *La tentation de Saint Antoine, Cahiers de la compagnie M. Renaud-J. L. Barrault* 59 (1967). 'Fantasia of the Library', trans. D. F. Bouchard, in *LCMP*.

'Nietzsche, Freud, Marx', followed by a discussion; in *Nietzsche* (Cahiers de Royaumont, Paris, 1967).

'La grammaire générale de Port-Royal', excerpt from Preface of 1969, *Langages* 7 (1967).

* 'Ceci n'est pas une pipe', on Magritte, Klee and Kandinsky, *Les cahiers du chemin* 2 (1968). Reprinted (Montpellier, 1973). See under Books. 'This is not a pipe' trans. in *October*.

* 'Réponse à une question', *Esprit* 5 (1968). 'History, discourse and discontinuity' trans. A. M. Lazzaro, *Salmagundi* (Spring, 1972). 'Politics and the study of discourse' revised trans. C. Gordon, *Ideology and Consciousness* 3 (London, 1978).

* 'Réponse au Cercle d'épistémologie', *Cahiers pour l'analyse* 9 (1968). 'On the Archaeology of the Sciences' (slightly truncated translation), *Theoretical Practice* 3/4 (London, 1971).

'Les déviations religieuses et le savoir médical', followed by a discussion; in J. Le Goff ed. *Hérésies et sociétés* (Paris-La Haye, 1968).

'Ariane s'est pendue', review of G. Deleuze: *Logique du sens, Le Nouvel Observateur* 229 (31 March 1969).

* 'Qu'est-ce qu'un auteur?' followed by a discussion, *Bulletin de la Sociéte Française de Philosophie* Vol. 63 (1969). 'What is an Author?' trans. D. F. Bouchard, in *LCMP*.

'Jean Hyppolite (1907–1968)', *Revue de Métaphysique et Morale* 74 (1969).

'Il y aura scandale mais . . .', on P. Guyotat: *Eden, Eden, Eden, Le Nouvel Observateur* 304 (7 September 1970).

'La situation de Cuvier dans l'histoire de la biologie', followed by an extended discussion, *Revue d'histoire des sciences et de leurs applications* 23 (1970).

'Croître et multiplier', review of F. Jacob: *La logique du vivant, Le Monde* 8037 (15–16 November 1970).

* 'Theatrum philosophicum', on G. Deleuze: *Difference et repetition, Logique du sens, Critique* 282 (1970). 'Theatrum philosophicum' trans. D. F. Bouchard, in *LCMP*.

* 'Histoire des systèmes de pensée', résumés of courses of lectures, *Annuaire du Collège de France,* yearly 1971–. Résumés for years 1970–1 to 1973–4 reprinted in A. Kremer-Marietti, *Michel Foucault* (1974). 'History of Systems of Thought' (1970–1 only) trans. D. F. Bouchard, in *LCMP*.

* 'Monstrosities in Criticism', on G. Steiner, *Diacritics* Vol. 1 (Fall 1971).

'Le discours de Toul', *Le Nouvel Observateur* 372 (27 December 1971).

* 'Nietzsche, l'histoire, la généalogie' in *Hommage à Jean Hyppolite* (1971). 'Nietzsche, genealogy, history' trans. D. F. Bouchard, in *LCMP*; also in *Semiotexte* 3.

* 'Response', *Diacritics* Vol. 2 (1972).

'Mon corps, ce papier, ce feu' (response to J. Derrida) in *Histoire de la folie à l'âge classique* (2nd edn.) (1972).

'Piéger sa propre culture', *Le Figaro* (30 September 1972).

'Les deux morts de Pompidou', *Le Nouvel Observateur* 421 (4 December 1972).

'Bachelard, le philosophe et son ombre . . .' *Le Figaro littéraire* 1376 (30 September 1972).

'Medecine et lutte de classe', in collaboration with Groupe Information Santé, *La Nef* 49 (1972).

'La force de fuir' in *Rebeyrolle—Derrière le miroir* (1973).

'En guise de conclusion', *Le Nouvel Observateur* 435 (13 March 1973).

* 'Présentation' in *Moi, Pierre Rivière (. . .)* (1973). See above, under Books for full title and translation. Excerpts: 'Un crime fait pour être raconté', *Le Nouvel Observateur* 464 (1 October 1973).

* 'Les meurtres qu'on raconte' in *I, Pierre Riviere (. . .)* (1973). See preceding item.

'Convoqués à la P.J.' in collaboration with A. Landau and J.-Y. Petit, on the Groupe Information Santé and the abortion law. *Le Nouvel Observateur* 468 (29 October 1973).

'Les rayons noirs de Byzantios', *Le Nouvel Observateur* 483 (11 February 1974).

'Un pompier vend la meche', review of J.-J. Lubrina: *L'enfer des pompiers*, *Le Nouvel Observateur* 531 (13 January 1975).

'La casa della follia' Italian trans. Cl. Tarroni in F. Basaglia and F. Basaglia Ongaro eds., *Crimini di Pace* (Turin, 1975).

* 'La politique de la santé au XVIIIe siècle' in *Les machines à guérir* (1976). See above, under Books. 'The Politics of Health in the Eighteenth Century', trans. C. Gordon, Ch. 9 in this volume.

* 'L'Occident et la vérité du sexe', *Le Monde* (5–6 November 1976). 'The West and the truth of Sex', *Sub/stance* 20 (1978).

* 'Corso del 7 gennaio 1976', lecture at the Collège de France, (7 January 1976), edited, and Italian trans. A. Fontana and P. Pasquino, in M.F., A. Fontana and P. Pasquino eds., *Microfisica del Potere* (Turin, 1977); in 'Two Lectures' trans. K. Soper, Ch. 5 in this volume.

* 'Corso del 14 gennaio 1976', lecture at the Collège de France (14 January 1976). See preceding item for details and translation.

'L'asile illimité', review of R. Castel: *L'Ordre psychiatrique*, *Le Nouvel Observateur* 646 (28 March 1977).

'La grande colère des faits', review of A. Glucksmann: *Les Maîtres Penseurs*, *Le Nouvel Observateur* 652 (9 May 1977).

'Va-t-on extrader Klaus Croissant?', *Le Nouvel Observateur* 679 (14 November 1977).

* 'La vie des hommes infâmes', *Les Cahiers du chemin* (Paris, 1977). 'The Life of Infamous Men' in M. Morris and P. Patton eds., *Michel Foucault; Power, Truth, Strategy* (Sydney, 1979).

* 'La "governamentalità" ', lecture at the Collège de France (February 1978), edited, and Italian trans. P. Pasquino. *Aut Aut* 167–168 (Florence, September–December 1978). 'Government-ality' trans. R. Braidotti, *Ideology and Consciousness* 6 (London, 1979).

'Le Citron et le Lait', review of Ph. Boucher: *Le Ghetto judiciaire*, *Le Monde* (21–22 October 1978).

'Des hommes qui ne voulaient pas devenir des fauves', *Libération* (22 March 1978).

'Du bon usage du criminel', review of G. Perrault: *Le Pull-over rouge*, *Le Nouvel Observateur* 722 (11 September 1978).

'A quoi rêvent les Iraniens?', *Le Nouvel Observateur* 727 (16 October 1978).

Articles on Iran, *Corriera della Sera* (Milan 5 November 1978), (7 November 1978), (19 November 1978), (26 November 1978).

'Manières de justice', *Le Nouvel Observateur* 743 (5 February 1979).

'Un plaisir si simple', *Le Gai Pied* 1 (April 1979).

'Lettre ouverte à Mehdi Bazargan', *Le Nouvel Observateur* 752 (9 April 1979).

'Pour une morale de l'inconfort', review of J. Daniel: 'L'ère des ruptures', *Le Nouvel Observateur* 754 (23 April 1979).

'Vivre autrement le temps', necrological notice on M. Clavel, *Le Nouvel Observateur* 755 (30 April 1979).

'Inutile de se soulever?', on Iran, *Le Monde* (11–12 May 1979).

'La stratégie du pourtoir', *Le Nouvel Observateur* 759 (28 May 1979).

'La Poussière et le Nuage', *Annales Historiques de la Révolution Française* (forthcoming).

4 Discussions and interviews

'Débat sur le roman', *Tel Quel* 17 (1964).

Interview on *Les Mots et les Choses* with R. Bellour, *Les Lettres Françaises* 1125 (31 March 1966).

Interview on *Les Mots et les Choses* with M. Chapsal, *La Quinzaine littéraire* 5 (16 May 1966).

'L'homme est-il mort?', interview on *Les Mots et les Choses* with Cl. Bonnefoy, *Arts et loisirs* 38 (15 June 1966).

Interview on André Breton with Cl. Bonnefoy, *Arts et loisirs* 54 (5 October 1966).

'Sur les façons d'écrire l'histoire', interview with R. Bellour, *Les Lettres Françaises* 187 (15 June 1967).

'Foucault répond à Sartre', interview with J.-P. El Kabbach, *La Quinzaine littéraire* 46 (1 March 1968). But see also 'Mise au point', *ibid.* 47 (15 March 1968).

'Correspondance à propos des entretiens sur Foucault', *La Pensée* 139 (1968).

'Conversazione con Michel Foucault' in P. Caruso, *Conversazioni con Levi-Strauss, Foucault, Lacan* (Milan, 1969).

Interview on *L'Archéologie du savoir* with J.-J. Brochier, *Magazine littéraire* 28 (1969).

'La naissance d'un monde', interview with J.-M. Palmier, *Le Monde* (3 May 1969).

'La piège de Vincennes', interview with P. Loriot, *Le Nouvel Observateur* 274 (9 February 1970).

* Interview with J. K. Simon, *Partisan Review* Vol. 38 No. (New York, 1971).

* 'Par delà le bien et le mal', discussion with lycée students, *Actuel* 14 (1971). Modified version in *C'est demain la veille* (1973). 'Revolutionary Action: "Until Now" ' trans. D. F. Bouchard, in *LCMP*.

* 'Sur la justice populaire. Débat avec les Maos', *Les Temps Modernes* 310bis (special issue): *Nouvelle fascisme, nouvelle démocratie* (1972). 'On Popular Justice. A debate with Maoists' trans. J. Mepham, Ch. 1 in this volume.

* 'Les intellectuels et le pouvoir', discussion with G. Deleuze, *L'Arc* 49 (Aix-en-Provence, 1972). 'The Intellectuals and Power' trans. M. Seem, *Telos* 16 (1973). 'Intellectuals and Power' trans. D. F. Bouchard, in *LCMP*.

'Table ronde', discussion on social work, *Esprit* (special issue): *Pourquoi le travail social?* (April–May 1972).

'Pour une chronique de la mémoire ouvrière', *Libèration* (22 February 1973).

* 'On Attica: an interview' (with J. K. Simon), *Telos* 19 (Spring 1974).

* 'Anti-Rétro', *Cahiers du Cinema* 251–2 (July–August 1974). 'Film and Popular Memory' trans. M. Jordin, *Radical Philosophy* 11 (London, 1975); also in *Edinburgh '77 Magazine* 2.

'Des supplices aux cellules', interview on *Surveiller et punir* with R.-P. Droit, *Le Monde* (21 February 1975).

Interview on *Surveiller et punir* with J. L. Ézine, *Les Nouvelles Littéraires* (17 March 1975).

* Interview on *Surveiller et punir* with J.-J. Brochier, *Magazine littéraire* 101 (June 1975). Reprinted as 'Les jeux du pouvoir' in D. Grisoni ed., *Politiques de la Philosophie* (1976). 'Prison talk' trans. C. Gordon, *Radical Philosophy* 16 (London, 1977); Ch. 2 in this volume.

* 'Pouvoir et Corps', *Quel Corps?* 2 (September–October 1975). Reprinted in (the book) *Quel Corps?* (1978). 'Body/Power' trans. C. Gordon, Ch. 3 in this volume.

* 'Questions à Michel Foucault sur la géographie', *Hérodote* 1 (January–March 1976). 'Questions on Geography' trans. C. Gordon, Ch. 3 in this volume.

* 'Crimes et châtiments en URSS et ailleurs', interview with K. S. Karol, *Le Nouvel Observateur* 585 (26 January 1976). 'Politics of Crime' trans. M. Horwitz (heavily cut), *Partisan Review* Vol. 43 No. 3 (1976).

'Sorcellerie et folie', interview on Th. Szasz: *The Manufacture of Madness* with R. Jaccard, *Le Monde* (23 April 1976).

Questions on strategy, geography, science and power in 'Des réponses aux questions de Michel Foucault', *Hérodote* 4 (October–December 1976). See also *ibid.* 6 (1977).

* 'La fonction politique de l'intellectuel', excerpt from French version of 'Intervista a Michel Foucault' (1977) q.v. below. *Politique-Hebdo* 274 (29 November 1976). 'The political function of the intellectual' trans. C. Gordon, *Radical Philosophy* 17 (London, 1977).

* 'Les rapports de pouvoir passent à l'intérieur des corps', interview on *La volonté de savoir* with L. Finas, *Quinzaine littéraire* 247 (1 January 1977). 'Interview with Lucette Finas' in M. Morris and P. Patton eds., *Michel Foucault: Power, Truth, Strategy* (Sydney, 1979). 'The History of Sexuality' trans. L. Marshall, Ch. 10 in this volume.

* 'Pouvoirs et stratégies', *Les Révoltes Logiques* 4 (1977). 'Powers and Strategies: an interview' in M. Morris and P. Patton eds., *ibid.* 'Powers and Strategies' trans. C. Gordon, Ch. 7 in this volume.

* 'Non au sexe roi', interview on *La volonté de savoir* with B.-H. Lévy, *Le Nouvel Observateur* 644 (12 March 1977). 'Power and sex: an interview', *Telos* 32 (1977).

'L'angoisse de juger', discussion on capital punishment with J. Laplanche, R. Badinter, *Le Nouvel Observateur* 655 (30 May 1977).

* 'Le jeu de Michel Foucault', interview/discussion on *La volonté de savoir*, *Ornicar?* 10 (July 1977). 'The Confession of the Flesh' trans. C. Gordon, Ch. 11 in this volume. See above, 'Note on Translations and Sources'.

'Dialogue sur l'enfermement et la répression psychiatrique', with V. Fainberg, D. Cooper, J. P. Faye and others, *Change* 32–33 (October 1977). Excerpt in *La Quinzaine littéraire* 265 (16 October 1977).

Interview on the Croissant affair. *Le Matin* (18 November 1977).

* 'L'Oeil du Pouvoir', discussion with M. Perrot and J.-P. Barou in J. Bentham, *Le Panoptique* (Paris, 1977). 'The Eye of Power' trans. C. Gordon, Ch. 8 in this volume. 'The Eye of Power', *Semiotexte: Schizo-culture* (1979).

* 'Intervista a Michel Foucault', interview with A. Fontana and P. Pasquino in Fontana and Pasquino eds., *Michel Foucault, Microfisica del Potere* (Turin, 1977). For excerpt and translation see above, 'La fonction politique de l'intellectuel' (1976). 'Vérité et pouvoir' (French version, shortened and scrambled), *L'Arc* 70 (Aix-en-Provence, 1977). 'Truth and Power' trans. C. Gordon, Ch. 6 in this volume. 'Truth and Power: an interview' (omitting excerpted part) in M. Morris and P. Patton eds., *ibid.*

'Table ronde sur l'expertise psychiatrique' in "Actes", *Delinquances et ordre* (1978).

'Precisazioni sul potere. Risposta ad alcuni critici', interview with P. Pasquino, *Aut Aut* 167–168 (Florence, September–December 1978).

Discussion on Iran with the authors, in C. Brière and P. Blanchet, *La Révolution au nom de Dieu* (1979).

'Table ronde autour de deux textes, "L'Historien et le Philosophe" de Jacques Léonard et "La Poussière et le Nuage" de Michel Foucault' (provisional title), *Annales Historiques de la Révolution Francaise* (forthcoming).

About the Author

Michel Foucault was born in Poitiers, France, in 1926. He has lectured in many universities throughout the world and served as director of the Institut Français in Hamburg and the Institut de Philosophie at the Faculté des Lettres in the University of Clermont-Ferrand. He writes frequently for French newspapers and reviews, and is the holder of a chair at France's most prestigious institution, the Collège de France.

M. Foucault is the author of *Madness and Civilization, The Order of Things, The Archaeology of Knowledge, The Birth of the Clinic, Discipline and Punish: The Birth of the Prison,* and *The History of Sexuality,* vol. 1. In addition, he has edited two documentary studies, *I, Pierre Rivière* and *Herculine Barbin.*